American Wildlife
in Symbol and Story

American Wildlife in Symbol and Story

EDITED BY
ANGUS K. GILLESPIE
AND JAY MECHLING

THE UNIVERSITY OF TENNESSEE PRESS / KNOXVILLE

The paper in this book meets the minimum requirements of the
American National Standard for Permanence of Paper for Printed
Library Materials. ∞   The binding materials have been chosen for
strength and durability.

Library of Congress Cataloging-in-Publication Data

American wildlife in symbol and story.

  Bibliography: p.
  Includes index.
  1. Folklore—United States. 2. Animals—United States—Folklore.
3. Ethnozoology—United States.
I. Gillespie, Angus K., 1942–   . II. Mechling, Jay, 1945–
GR105.3.A47   1987   398'.369'.0973   86-19315
ISBN 0-87049-522-4 (alk. paper)

For Archie Green
—A.K.G.

For my parents
—J.M.

Contents

Illustrations

Original Line Drawings by Ruth Strohl Palmer

Introduction

JAY MECHLING AND ANGUS K. GILLESPIE

Animals are nothing but the forms of our virtues
and vices, wandering before our eyes, the visible
phantoms of our souls.
                                    —*Victor Hugo*

The essays collected here take as their "texts" wild animals that seem
to be especially attractive symbols for Americans' thinking about
everyday life. In some cases the animal is unique to the Americas. In
others the animal is known elsewhere but here appears in a New
World context loaded with a legacy of European understandings, as
in the cases of the bear, the fox, and the crocodile. The challenge for
each author is to describe the pattern of symbolic uses of a given
wild animal and to decipher from those patterns the particular
meanings of that animal for Americans. Fundamental to this approach is the assumption that American symbolic discourse about a
wild animal is, simultaneously, American symbolic discourse about
human social relations. In a sense, each author is engaged in the interpretation of Americans' interpretations of a wild animal.

But what, exactly, does it mean to "interpret" a thing or a person
or an event? Although there is a substantial scholarly literature on
interpretation in the humanities and the social sciences, we like Gregory Bateson's simpler approach as demonstrated by the little story

he tells in his introduction to *Mind and Nature.* A certain computer programmer wondered if his computer would ever "think like a human being," so he posed that question to the machine. After a suitable interval of analyzing its own computational habits, the computer printed out the answer on a piece of paper. Running expectantly to the printer, the programmer found, neatly typed, the words: THAT REMINDS ME OF A STORY.[1]

Bateson's point, of course, is that to think like a human being is to think in terms of stories, to think in terms of coherent sequences and patterns of elements. Bateson had a larger point to make (namely, that all living systems share the quality of mind of thinking in terms of stories), but we can take from his anecdote the insight that one way to think about culture is as the repertoire of all those "stories" humans use to think about the world. To "interpret" a thing or a person or an event, in other words, is to find the story that makes best sense of the thing, person, or event. The meaning of a "text" lies therefore in its "context," in its relation to the other elements of the story of which it is a part. We take culture to be the public, patterned systems of symbols and stories that people use to communicate and to establish shared meanings. Culture creates discrete categories from the continuous stream of experience, names those categories, and comments upon the relationships among them.

Babcock-Abrahams summarized this rationale over a decade ago, naming in the canon of work on classification and taboo selected work by Claude Lévi-Strauss, Edmund Leach, Mary Douglas, Victor Turner, and others.[2] By all accounts, Leach's famous 1964 essay on "Animal Categories and Verbal Abuse" established the research agenda for those in pursuit of "why animals are good to think." Concerned with A. R. Radcliffe-Brown's problem of the "ritual value" of animal categories, Leach developed in that essay a general theory of taboo. Leach's great insight was to pose as the central interpretive question the correlations between three verbal category sets:

(a) Self——Sister——Cousin——Neighbor——Stranger
(b) Self——House——Farm——Field——Far (Remote)
(c) Self——Pet——Livestock——'Game'——Wild Animal

"The way we employ the words in set (c), a set of animals," reasoned Leach, "allows us to make statements about the human relationships which belong to set (a)."[3] Discourse about animals is, in effect, discourse about human relationships, just as discourse about the human body and the food and excrements that cross its boundaries is discourse about the social group.[4] Leach and others have been particularly interested in the ritual and verbal associations between eating and sexual intercourse (that is, rules about incest) as expressing the connections between the taboos in the category sets of animals and humans. Leach's and others' analysis on this point focuses mainly upon the ambiguous, middle terms of "pet, livestock, and game," treating the remote wild animals as "not subject to human control, inedible."[5]

Many of our authors rely upon notions of "ambiguity," "anomaly," and "ambivalence." The human necessity of perceiving meaning-through-difference and the human tendency to rely upon binary thinking as the simplest strategy of creating meaning-through-difference require the introduction of a third category of middle terms to bridge the original categories.[6] "Such abnormal middle forms," writes Babcock-Abrahams, "are regarded as dangerous and powerful and are typically the focus of taboo and ritual observance."[7] The anomalous middle terms "mediate" between binary oppositions, providing a culturally acceptable way to deal with the anxieties and uncertainties created by the ambiguity of the middle. Barbara Babcock-Abrahams borrows from Douglas to identify "five cultural strategies for dealing with ambiguity":

> 1. Ambiguity is reduced by settling on one or other
> interpretation. . . . 2. The existence of an anomaly can be
> physically controlled. . . . 3. A rule of avoiding anomalous things
> affirms and strengthens the definitions to which they do not
> conform. . . . 4. Anomalous events may be labeled
> dangerous. . . . 5. Ambiguous symbols can be used in ritual. . . to
> enrich meaning or call attention to other levels of existence.[8]

The reader will see in the essays that follow instances of all five of these strategies, as Americans use the ambiguities of certain wild animals to reflect upon the ambiguities and uncertainties of American experience.

One source of anxiety among Americans is the differences between people categorized as "Americans," differences along lines of gender, race, ethnicity, age, and social class. The semiotic view that culture consists of the *public* systems of symbols and stories permits us to take a view of culture as a strategy for "the organization of diversity," rather than as a strategy for "the replication of uniformity."[9] It is the public system of symbols and stories—not some putative core personality—that may be shared by large numbers of Americans over space and time.

This view of American culture allows for systems of cultural discourse at all levels of generalization, from the intimate folk group of the family to the large television audience watching a presidential inaugural or the halftime show at the Superbowl. This view also posits the individual as a relatively autonomous actor who learns to move back and forth between and among these discrete cultures, able to discriminate between the extremely efficient discourse of a "high context" folk group, who have a substantial tradition of shared experiences, and the necessarily more denotative public discourse of, say, a public school classroom or a bureaucratic workplace, composed of people who might not share many life experiences and who, therefore, do not have shared contexts or "stories" for making sense of public events.[10] Thus, there are American cultures described in the following essays, and it will not surprise us to discover that an important use of wild animals is to symbolize the "alien other," to mediate somehow the anxieties created at those uneasy borders where American cultures meet. For similar reasons, the wild animal is also a richly ambiguous symbol for American discourse about matters sexual, as the following essays on the rattlesnake, the alligator, and the fox demonstrate.

Our main claim in these essays, then, is that "wild animals are good to think," that certain wild animals provide Americans rich, ambiguous symbols for thinking about their own experiences as Americans. The sources of the ideas, images, and stories (myths) about wild animals are many, but we may distinguish seven sorts of sources: conversational genres, oral narratives, children's literature, popular (mass-mediated) culture, participatory performances, elite culture, and scientific writing. We shall briefly introduce these seven in this order, moving from the most "folk" level of storytelling to the most elite level.

First are the shorter folk *conversational genres* most central to our commonsense knowledge of the world.[11] These are the jokes, proverbs, riddles, children's rhymes, songs, folk beliefs, superstitions, and so on, that constitute much of the everyday discourse by Americans about wild animals. Embedded in and expressed by these genres are "folk ideas," the basic units of belief about objects in the world.[12] This source of ideas about wild animals is likely to be primary, so much taken for granted are folk ideas. Gillespie finds in armadillo jokes and Mechling in alligator jokes, for example, folk ideas that provide the basic understanding for the appearance of those animals elsewhere in American symbolic culture. Proverbial expressions, including the humorous versions such as Tuleja's "It's hard to soar with Eagles when you work with Turkeys" or Mechling's "up to your ass in alligators," similarly encode metaphorical connections between folk ideas about the animals and human social situations.

Also a folk genre is *oral narrative,* the second major source of ideas about wild animals in America. This genre is worth its own category because, unlike the shorter, conversational genres listed above, this genre includes the true "stories" people pass on to explain to one another the meaning of a wild animal. It is also the category that has been treated to the most folklore scholarship. Myths are the longest genre of this sort, and several of the authors of these essays include Native American myths involving, say, the coyote, armadillo, or bear. For some animals, there exist folktales from Native American, Afro-American, and European traditions. And for all of these animals there are urban beliefs legends or personal memorates that work to put the "accent of reality" (as William James put it) upon the teller's and listeners' understanding of the animal. Many of the essays included here examine "encounter stories" relating the narrator's encounter with an alligator, rattlesnake, bear, or coyote. Gillespie gives considerable attention to Texas legendry about the armadillo, and Mechling shows how the alligator entered American urban legendry. We find these longer narratives among amateurs and professionals alike. A park ranger is as likely to have a repertoire of stories as is a tourist attraction announcer or a hunter holding forth in a local tavern.[13]

A third source of our ideas about wild animals is *children's literature,* the printed stories and accompanying illustrations that provide a repertoire of ideas and images for making sense of all sorts of animals. Some children's literature is little more than a printed version of the traditional oral narratives, and some is original. Authors of children's books seem especially disposed to use animal characters in lieu of human ones.[14] Like the folk genres, this written, visual source of ideas is powerful because its influence begins so early in the creation of the child's map of the everyday world. It is powerful, too, because of its visual component, the illustrations accompanying children's stories. All the more powerful is the transformation of animal illustrations into three-dimensional toys, such as the Teddy Bear or Winnie-the-Pooh. Thus, a persistent problem for the rangers at Yosemite and Yellowstone National Parks is that Americans tend to approach real bears as if they were the storybook kind. Rangers refer to this phenomenon as "the Bambi complex"—which brings us to our fourth main source of ideas and images of wild animals.

Popular culture (also known as mass-mediated culture or commercial culture) is an increasingly important locus of such ideas and images. Included in this category are such genres as postcards, souvenirs, cartoons, comics, television commercials, print advertising, theatrical films, television programs, and mass-circulation magazines. Popular culture provides a repertoire of stories and images accessible to a wide audience, crossing gender, ethnic, and social class divisions. Popular culture is the most "public" of the cultural systems, in this sense, and the commercial success of a particular wild animal image may be an index to its pervasiveness among diverse American cultures.

These popular materials from commercial culture appear prominently in the essays that follow, from Meléndez's Wile E. Coyote to advertisements for Wild Turkey bourbon to a theatrical film, *Alligator* (1980). The richness of these materials reminds us that the usual analytic distinctions are somewhat misleading, and that the folk, popular, and elite levels of culture really are in a dialectical relation to each other, with individual items and genres moving within and across these boundaries. One folklorist coined the term "folklure" to describe the use of folkloric motifs in advertising, the important premise being that some advertising "works" because it is tapping a largely unconscious set of meanings and emotional responses learned originally in the folklore.[15] Gillespie explores this phenomenon in the saga of Lone Star Beer's use of the armadillo in its advertising, and the essays on the turkey and the alligator touch upon aspects of "folklure."

The fifth source of ideas, images, and stories are the *performances* that involve somehow an interpretation of a wild animal. We have in mind here the participatory, drama-like events that would include tourist attractions, festivals, museum and zoo programs, hunting expeditions, cooking and foodway events, and the like. Oldest in this category are the Native American performance rituals and dances that involve the armadillo, the coyote, the bear, and the rattlesnake. The snake handling in the white religious communities described by Wilson is a related phenomenon. Important, too, are the folk healing customs involving wild animals, tapping the power of a dangerously ambiguous creature like the alligator to effect a cure.[16]

Rangers and zoo curators often are our most available interpreters, but in the same class are, for example, the alligator tourist attractions in Florida. Armadillo races in Texas, the annual National Turkey Calling Contest in Yellville, Arkansas, and the annual Rattlesnake Roundup are other wonderful examples of participatory festivals that are largely "about" the symbolic meanings of these wild animals. Not least important as a performance of the meaning of one of these animals is the Thanksgiving dinner.

The power of these performance genres lies in their combination of verbal and nonverbal discourse, their appeal to all five human senses. They muster all the power of ritual and of play.[17] And they are collective, usually involving relatively large groups of people conspiring toward a shared interpretation of the wild animal.

The sixth source of our notions about animals is *elite culture*, the body of fine literature and fine arts that is the usual subject matter of humanistic study. Fine painting, poetry, novels, and short stories in America often feature wild animals as central symbols in the moral, imaginative landscape of their fictive worlds. Melville's white whale and Faulkner's bear are only the most well-known cases. Poets Gary Snyder and Simon Ortiz find the coyote an especially attractive figure, and novelist Thomas Pynchon uses the alligators–in–the–sewers legend for his own artistic purposes in *V*.[18] In American elite art, we can trace the iconography of American wildlife from the earliest European renditions through the likes of Audubon and Sargent, up to the present.[19]

It will surprise some to learn that *scientific* discourse is the seventh source of American ideas about wild animals. So accustomed are we to thinking of scientific writing as "fact," opposed to folk and popular "fiction," that we fail to appreciate how cultural is the his-

tory of American scientific writing about wild animals. Some scientific writing is either the source of or, at least, perpetuates the oldest
folk ideas about animals. And even when a scientific treatise takes
space in its historical treatment of a wild animal to "debunk" the
"myths and fallacies" about the animal (as in the cases of the meticu-
lously thorough books by Klauber on the rattlesnake and Neill on
the alligator), the author is acknowledging tacitly that the starting
point for American understanding of the beast is a repertoire of folk
and popular beliefs concerning it. American zoology and "ethnozoology" are probably a good deal more continuous than discontinu-
ous. It would be interesting to explore, for example, the social and
cultural variables at work in a scientist's selection of a particular
wild animal for study. We suspect that the testimony from scientists
would reveal that a certain underlying set of beliefs attracts a given
scientist to a given wild animal. Even a cursory look at the rhetoric
of American naturalists, from Catesby to Seton to Eisely, reveals all
sorts of human traits being projected onto the animal.

The point of distinguishing these seven sources of American ideas
about wild animals is to help alert us to the many ways in which we
gain our commonsense knowledge about things. But we want to emphasize that it is the tangle of genres, the dialectic between these
sources of symbols and stories, that interests us. All of these sources
provide interpretations of the wild animals, and interpretations of
the interpretations. We are interested in the fact that folk ideas about
an animal seem to underlie both popular images and scientific writing, that popular images may enter folk genres, that elite artists like
Faulkner, Hawthorne, and Pynchon dip into folk and popular genres for stories about animals. Culture is never frozen, never static,
and it is the fascinating movement of images, symbols, stories, and
their attendant ideas across genres, space, and time that demonstrates for us the dynamism of culture. There is no simple linear
cause-and-effect relationship at work here, and we are reminded of
Geertz's point about the "doubleness" of cultural symbols: that they
are simultaneously "models of" and "models for" action in the
world.[20]

These essays and our shared interpretive approach to American
cultural materials also remind us that interpretation is a social, political, and moral act. [21] No interpretation is objective, isolated, neu-

tral, not even the so-called scientific one. All interpretations are ideological, are socially located, and serve (even unintentionally) some end. People often struggle over interpretations, knowing at some level that to capture the interpretive high ground is to capture the definition of a reality.

Gillespie's discussion of the Armadillo World Headquarters and the Texan counter-culture's adoption of the armadillo as its icon is an example of the sort of interpretive struggle we mean, as is Mechling's discussion of the racial struggle over the interpretation of the alligator and Meléndez's discussion of Anglo versus Chicano and Native American interpretations of the coyote. We would like to think that the essays collected here contribute to our understanding of the cultural bases of our responses to wild animals, help us see more clearly how the ideological and commercial uses of these animal symbols by others may be manipulating us by touching our subconscious and forming our commonsense understanding of the world. Wilfred Neill worries in his rich book on the alligator that folk ideas about certain endangered species will threaten conservation efforts, so it is the animals as well as the humans that stand to suffer if we fail to examine the entire range of meanings we hold regarding wildlife. The authors of the essays in this volume by no means speak unanimously on these questions of ideology and theoretical orientation, but we think they all offer exciting insights into the social and psychological complexes surrounding these wild animals.

Wild animals may be "good to think," but they are "fun to think," too, and we hope the reader will find enjoyable the playful approaches we encouraged our contributors to take. We invited our authors to consider the entire range of symbolic treatments of their animal subjects, including Native American uses, reports by early explorers and naturalists, scientific writing, and the popular accounts one finds in natural history or outdoor-life magazines. Most contributors did field work, interviewing park rangers, hunters, tourist-attraction managers, animal scientists, and, in at least one instance, a colorful bartender. And we know that our contributors became voracious collectors of postcards, bumper stickers, ashtrays, keychains, posters, pamphlets, and other assorted "artifacts" featuring their particular animal icon. Clearly, each of us was attracted to a particular animal for reasons that must be partly cultural and partly personal, and therein probably lies many a tale. But we shall let our contributors speak for themselves.

We had a problem settling upon an order in which to present these essays. Several ordering principles crisscross here, so the reader may choose to read the chapters out of sequence according to his or her own interests. The opening essay by Tad Tuleja on the turkey and the next by David Scofield Wilson on the rattlesnake take on two animals that were early candidates for national symbols. Mechling's essay on the alligator and Gillespie's on the armadillo deal with immensely ambiguous animals whose ambiguity contributes to their usefulness as cultural symbols (the two vied in sixteenth-century European iconography for the role as quintessential symbol of North America). The essays by Dan Gelo, Mary Hufford, and Theresa Meléndez explore the symbolic uses of three familiar mammals—bear, fox, and coyote—that seem to have a long and complex history of relationship with human cultures in North America.

There are important wild animals we have omitted, of course, partly because of limitations of space but also because there is no clear place to draw the line. Consequently, our volume leaves out certain obvious candidates, like the bison, the manatee, the shark, the crayfish, the raccoon, or the salmon. Other potentially fascinating candidates are the prairie dog, the wolf, the raven, the moose, and the opossum. Our hope is that this volume will inspire other scholars to add to our analysis of the "American bestiary."[22]

Finally, although each contributor acknowledges assistance from and offers thanks to friends, colleagues, and informants, we two editors wish to thank Jan Brunvand and Barre Toelken for their careful and helpful readings of the entire manuscript. And Carol Orr, director of the University of Tennessee Press, sustained her faith in this project over its long gestation.

University of California   Rutgers University
Davis, California   New Brunswick, New Jersey

NOTES

1. Gregory Bateson, *Mind and Nature: A Necessary Unity* (New York: Dutton, 1979). We are describing here what may be called the "interpretive" approach to American culture, still a loose skein attempting to bind together various phenomenological theories of social reality, but most especially the semiotic and hermeneutic traditions. What is so attractive about this approach for American studies people is that the problems of "interpretation" are shared by humanists and social scientists alike, thus breaking down the artificial barriers between the theories and methods of the humanities on one hand and of the social sciences on the other. Accordingly, the scholars whose work most informs these essays are humanistic anthropologists such as Clifford Geertz, Mary Douglas, and Victor Turner. The two best introductions to this approach are Clifford Geertz's *The Interpretation of Cultures* (New York: Basic Books, 1973), especially chapter 1, "Thick Description: Toward an Interpretive Theory of Culture"; and Victor Turner's lucid survey, "Process, System and Symbol: A New Anthropological Synthesis," *Daedalus* 106 (1977): 61–80.

2. Barbara Babcock-Abrahams, "Why Frogs Are Good to Think and Dirt Is Good to Reflect On," *Soundings* 58 (1975): 167–81. See, also, Roy Willis, *Man and Beast* (London: Hart-Davis, MacGibbon, 1974).

3. Edmund Leach, "Anthropological Aspects of Language: Animal Categories and Verbal Abuse," in *New Directions in the Study of Language,* ed. Eric. H. Lenneberg (Cambridge, Mass.: MIT Press, 1964), 37.

4. Mary Douglas, *Natural Symbols: Explorations in Cosmology* (1970; rpt., New York: Pantheon Books, 1982). Douglas urges us to consider how members of a society come to see the human body, its boundaries, the food crossing the boundary into the body, and the excrement crossing the boundary out of the body as symbols of society, of purity and pollution. For an application of Douglas's approach on American materials, see Elizabeth Walker Mechling and Jay Mechling, "Sweet Talk: The Moral Rhetoric Against Sugar," *Central States Speech Journal* 34 (1983): 19–32.

5. Leach, 44. Most scholarship on the symbolic meanings of animals to Americans has been on those same, middle terms—livestock and pets. Anthropologist Marshall Sahlins (*Culture and Practical Reason* [Chicago: Univ. of Chicago Press, 1976], 170–79), for example, analyzes American food taboos regarding "the domesticated series cattle-pigs-horses-dogs" as a way of understanding our world view, and Page Smith and Charles Daniel's *The Chicken Book* (San Francisco: North Point Press, 1982) has become a minor classic in the exhaustive, interdisciplinary study of a domesticated animal.

Similarly, there is a considerable literature on the meanings of pets in American culture, with some of the best insights provided by animal rights scholars who are attuned to the symbolic meanings of pet animals and food animals. See Yi-fu Tuan, *Dominance and Affection: The Making of Pets* (New Haven: Yale Univ. Press, 1984) and Maria Leach, *God Had a Dog: Folklore of the Dog* (New Brunswick, N.J.: Rutgers Univ. Press, 1961). In quite a different category, but still addressing the meanings of animals in the American symbolic landscape, is the scholarship on imaginary, fantastic, and legendary beasts, such as Richard M. Dorson's *Man and Beast in American Comic Legend* (Bloomington: Indiana Univ. Press, 1983) and Roger L. Welsch, *Tall-Tale Postcards: A Pictorial History* (South Brunswick and New York: A.S. Barnes and Company, 1976).

Pursuing Leach's point about sexuality and edibility, we believe that notions about the edibility of wild animals may be as important as ideas about the edibility of the middle terms. Indeed, the edibility of some of the wild animals in the following essays, and the special ritual circumstances of their edibility, are important clues to their meaning. Gillespie's discussion of ideas about the edibility of the armadillo, Mechling's analysis of the ethnic coding in patterns of eating alligator meat, Wilson's comments on the meanings of eating a rattlesnake, Gelo's discussion of attitudes toward bear meat, and Tuleja's portrait of the Thanksgiving turkey all testify to the power and danger loaded into our consumption of the flesh of wild animals. And it is relevant that two of these animals, the alligator and the bear, sometimes eat humans.

6. It is absolutely central to Gregory Bateson's cybernetic, information-theory approach to culture that meaning lies only in the discovery of difference. See his various essays in *Steps to An Ecology of Mind* (New York: Ballantine, 1972), but especially the essay "Form, Substance, and Difference," 448–65. Claude Lévi-Strauss makes somewhat the same point in his structuralist work, though Bateson would find too limiting Lévi-Strauss's focus upon binary opposition as the principal form of difference.

7. Babcock-Abrahams, 169.

8. Ibid., 173–74. See, also, Mary Douglas, *Purity and Danger: An Analysis of Concepts of Pollution and Taboo* (London: Routledge and Kegan Paul, 1966).

9. Anthony F.C. Wallace, *Culture and Personality,* 2nd ed. (New York: Random House, 1970).

10. Douglas, Geertz, Victor Turner, Kenneth Burke, Alan Dundes, Roger Abrahams, and others in the tradition of "interpretive" anthropology urge us to take the point of view of the human actor in the social drama. Turner probably has best played out the dramatistic metaphor, as

in his *Dramas, Fields and Metaphors: Symbolic Action in Human Society* (Ithaca, N.Y.: Cornell Univ. Press, 1974). E.T. Hall discusses "high context" and "low context" in his *Beyond Culture* (Garden City, N.Y.: Anchor Press/Doubleday, 1976), 85–116.

11. For excellent treatments of the folk genres of everyday life, see Roger D. Abrahams, "A Rhetoric of Everyday Life: Traditional Conversational Genres," *Southern Folklore Quarterly* 32 (1968): 44–59, and Alan Dundes, "Some Minor Genres of American Folklore," *Southern Folklore Quarterly* 31 (1967): 20–36.

12. Alan Dundes, "Folk Ideas as Units of World View," in *Toward New Perspectives in Folklore,* ed. Américo Paredes and Richard Bauman (Austin: Univ. of Texas Press, 1972), 93–103.

13. The quantity of folklore scholarship on legend is large, but a good place to begin is Wayland D. Hand, ed., *American Folk Legend* (Berkeley: Univ. of California Press, 1971). Easily accessible introductions are Jan Harold Brunvand's *The Vanishing Hitchhiker: American Urban Legends and Their Meanings* (New York: Norton, 1981) and *The Choking Doberman and Other "New" Urban Legends* (New York: Norton, 1984).

14. Two surveys of this genre are Margaret Blount, *Animal Land: The Creatures of Children's Fiction* (New York: William Morrow & Company, 1975), and Mary Lystad, *From Dr. Mather to Dr. Seuss: 200 Years of American Books for Children* (Boston: G.K. Hall and Company, 1980).

15. Priscilla Denby, "Folklore in the Mass Media," *Folklore Forum* 4 (1971): 13–25.

16. See Don Yoder, "Folk Medicine," in *Folklore and Folklife: An Introduction,* ed. Richard M. Dorson (Chicago: Univ. of Chicago Press, 1972), 191–215.

17. Especially helpful in thinking about rituals is the introduction, "Secular Ritual: Forms and Meanings," Sally F. Moore and Barbara G. Myerhoff wrote for the volume they edited jointly, *Secular Ritual* (Amsterdam: Van Gorcum, Assen, 1977), 3–24.

18. A good example of an investigation of an American author's use of folk ideas is Daniel R. Barnes, "The Bosom Serpent: A Legend in American Literature and Culture," *Journal of American Folklore* 85 (1972): 111–22.

19. See, for example, David Scofield Wilson, *In the Presence of Nature* (Amherst: Univ. of Massachusetts Press, 1978), on the connection between the ideas and iconography of American wildlife.

20. Geertz, 93.

21. The two people who have done the most to bring to our attention the "politics" of the interpretation of everyday life are Clifford Geertz and Erving Goffman. See Geertz's, "Thinking as a Moral Act: Ethical Dimen-

sions of Anthropological Fieldwork in the New States," *The Antioch Review* 28 (1968): 139–58, and Goffman's *Frame Analysis* (New York: Harper Colophon Books, 1974).

22. Using wild animals as our "texts"—in effect, as our ambiguous stimuli for cultural projective testing—would lead to some new understandings in comparative culture research, both among cultures in the United States and between our and foreign cultures.

General Note

Several of the essays in this volume refer to two standard folklore indexes: Antii Aarne and Stith Thompson, ed., *The Types of the Folktale,* 2nd rev., *Folklore Fellows Communications,* no. 14 (Helsinki, 1961), and Stith Thompson, *Motif-Index of Folk Literature* (Copenhagen and Bloomington: Indiana Univ. Press, 1955–58), 6 vols. Motif numbers throughout the book refer to Aarne/Thompson (AT #) tale type numbers and to Thompson motif numbers.

The Turkey

TAD TULEJA

In the winter of 1784, writing from France to his daughter, Benjamin Franklin chided the American Order of the Cincinnati for choosing the bald eagle as their emblem. In the elder statesman's view, this creature, which two years earlier had also become the emblem of the United States, was "a bird of bad moral character," addicted to stealing the osprey's catch rather than hunting for himself. "Like those among men who live by sharping and robbing," said Franklin, "he is generally poor, and often very lousy. Besides, he is a rank coward." To those who had commented that the Cincinnati emblem looked more like a turkey than an eagle, Franklin's rejoinder was a wry Amen.

> I am...not displeased that the figure is not known as a bald eagle, but looks more like a turkey. For in truth, the turkey is in comparison a much more respectable bird, and withal a true native original of America. Eagles have been found in all countries, but the turkey was peculiar to ours;...He is, besides, (though a little vain and silly, it is true, but not the worse emblem for that), a bird of courage, and would not hesitate to attack a grenadier of the British guards, who should presume to invade his farmyard with a red coat on.[1]

This defense has been cited frequently as evidence that Franklin championed adopting the bird as a national symbol. Considering his notoriously waggish nature, this conclusion is speculative at best. Franklin, it might be recalled, had once "proposed" in the *Pennsylvania Gazette* that rattlesnakes be exported to England as "the most suitable Returns for the Human Serpents sent us by our Mother Country." In addition, as a member of the committee appointed by the Continental Congress in 1776 to propose designs for a national Great Seal, he had suggested not the whimsical turkey but a staid Biblical tableau: Moses closing the Red Sea over Pharaoh, with the motto "Rebellion to tyrants is obedience to God."[2]

But however playful Franklin's championship of the turkey may have been, he was clearly genuinely attracted to the bird, on two counts. The first—its supposed courage—may be dismissed as literary license, employed by an inveterate jester as a barb for Mother England. The second—its American origin—is more to the point he was making: that a proper emblem of this nation ought to be American itself. Whatever Franklin's real feelings about the turkey, he correctly stressed its indigenousness as the bird's special claim to our attention.

He was not the first, nor the last, to do so. From the sixteenth century onward, commentators noted that the turkey, like the armadillo and the rattlesnake, was peculiar to the New World. The later association of the bird with the Pilgrim thanksgiving reinforced its image as an American symbol, and it remains an unofficial national mascot. Among many hunters, moreover, the wild turkey is still considered the most intelligent of woodland adversaries, the preeminent American quarry.

In popular idiom, however, the bird has a different meaning. The sophomoric jibe "turkey" means "loser"; it signifies the kind of hapless incompetent that teenagers since the 1950s have also called "nerd." In this essay I will suggest that this contemporary low image is a paradoxical outgrowth of the bird's former eminence. The turkey's fall from idiomatic grace, far from being accidental, should be seen as a predictable concomitant of American social and economic trends. In the two hundred years since Franklin wrote his encomium, the bird has degenerated from an image of the New World frontier to one of domestic buffoonery. This decline, I will try to demonstrate, sheds light on the American attitude toward wildness, and on our national genius for transforming wildness into goods.

Although Franklin correctly identified the New World as the original home of the turkey, not all early observers were as well informed. The first Spanish reports of the bird reached Europe early in the sixteenth century; captive wild imports reached European tables shortly thereafter, along with domesticated birds that had been given to Cortés by the Aztecs. Yet as late as the mid-eighteenth century, the erroneous notion persisted that the turkey had come from the East. The French common name was *dindon*, a contraction of *poule d'Inde*, and even the erudite Dr. Johnson, in his 1755 dictionary, defined it as "a large domestick fowl brought from Turkey." It is uncertain whether he was referring to the distinctively American gobbler or to one of the many other gallinaceous birds which, since the Middle Ages, the English had wrongly viewed as Turkish products. With modern taxonomy still an infant science, Johnson's contemporaries frequently confused American turkeys, peafowls, capercaillies, and guinea fowls; all were indiscriminately identified as turkeys, although today only the American variety retains the misnomer.[3]

The American wild turkey, which is no more Turkish than its cousins, bears the Latin name *Meleagris gallopavo*. Six major subspecies inhabited pre-Columbian North America, but the technical distinctions among them are less significant for our purposes than the shared characteristics of the males. All possess a vivid head and throat ornaments (the fleshy wattles and caruncle), all have bristly pectoral appendages known as "beards," and all engage in characteristic gobbling and fan-tailed courtship displays.[4]

These characteristics were a source of wonder even to the American Indian tribes, many of which hunted the bird and used its feathers and bones for ornamental and religious purposes. The strikingly striated tail feathers of the mature male were used by many people in fletching arrows, making robes and mantles, and general adornment. Among the Southwest Pueblo tribes, the feathers of domesticated turkeys were used to adorn prayer sticks, and even among the Cheyenne, who would not eat the bird for fear of becoming cowardly, its feathers were the characteristic fletch material. Other peculiarities of the animal also evoked curiosity. A Cherokee myth, for example, explains the frontal beard by saying it was originally a scalp carried by Turtle and given by him to Turkey. A charming Hopi myth explains the bird's bald red head as a consequence of its attempt to help the people by pushing the sun up into the sky. Such stories suggest that, even among the southwestern tribes, who had domesticated the bird probably around 700 A.D., its physical peculiarities remained a source of fascination.[5]

This fascination was even more evident among the first European visitors. Few of them failed to comment on the likeness of the turkey's mating display to that of the peacock, or on the changing coloration of the head ornaments among wild birds in heat. In the sixteenth and seventeenth centuries, with the American continents still anomalous for Europeans, observers predictably emphasized the oddity of the flora and fauna to be found there. Animals unknown in the Old World presented themselves as suitable emblems, and European artists, alert to the visual possibilities of hitherto unseen species, quickly adopted the turkey as the New World motif.

The earliest European depictions of the bird appeared in 1555, a generation after Cortés had brought specimens back from Mexico. In that year the French ornithologist Pierre Belon drew a trio of turkeys in his *L'histoire de la nature des oyseaux* (fig. 1.1.) and the Swiss naturalist C. Gesner included one in his *Historia Animalium*. Sixteenth-century maps occasionally employed the bird as an emblem for the new *terra incognita*. Hugh Honour mentions the French cartographer Pierre Desceliers in this regard, although a better known example is provided by the artist Jacques LeMoyne, whose scene of South Carolina appeared in J. T. DeBry's 1590 volume of *America*: the flock of turkeys shown there, although clearly modeled on the domestic variety, is a typical visual locator of the exotic. As late as 1664, on an English map of New Jersey (fig. 1.2.), the bird is still serving this identifying cartographic function.[6]

In the seventeenth century, too, it enters the inventory of motifs employed by decorative artists. Art historian Albert Roe, citing examples from French engraving, Dutch painting, and English silver and gold work, notes that the turkey appears "reasonably frequently in the ornamental vocabulary of the decorative arts" in the late sixteenth and seventeenth centuries. In an article on a silver cup designed by New England craftsman Robert Sanderson, Roe suggests that the embossed turkey decorating its face was by the mid-seventeenth century a common emblem for America among the English silversmiths who were Sanderson's mentors. A typical Eng-

1.1. This drawing by French ornithologist Pierre Belon for his 1555 volume, *L'histoire de la nature des oyseaux*, was one of the first European representations of the American bird. Courtesy of the History of Science Collections, Cornell University Libraries.

lish example of the same period—a cup and stand set from Leeds—displays four such embossed emblems: a peacock representing Europe, a lion for Africa, a camel for Asia, and a turkey, with fan raised, for America. So a century before Franklin's observation, the turkey was already functioning, on both sides of the Atlantic, as a symbol for the New World.[7]

By Franklin's time, however, the bird's iconographic function had begun to dissipate. As the turkey became more widely known and as the New World itself lost much of its exotic allure, an appreciation of the turkey's distinctively national appeal became a minority impression. In their zeal to adopt a "dignified" symbol of the new nation, Congress chose the safe, conventional eagle—an emblem sure

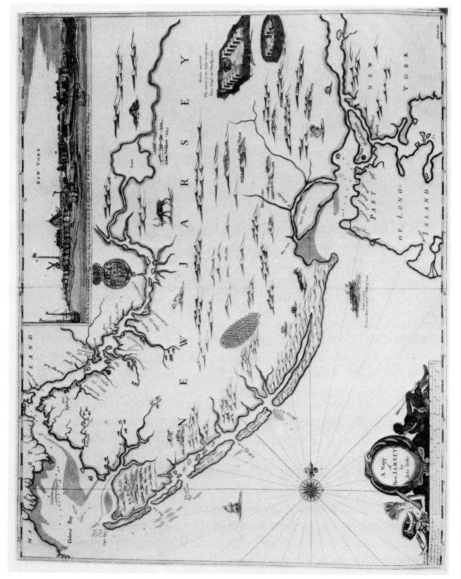

1.2. Turkeys often served in 16th and 17th century art as emblems for the New World. On this 1664 English map a male bird displays its plumage just west of Manhattan island. Courtesy of The Henry Francis du Pont Winterthur Museum.

to impress European heads of state; Franklin's support for the turkey was seen as characteristically quirky. Although many eighteenth century artists depicted the bird, few seemed to share Franklin's understanding of its indigenousness as a significant trait.[8]

A notable exception was provided in 1826 by the naturalist John James Audubon. To Audubon the wild turkey was so appropriate an emblem of America that he chose it as the opening subject for his pioneering work *Birds of America*. Plate I of that celebrated volume, the "Great American Cock," has always been the most famous (and most expensive) of his avian paintings. On a personal level as well, Audubon recognized the symbolic value of the bird; his seal ring bore an engraving of the male over the motto "America My Country."[9]

After about 1800, however, such usages were increasingly rare, as the eagle—that favorite of European royalty—gradually supplanted the turkey as national emblem. Or at least as a public emblem. For while the eagle in the nineteenth century became the dominant "official" symbol of national destiny, the turkey remained a sentimental favorite: a kind of resilient *Volksvogel* whose usefulness as a symbol of America, while denied public expression, thrived in the folk "underground." The principal reason for its continued, if hidden, popularity was that it symbolized two interrelated aspects of the American frontier: wildness and abundance. Throughout the Age of Progress, the bird functioned far more effectively than the eagle could as a representative of natural richness, and of the unspoiled wild which Progress, to get at that richness, was turning into railroads and towns.

An early twentieth-century ornithologist wrote that among early settlers and travelers to this country, "the wild turkey, 'America's noblest game bird,' probably receives more extended notice...than any other North American avian form."[10] This was to be expected, for in the colonial period, the wild turkey itself was vastly "extended" in range and density. If the writers of the sixteenth and seventeenth centuries were amazed at the mere fact of turkeys, those of the eighteenth and nineteenth were most astonished by their numbers. The bird was an ideal symbol for New World abundance. Numerous accounts mentioned flocks of several hundreds, even thousands, of the birds. In 1775 a Kentucky observer mentioned a gathering so dense that "they appeared to be one flock, universally scattered in the woods." A British traveler to Ohio in 1784 called the flocks there "numberless," and estimated one to have contained five thousand birds. An Indiana traveler in 1823 said they roosted in "sickening abundance." In the Texas and Oklahoma area—an especially prolific range—hunters as late as the 1870s spotted flocks of up to three thousand. The pre-Columbian population has been estimated at 10 million birds.[11]

This profusion was tempting to hunters, and they answered it with an extravagance of their own. Nineteenth-century turkey hunting seems to have been imbued with the same myopic gusto and the same disregard for utility that infected buffalo hunting on the Plains. An 1808 traveler to Kentucky suggested that only a very poor sportsman could fail to shoot a dozen birds in a day. In Indiana a reasonable tally was considered fifteen to twenty a day. In Ohio, during an 1823 "circular hunt," four square miles were enclosed and sixty to seventy turkeys were killed—a modest harvest for these popular enclosure hunts. And along the Canadian River in 1878, a hunting party including Union general Philip Sheridan succeeded in taking 175 birds in the span of only a few hours' shooting.[12]

William Strong kept a journal of the Canadian River hunt. His account of the party's "magnificent bag" reveals contemporary hunting passions to have been less informed by a desire to put meat on the table than a mania for counting coups. He describes a bizarre slaughter in which roosting turkeys are picked off one by one from branches over the shooters' heads.

> Who ever heard of anything like it! What a story to tell one's children,—and how amazed one's sporting friends at home would be, at the recital of such unequaled success! It seemed, for a moment, quite cruel and unsportsman-like, to shoot the poor birds from the lower limbs of small growth cottonwoods—the shooter standing right under them. . . . it occurred to me it would be better to walk back twenty-five or thirty yards, and give the birds a chance; and the propriety of shooting them on the wing, suggested itself; . . . I then remembered, that it was regarded, among honorable sportsmen, as perfectly legitimate to shoot turkeys while sitting at night; and inasmuch as I had only seventy-five, or at most, a hundred shells, and wanted a bird for every shot, couldn't afford to take chances.[13]

Strong is notably incurious about what he can *do* with seventy-five dead turkeys, and a similar lack of reflectiveness infuses many contemporary hunting accounts. Because of a widespread shooting-gallery mentality among sportsmen, many turkeys never made it to the table. Vast numbers spoiled where they fell. More rotted in market hunters' wagons, and others starved in capturing pens. Even those birds that were eaten were often underutilized. Frequently only the breast was consumed; in many parts of the country, it was used—dried or made into a flour—as a substitute for bread. In an era of material abundance, cavalier waste was the norm. By the end of the century Franklin's true native original, to supply the wants of a people of plenty, was being threatened with extinction.[14]

This cannot be blamed entirely on hunters. Conservationists agree that loss of habitat, rather than wanton "harvesting," is the most serious threat to animal populations, and this was true in the case of the turkey. The axe and the plow, not the gun, were the chief causes of its decline, although that decline was certainly abetted by indiscriminate sport shooting. Whatever the combination of causes, by the early years of this century, the decline was almost complete. Originally abundant from Maine to Arizona, the turkey was gone from Connecticut by 1872, Indiana by 1900, and Nebraska by 1915. In 1920 the species had been obliterated from half of the thirty-six states in which it had once flourished. Since then, live trapping and transplanting projects undertaken by state game agencies have dramatically reversed the downward trend, and today the wild bird has been restored in most of its original range. It is also available for harvesting in ten nonindigenous states, including Hawaii. The current wild population is approximately 2 million—a meager figure compared to colonial populations, but still impressive restoration.[15]

Not surprisingly, sportsmen are among the most vocal enthusiasts of continued restoration. In a 1958 article, Pennsylvanian John Stuart Martin called the return of the wild turkey to his state "the best conservation news since the salvation of the beaver." Praising the renewed availability of the bird for hunters, he said, "To me the wild turkey symbolizes our primal wilderness as the white settlers first found it. Indigenous only to this continent, these gobblers were the feathered emperors not only of the South's dismal swamps but also of the northeastern forests." The adulatory strain found here is typical in hunters' descriptions of the bird, and the attribution of nobility is a frequent element of that strain. Wright calls the turkey "America's noblest game bird." Vermont storyteller Archibald Rutledge refers to "the royal bird," the "king of the pineland wilderness." A recent magazine report on the return of Merriam's turkeys to the Southwest calls the turkey "king of the game birds."[16]

Such flattery, it must be remembered, is reserved for the wild turkey only, never its domesticated cousin. In fact the barnyard variety frequently appears as a foil. *Texas Monthly* contrasts the wild bird with the "dim-witted, lumbering loser" we eat on Thanksgiving Day. North Carolina hunter Earl Groves says the wild turkey is "a remarkable bird, as different from the domestic turkey as a race horse is from a donkey." In all encomiums on the turkey, domesticity is seen as a blemish.[17] The reason generally given is that the barnyard bird is stupid and slow, while the wild bird is immensely intelligent—that is, woods-smart or wary. Wariness, at least towards humans, is an acquired trait in turkeys. The ease with which the birds were felled in the early roost shoots attests to their primitive ignorance in this matter; because turkeys were inattentive to sound, some early travelers considered even the wild variety stupid. But today's birds have learned to fear humans, and in the words of one authority, "None of our nation's animals is more wary than the 'educated' wild turkey."[18]

The bird's intelligence is the substance of many legends. The Yankee vernacular writer Archibald Rutledge provides an early twentieth century example. In the tale "Joel's Christmas Turkey" he calls his hero Joel, a modern Leatherstocking, "the best woodsman in his county."

> But for all his craft, there was a wild turkey living in the tupelo swamp behind his cabin that made Joel stretch himself, and, so far, stretch himself in vain. It seemed to the hunter that he had used every whit of his strength, woodcraft, patience, and tireless energy of pursuit in the attempt to win this royal prize; . . . This turkey could not speak human speech as can some of the creatures about which our fanciful naturalists write. He could not put his finger to his nose and scoff at Joel, saying, "O sad brother, I am the Wise One. Booloo is my friend. I shall meet him at the Council Tree at midnight, and you will never find us any more." He was just a plain turkey; but when that has been said all has been said that

need be mentioned; for if a plain wild turkey is not the most
intelligent bird afoot or awing, then the dodo isn't dead.[19]

Although this was written in 1921, its implicit attitude of respect for
the wild is still widespread today. J.C. Lewis, to illustrate the extraordinary vision which is a chief component of the bird's wariness,
says that the oldtimers claimed "a turkey could detect the human eye
looking through a knothole from inside a hollow tree." Florida
hunter Tom Gaskins bestows on "one of the smartest gobblers I ever
knew of" the honorific title The Phantom. Sports writer Jim Carmichael admits, "Every turkey hunter has a hard luck tale to tell. My
personal catalogue would make *Websters Unabridged Dictionary*
look like a dime novel."[20]

Most attempts to debunk this notion of the ever-vigilant turkey
focus on one of three behavioral peculiarities. The first—the bird's
intermittent inattention to sound—I have already mentioned. It was
this inattention that made it possible for nineteenth-century roost
shooters to slaughter dozens of birds at a sitting, for Appalachian
marksmen such as World War I's Alvin York to pick off long
columns of the birds by working up the line from the rear, and for
"turkey shoot" to enter the language in the 1840s as an approximate
equivalent of "shooting fish in a barrel."[21]

The second peculiarity is the bird's supposed habit of opening its
mouth to catch rain and continuing to drink until it drowns. I have
heard this canard leveled against domestic turkeys on several occa-
sions. A friend raised in the 1950s on an upstate New York farm tells
me it was widely believed there at that time. In Ohio folklore, a turkey stretching its neck is a portent of rain. It has even been suggested
that mass drownings are responsible for the population drops common in turkey flocks after rainy springs. Although none of this has a
basis in biological fact, the legend persists. When I asked the owners
of a Massachusetts turkey farm about the drowning turkey problem,
they laughed in exasperation, recognizing a barnyard fiction that
would not die.[22]

The third peculiarity is the bird's inability to reason its way out of
an obviously "open" pen. This proof of imbecility was remarked
upon as early as 1815 by an Ohio traveler cited in Wright. "Wild turkeys are very plenty," he reported. "I have often set a square pen
made of rails, then scattered a little corn about it and into it, and

caught eight or ten fine ones at a time. The pen being covered at the top the turkeys could not fly out, and they never thought of ducking their heads to get out by the same passage they came in."[23]

This method of pen capture was common in the nineteenth century. It depends for its efficacy on the fact that birds are loath to look down once they have been enclosed. Domestic poultryman G.T. Klein laments that poults sometimes actually starve because they "walk over feed with their head in the air," unwilling or unable to look down. The reason for this reluctance is unclear, but it coincides with other indications of the animal's bewilderment about space and particularly about barriers. Lewis and others note that turkeys balk at flying over wire fences. And hunter Larry Dablemont claims, "I've seen them cornered against a fence they could easily fly over, frantically trying to go through it just because they could squeeze their heads through an opening."[24]

Whatever oddities of spatial perception may be involved in this barrier-specific dementia, and whatever aural inadequacies may account for the turkey's occasional insensitivity to gunfire, hunters agree that these marks of stupidity do not make the bird any less elusive a quarry. Even Dablemont, whose article "Spring Gobblers Are Dumb" purports to debunk the myth of turkey wisdom, ends in a rueful quibble: "Intelligent? Not the wild turkey. He stays alive because he is a walking example of fear and caution."[25]

Because wild turkeys are wary prey, and because their now diminished numbers make them far more difficult to locate than they were a century ago, modern turkey hunters seem to consider themselves a select breed; their lore resembles not so much a collection of yarns as it does the hermetic knowledge of a cult. In a foreword to Earl Grove's guide, H. Lea Lawrence coyly applauds the hunters of "this most elusive and intelligent of American game birds." "Turkey hunting has been variously defined as an addiction, an affliction, an art closely paralleling black magic or voodoo, an excuse for seclusion, and plain damn foolishness. Probably all of these are correct to some degree." In his collection of tips to turkey hunters, Tom Gaskins is even more blatant about the arcane aspects of his avocation. Addressing the reader as "Comrade of the Cult," he scoffs at the ignorance of a novice who mistakes a turkey buzzard for a turkey, and confides to his fellow "real turkey hunters" that wild turkeys have long been "the ultimate, the acme, the very top in my hunting world dreams." John Randolph echoes this confidence with a blunt boast in *Field and Stream*: turkey hunting, he writes, is "not the only game in town—just the best."[26]

The clannishness of the sport is especially evident in commentaries on turkey calls. Hunters hold various and vociferous opinions on the propriety of individual calls (a "cack-cack-cack" sound will never do when the situation calls for a "putt") and also on which type of "instrument" best simulates the bird's vocalizations. Some hunters still swear by the old Indian standby, a hollowed-out turkey wing bone; some call only with the unaided mouth; and others use one or more of the various diaphragm, horn, and box calls available commercially to cult members. Gaskins has run a cottage industry for years manufacturing a box call (fig. 1.3.), and he swears by it with as much fervor as any bass fisherman ever swore by a "popper."

But the ability to call the birds to your blind is only one aspect of the arcana. That arcana also includes general woods lore; the successful turkey hunter is as comfortable in the wild as the bird he means to bring home. He should also be as "intelligent" as his prey; as a Nebraska turkey expert advises newcomers to the sport, "You've got to do some thinking out there in the woods."[27]

Of course, all hunting fraternities emphasize the importance of knowing the prey and the terrain, but among turkey hunters this knowledge takes precedence over other attributes. Because the turkey is not dangerous game, the heroic qualities of courage, strength, and endurance are deemphasized in hunting narratives, and savvy comes to the fore: the turkey shoot becomes in effect a "thinking man's game." Ideally the hunt is a learning experience in which the secrets of the woodland art are passed on not only from elders to novices but to all hunters from the wilderness itself. As a symbol of a fading natural abundance and of the wildness that supported it, the Great American Cock comes to represent a lost possibility, a natural, exotic virginity that habitat encroachment, and the dictates of a market culture, have long since relegated to myth. That myth is recaptured in turkey season, when mechanics or insurance salesmen, miraculously transformed into frontiersmen, can be joined by "intelligence" and blood to the "feathered emperor" of a fading realm.

The activities of the turkey clan thus display elements not only of play-acting, but of a national, and nationalizing, ritual. In tracking the elusive bird, sportsmen today reinvent the "primal wilderness as

1.3. In an amusing gloss on the bird's notorious intelligence, this contemporary postcard shows a wild turkey stealing a hunter's box call. The call's maker, Tom Gaskins of Palmdale, Florida, explains, "John Murray dreamed it up and Russ Smiley painted it, because Ed English told me a gobbler came in his camp and stole his turkey call. There are other such rumors."

the white settler first found it." It is no wonder that they are in the forefront of efforts to preserve the wild breed; hunting it today has become a link to an untamed antediluvian reality which is, in the words of a current Wild Turkey bourbon ad, "part of our national heritage." In Ken Davies's luxurious paintings for the Kentucky distillers of that bourbon, (fig. 1.4.) we see the bird as it was originally envisioned—a majestic russet giant in command of untracked fields. And we begin to understand the hunt as a game that brings psychic survival, a ritual that restores a lost Eden. Nebraska hunter Greg Kuzma asks himself the question "Why do I hunt?" and discovers both envy and awe. It is, he says, because "I am jealous of the sky, the wind...of creatures that work their way in it, are designed for it...of that immense and lovely freedom."[28] If the turkey no longer symbolizes the United States that is, it does continue to suggest, from Kentucky to the Great Plains, the idea of an America that was.

Part Of Our National Heritage

In 1776, Benjamin Franklin proposed that the Wild Turkey be adopted as the symbol of our country. He pointed out that this majestic bird is native only to the American Continent.

It seems only fitting that the Wild Turkey later became the symbol of our country's greatest native whiskey.

WILD TURKEY®/ 101 PROOF / 8 YEARS OLD

AUSTIN NICHOLS DISTILLING CO. LAWRENCEBURG, KENTUCKY © 1982

1.4. The "feathered emperor" of the American virgin land appears with appropriate bearing in this 1982 advertisement for Wild Turkey bourbon. The copy perpetuates the charming myth that Benjamin Franklin endorsed the bird as a national symbol. Wild Turkey by Ken Davies, courtesy of Austin, Nichols & Co., Inc.

Yellville, Arkansas, home of the annual National Turkey Calling Contest, is also the site of an annual turkey "drop" designed to call attention to the plight of the wild bird and to generate support for its protection. In a bizarre variation on the turkey shoots which were so popular in nineteenth-century America, captive wild birds are released from an airplane over the town square, to become the property of anyone who can catch them. As Jessie Adams, the Yellville town secretary, told me, "The hopes were that some of the turkeys released would escape and return to the wild and help repopulate the area for hunting." The drop has generated some unwelcome publicity among people unfamiliar with Ozark ways—such as the National Public Radio broadcast which made much of an unforeseen incident that enlivened the 1982 event. In that year, as hundreds of spectators awaited the unfolding of magnificent wings, a practical joker in the plane released not wild turkeys, or even their farm-bred cousins, but a "flock" of frozen birds, liberated from a nearby market.[29]

The droll incident suggests something significant about the current status of the bird. A hundred years ago, the word "turkey" evoked images of crisp autumn dawns, of fugitive forest kings shrouded in maple and fir. To most Americans today, it evokes pictures of Thanksgiving tables, with the bird a mute centerpiece that only a day before had been gracing the grocer's deep freeze. Few Americans now alive have ever seen a turkey in the wild; nearly everyone has cracked a turkey wishbone. The symbolic value of the bird as an image of feral independence has long since given way to a practical value within the American food economy. This shift is of course most evident in late November, when the former image of natural abundance, now domesticated, cooked, and stuffed, serves to remind us of the efficiency of our food delivery system.

This efficiency is a fairly recent development, but then so is the American Thanksgiving. Contrary to popular belief, Thanksgiving did not become a national tradition under the Massachusetts Pilgrims; nor was turkey the *pièce de résistance* at the famous 1621 meal (turkeys were served, but far more sustenance was provided by several deer contributed by the Indians). Until the late nineteenth century, Thanksgiving days were celebrated only intermittently in the United States, in response to presidential proclamations. Turkeys were popular fare on these days, but they were also popular on

Christmas and other feast days. Schorger conservatively estimates, "It is doubtful that a turkey became a common adjunct to a Thanksgiving dinner until about 1800."[30]

The bird's identification exclusively with that holiday did not come about until after 1863, when the redoubtable Sarah Josepha Hale, after years of editorial lobbying, succeeded in convincing President Lincoln to proclaim Thanksgiving an annual feast. In a study of American holidays, Maymie Krythe lists an 1863 Thanksgiving Day menu which already includes the traditional items of roast turkey, cranberry sauce, and pumpkin pie. She also cites an English traveler's comment that Thanksgiving Day in the 1870s was especially "rough" on the birds, since on that day prisoners, the destitute, and the ill were all fed turkey at public expense.[31]

The idea of a "Turkey Day," however, seems to have taken root slowly. In searching for Thanksgiving and turkey memorabilia appearing before World War II, Bella Landauer discovered only an 1875 illustration of a family dinner, an 1898 label advertising "Yankee Bird" tobacco, and four Thanksgiving greeting cards, none earlier than 1909. She called this, justly, "a meager showing for one of our great national holidays."[32] By midcentury that showing had greatly improved, thanks less to restoration of the wild bird (which only began to be successful in the 1950s) than to changes in the poultry farming industry.

Turkey growers in the 1940s had begun to perfect hybrid strains, such as the Bronze and the Beltsville White, that were smaller and more tender than the wild varieties. At the same time they adopted a more aggressive marketing policy that lowered the price of the birds and established them in the public mind as the "traditional" Thanksgiving main course. By midcentury illustrations of the holiday began to include an obligatory stuffed bird. Wilfred Jones's frontispiece to the 1946 story collection *The Harvest Feast* is an early example. It depicts the now-familiar First Thanksgiving scene with the stuffed turkey as a prominent centerpiece; none of the deer is in sight. Norman Rockwell's famous "Freedom from Want" poster reprised this traditional scene in a modern setting, as have dozens of November advertisements ever since. By the mid-1950s, the turkey and Thanksgiving had become fused in popular iconography; as the poultry industry expanded, so too did the use of the bird as a symbol of American abundance.[33]

Of course that abundance was now domesticated and rational-ized. Marketing has done more, in a shorter amount of time, to put turkey on the American table than roost shooting and circular hunts ever did. Between 1950 and 1980, according to the Department of Agriculture, U.S. per capita consumption of domestic birds rose over 250 percent. The meat-packing giant Swift Premium now maintains a toll-free Butterball Turkey Talk-Line to handle customer inquiries in the holiday season. A turkey industry newsletter, which describes the noble bird as "a remarkable meat-producing 'machine,' " com-plains that "the problem with . . . profitability is an oversupply of frozen hens in the third quarter." Hardly a problem that would have bothered the nineteenth century roost shooter.[34]

The conjunction I am suggesting between marketing aims and popular imagery is not in itself surprising: recently, products as di-verse as cigarettes (Marlboro), soft drinks (Coke and Pepsi), auto-mobiles (all of the major U.S. manufacturers), pantyhose (Underalls), and telephone service (Bell) have been hawked by ap-peals to sentimental patriotism. What is strange is that, in the very period in which the turkey is becoming renationalized, it is also coming to be seen as an emblem of ignominy and failure. At just the time when a turkey on every table is becoming a social ideal, "tur-key" is becoming a synonym for "loser" or "fool." How can we rec-oncile these apparently contradictory developments?

The current low estimate of the turkey is ubiquitous in popular culture. Novelty shops feature coffee mugs and buttons depicting a doddering fantail and the legend "It's hard to soar with eagles when you work with turkeys." A humorously self-deprecating greeting card wishes the recipient Happy Thanksgiving "on behalf of all the great turkeys of the world." A manufacturer of bulletin boards mim-ics a prohibitive traffic sign by announcing "No Turkeys Allowed" (fig. 1.5.). Country singer Lacy J. Dalton, confronted by an obstrep-erous barfly, spurns him with the line, "I'll be damned if I'll go home with a wild turkey like you."[35]

Used in personal derision, the word refers, according to a stan-dard dictionary of slang, to "an ineffective, incompetent, objection-able, or disliked person." The earliest example of this usage is 1951, although "square" as an equivalent to turkey is found six years be-fore. The same dictionary also gives "any worthless, useless, unsuit-

1.5. This contemporary, anonymous bulletin board sign presents the turkey in its modern guise of loser or fool. Photograph courtesy of Daniel Martinez.

able thing," and cites as the first example of this usage a passage from James Cain's *Mildred Pierce* (1941), where a beach, of all things, is so described. A third definition is theatrical. Beginning around 1944, a turkey is "an inferior entertainment. . .a financial failure, a flop."[36]

The theatrical usage, probably the oldest, is still common, and it has been extended in recent years to failures in all performance media. The *National Lampoon* staff styled its 1969 parody of Tolkien, *Bored of the Rings*, "a gobbler," and its 1975 "greatest hits" album *Gold Turkey*. Harry and Michael Medved retained the usage in 1980, calling their compendium of dreadful Hollywood productions *Golden Turkey Awards*.[37]

The association of the turkey with theatrical failure, and by extension with failure in general, may be seen on one level as a mere linguistic accident. Wilfred Granville, in his dictionary of theatrical terms, defines a "turkey show" as "one played to country audiences; in reference to turkeys (rustics)." Here the audience itself is the turkey, although the sense of denigration is slight. Another dictionary of theater terms has "turkey" as "a show which fails deservedly," and suggests that it was originally applied to actors (called "turkey actors") "who got up weak Thanksgiving productions which the indulgent public patronized as an annual tradition." This provocative thought, linking failure and Thanksgiving, hints that all those "Turkey Day" pageants designed to edify our youth may have had the opposite effect, by establishing a semantic connection between the holiday and wasted effort.[38]

But the linguistic explanation is unsatisfying: it defines the etiology of the usage without accounting for its potency today. For an explanation of that potency, let us go to the New York farmer's wife who in the 1930s took up a second career and became America's most famous primitivist painter. In the 1940s Grandma Moses did a piece called "Catching the Thanksgiving Turkey" which, because of its poignant recollection of a fading America and because of the artist's own gloss, provides an unscholarly but telling answer to why the turkey is considered a loser.

The scene is a rustic panorama, with the bulk of the canvas taken up by a vista of low rolling mountains. The ostensible subject of the painting—a Tom about to be beheaded—is confined to the lower left foreground, where it is being set upon by a farmhand while another turkey incongruously puffs himself up nearby. Moses's comments on the tableau only hint at the dramatic contrast between the barnyard genre scene and the expansive wilderness beyond; in doing so, however, they provide an apt summation of the turkey's fate in modern times: "Why do we think we must have turkey for Thanksgiving? Just because our forefathers did; they had it because turkeys were plentiful and they did not have other kinds of meat. Now we have abundance of other kinds of luxuries. Poor turkey. He has but one life to give to his country."[39]

Her history is of course wrong. Even in the richest days of wild turkey hegemony, there was no shortage of "other kinds of meat" for early hunters. But her sentimental main point is on target. It is that the turkey, our great national bird, whom she wryly compares to Nathan Hale, has become expendable—a means to an end. While the mountains brood beyond them, the men and women in the barnyard are intent only on "harvesting" an animal that was once such a part of those mountains. Thus reduced to mere usefulness, the bird becomes an object of pity. The elusive Phantoms and feathered emperors were kings of a wild frontier. Old Tom is merely a joke—a hybridized, unnaturally fattened buffoon whose destiny is to be stuffed with chestnuts and devoured.

And this devolution of his symbolic role has come about, ironically, precisely because he was once an appropriate image of American wildness, a fitting symbol of New World freedom and abundance. Americans learned to eat turkey long before "frozen hens in the third quarter" were imagined; but when the consumption of turkey meat became part of a vast, rationalized economic process, the bird lost—or rather was deprived of—the aura of expansiveness and abundance that had made it useful as an image in the first place. In a modern market culture, predictability is a key to success; the unpredictable wild turkey would make a poor symbol of modern, reliable abundance. The "Butterball" therefore supplants it, and the wild bird retains its nationalistic status only in the Wild Turkey ads.

In an old Bell Telephone cartoon ad, the contrast between the wild and the domestic turkey is implied with humorous acumen. A fattened Tom, seeing a farmer sharpening an axe, avails himself of the Yellow Pages to locate a reducing salon. In the final panel of the cartoon, as trim as a wild bird, he walks smugly past a window where the carcass of another turkey is cooling. The lesson—that well fed means soon dead—should be a telling one for a people who nearly exterminated its greatest game bird only to replace it in popular affection with one representing domesticity and doom. Perhaps what the history of the turkey as symbol really suggests is a growing resentment, on the part of a nation of consumers, at its own success.[40]

Critics of the American establishment in the 1960s used to deplore the "packaging of marginality." They were referring to the business community's expertise in translating potentially subversive social artifacts (rock music, blue denim) into homogenized versions of their former selves, and then selling them back to their creators (in this case, the country's youth) at inflated prices. The point can also be made about the turkey. The fugitive forest king, cornered by consumer specialists, becomes the symbol of the one true American holiday, but only in a form that will allow it to reach the widest and most predictable market. To continue to serve as an emblem for American culture, the turkey must become subject to mass production, processing, and quality control.

Bil-Mar Foods, a Michigan meat supplier, carries the transformation of the symbol to a logical conclusion in a clever marketing device. The company's "Mr. Turkey" logo (fig. 1.6.) is a sassy-looking young gobbler with a top hat, tuxedo, and cane. He advertises not wild turkey meat, or even domestic turkey parts, but a line of processed foods: turkey hamburger, turkey sausage, turkey ham. Thus, to meet the needs of an increasingly urban and sedentary population, the poultry industry succeeds both in taking the bird out of the country and in taking the country out of the bird.

The producers of Wild Turkey bourbon have decidedly kept the country in the bird, but with a significant twist. The Austin, Nichols Company, which distills and markets the Kentucky elixir, began as a backwoods venture put together by a group of turkey hunters; hence the brand name. But in 1972, perhaps with an eye on the Bicentennial, the company hired the New York firm of Nadler & Larimer to handle its advertising, and, thanks to an inspired campaign utilizing Davies's paintings and Franklin's supposed endorsement, Wild Turkey sales have quintupled in the past decade. As in other campaigns that trade on nationalist nostalgia, the evocation of a nearly lost "heritage" proves lucrative as well as enchanting.[41]

1.6. A Midwest meat packer carries the domestication of the turkey to an extreme and clever conclusion with its nattily dressed, self-assured "Mr. Turkey." This symbol is the Registered Trade Mark of Bil-Mar Foods, Inc., of Zeeland, Michigan.

Thus, in an oddly bifurcated evolution, the turkey is transformed not only into an object of ridicule but also into a symbol of that success against which the ridicule is secretly directed. The final irony is that, as an image rivaling the stuffed centerpiece, the wild turkey is being kept alive in the public eye by an Appalachian distillery which, with its highly professional marketing and enviable return on investment, is itself a willing victim of Progress.

NOTES

1. The letter to Mrs. Sarah Bache, dated January 26, 1784, appears in Franklin's *Works*, vol. 10, ed. Jared Sparks (Boston: Tappan, Whittemore and Mason, 1840), 58–65.

2. For the rattlesnake story, see John Bigelow, ed., *The Life of Benjamin Franklin*, vol. 1 (Philadelphia: Lippincott, 1905), 364–65. The Great Seal committee, composed of Franklin, Jefferson, and John Adams, was appointed on July 4 and brought in its report on August 20; see the *Journals of the Continental Congress* (Washington, D.C.: U.S. Government Printing Office, 1904–37).

3. European misidentifications of the bird are discussed in A.W. Schorger, *The Wild Turkey: Its History and Domestication* (Norman: Univ. of Oklahoma Press, 1966), 3–4. This is the most exhaustive general study of the bird.

4. Ibid., 42–89; and Lovett Williams, *The Book of the Wild Turkey* (Tulsa, Okla: Winchester Press, 1981).

5. Schorger, 354–64; Hamilton A. Tyler, *Pueblo Birds and Myths* (Norman: Univ. of Oklahoma Press, 1979), 85–106; James Mooney, *Cherokee Animal Tales*, ed. George F. Scheer (New York: Holiday House, 1968), 43–46.

6. For early views of the turkey see Schorger, 490 ff.; Hugh Honour, *The New Golden Land: European Images of America from the Discoveries to the Present Time* (New York: Pantheon, 1975), 39. Albert Roe, "Robert Sanderson's Silver Caudle Cup in the Winterthur Collection: The Turkey Motif in Seventeenth Century Design," *American Art Journal* 9 (May 1977): 61–77, mentions the New Jersey map.

7. Roe, 61–77.

8. Schorger, 490–501, discusses the turkey in art.

9. Alice Ford, *John James Audubon* (Norman: Univ. of Oklahoma Press, 1964), 183–84.

10. Albert Hazen Wright, "Early Records of the Wild Turkey," *The Auk* 31 (July 1914): 334.

11. See Schorger, 50–61, for population and density figures.

12. Ibid.

13. William Strong, *Canadian River Hunt*, ed. Fred. P. Schonwald (Norman: Univ. of Oklahoma Press, 1960), 21.

14. Schorger, 367, 403–4.

15. Figures from "Preserving a Heritage for America," promotional brochure of the National Wild Turkey Federation, Edgefield, South Carolina. I am indebted to James Kennamar, director of research for the federation, for sending me this information.

16. John Stuart Martin, "The Wild Turkey Comes Back," *Readers Digest* (Dec. 1958): 148–50; Wright, 334; Archibald Rutledge, "Joel's Christmas Turkey" in *Old Plantation Days* (New York: Frederick Stokes, 1921), 199–200; "Gobble, Gobble, Gobble" in *Texas Monthly* (April 1983): 110.

17. *Texas Monthly*, ibid.; Earl Groves, *Talking Tomfoolery* (n.p., 1977).

18. Schorger, 134–36, in discussing the Duke of Würrtemberg's opinion that the turkey, oblivious of the sound of river steamers, was a "stupid, unwary bird."

19. Rutledge, 199–200.

20. Tom Gaskins, "Tom Tells Tall Turkey Tales," privately printed

pamphlet (Palmdale, Florida, 1965), 26; Jim Carmichael, "Hunting Land Game with a Shotgun," in *The Experts' Book of the Shooting Sports*, ed. David Petzal (New York: Simon & Schuster, 1972), 240; James C. Lewis, *The World of the Wild Turkey* (New York: Harper & Row, 1973), 109.

21. Mitford Mathews, editor of *A Dictionary of Americanisms on Historical Principles* (Chicago: Univ. of Chicago Press, 1951), locates "turkey shoot" in 1845. Bella Landauer discusses the popular nineteenth-century pastime and York's marksmanship in "Yankee Bird," *New York Historical Society Quarterly Bulletin* 28, no. 4 (Oct. 1944).

22. My New York informant is Clint Coles, now of Kerrville, Texas. The Ohio belief is found in Wayland Hand, Anna Casetta, and Sondra Thiederman, eds., *Popular Beliefs and Superstitions: A Compendium of American Folklore* (Boston: G.K. Hall, 1981). The drowning myth, discredited by the owners of Bennett's Turkey Farm in Wilbraham, Massachusetts, is also debunked in Williams, 73.

23. Wright, "Early Records," *The Auk* 31 (Oct. 1914): 472.

24. G.T. Klein, *Starting Right with Turkeys* (Charlotte, Vt.: Garden Way Publishing Co., 1972), 5. The wire fence phobia is mentioned in Lewis and in Gary Oberbillig, "Wild Turkeys," *Small Farmer's Journal* 9, no. 1 (Winter 1984). Larry Dablemont, "Spring Gobblers Are Dumb," *Outdoor Life* 172 (Feb. 1983): 67.

25. Dablemont, 67.

26. Groves, vii; Gaskins, 2; John Randolph, "Seven Steps to Trophy Gobblers," *Field & Stream* 89 (Feb. 1985), 113.

27. From a cassette tape, "Hunting Nebraska's Wild Turkey," by Dick Turpin and Carl Wolfe of the Nebraska Game and Parks Commission.

28. Davies's paintings appear periodically in Wild Turkey magazine ads, as for example in *Texas Monthly* (April 1983), 59. Greg Kuzma's reflection "Why Do I Hunt?" is in *Nebraskaland* (Oct. 1982): 32–35.

29. Adams's comment was in a letter to me, May 12, 1983. The NPR show was a segment of "All Things Considered" aired in the fall of 1982.

30. Schorger, 369.

31. Maymie Krythe, *All About American Holidays* (New York: Harper & Brothers, 1962); the English traveler was George Augustus Sala, whose memoir of an 1879 journey, *America Revisited*, appeared in 1880.

32. Landauer, 129.

33. Wilhelmina Harper, ed., *The Harvest Feast* (1938; rpt., New York: Dutton, 1946).

34. *Nicholas Turkey News* 26, no. 1 (Jan. 1983) and nos. 9 and 10 (Sept.–Oct. 1983).

35. Dalton performs the Moffatt-Sebert song "Wild Turkey" on her 1981 Columbia album *Takin' It Easy*.

36. Harold Wentworth and Stuart Flexner, *Dictionary of American Slang* (New York: Thomas Crowell, 1975).

37. Henry Beard and Douglas Kenney, *Bored of the Rings* (New York: New American Library, 1969); *Gold Turkey* (Epic/CBS, 1975); the Medved book was published by Putnam in 1980.

38. Wilfred Granville, *The Theater Dictionary* (New York: Philosophical Library, 1952); Walter Bowman and Robert Ball, *Theatre Language* (New York: Theatre Arts Books, 1961).

39. Moses is quoted in Otto Kallir, ed., *Grandma Moses: American Primitive* (Garden City: Doubleday, 1947). I have regularized her idiosyncratic spelling and punctuation.

40. The Yellow Pages ad, drawn by J.B. Price, appeared in the *Saturday Evening Post* on November 26, 1960.

41. I am indebted to Nadler & Larimer's senior vice-president Bruce Bromley for background on the Wild Turkey campaign.

The Rattlesnake

DAVID SCOFIELD WILSON

A recent (1982) cartoon by Gary Larson for *The Far Side* shows three rattlesnakes, a baby and two adults, each poised in a classic coil with its head raised and its rattler aloft. One sour parent is saying to the other, relatively deadpan adult, "This is your side of the family, you realize." The object of their concern is the baby between them, its rattle raised but still, and its head "rattling" away foolishly. This mistake embarrasses them and amuses us who share with Larson, and with the parents, a number of understandings about how rattlesnakes work, how they are supposed to act, and what they signify.[1]

The baby's error is a double one in that it not only gets its movements wrong—all babies do that—but it gets them categorically muddled. To vibrate the wrong end means the rattle does not sound, and sounding lies at the heart of the tales told about this reptile, just as it lies at the root of both its common and scientific names. Furthermore, the sounding is so widely understood to function as a warning, and the warning beneficently to balance the danger the snake presents, that by getting its two ends muddled the rattler reminds us that the symmetry we have come to count on in creation may be no more than an artifact of our apprehension, a fiction, a convention.[2]

Human beings cannot afford, any more than baby rattlesnakes, to get their responses wrong, especially not categorically muddled, for at that level meaningfulness and meaninglessness hang in the balance. Newcomers to North America found it advisable to get the rattler right, and that turned out to be a double task. The rattler was both a new snake and a new sort of snake which suggested that it might signify something serious about the newness of the New World. Precisely what, remained problematic. Did it show that the design of the New World was benign? Was the creature essentially a mistake to be erased? In short, the new Americans found themselves obliged to figure out both what to make of the rattlesnake literally (a trophy, a meal, a stuffed specimen of nature, a hatband or handbag) and figuratively (a sign of the wild, a variety of vermin, an emblem of Providence, an omen of evil). Some of this they worked out in terms of tales told in the Old World, of course, but some they spun anew in response to the context of a new land and its evolving society. And the work goes on still in snake hunts and zoos and academic researches. To pursue the workings of mind and emotion in Americans' struggle to come to terms with real and symbolic rattlesnakes is to gain access to the "logic" and "aesthetic" lying deep within the several subsets of Americans who know and care about the snake: ranchers, naturalists, herpetologists, and others. We will find as well that the rattlesnake provides a natural nexus for the convergence of separate systems of meaning: science, sentiment, patriotism, folklore, literature, and art.

Rattlesnakes are found in the Americas only. They belong to the family of serpents now called *Crotalidae,* or pit vipers, which includes copperheads and water moccasins and the famous fer-de-lance and bushmaster, all venomous but without rattles, as well as two genera of rattlesnake, *Crotalus* and *Sistrurus.* Seventy species are found in North America and Mexico, but only a handful carry common names that nonspecialists would recognize ("timber rattlesnake," "diamondback," "sidewinder," etc.), and in most nontechnical literature and speech the generic term, "rattlesnake," serves for any species of rattler. The very earliest reports of rattlesnakes were by explorers of Central and South America who applied the term *cascabel* or *cascavel,* meaning "a small bell," to the tail and by synecdoche to the whole snake. The earliest English explorers adopted "rattle" for the sound and for the appendage, "rattlesnake" for the creature. "Rattler" appears later. Early writers in scientific Latin called the rattle *tintinabuli* and *crepitaculum,* but the first Latin name for the snake, *caudisona,* brings the sound and the tail together as a name for the creature. The root of *crotalus* means "little rattle" in Latin. The roots of *sistrurus* mean "rattle" and "tail." Vernacular denominations equally recognize the definitive significance of the sounding tail for the reptile's identity: "sizzle-tail," "buzz-tail," "chatter viper," and "rattletail snake," as well as the jocular "snattlerake."[3]

All species of rattlesnakes have rattles at all ages, even baby snakes, despite persistent beliefs to the contrary. How often they sound, what they sound like, and what the sounding means are matters of great interest and dispute. Traditional lore, tall tales, and science part on these matters, but all take for granted the central significance of this New World snake's caudal apparatus and its unique sound.

If the tail distinguishes the rattlesnake from other serpents, its venom and fangs affiliate it with other dangerous vipers and pit vipers. Much of the lore and literature and commercial exploitation of people's interest in rattlesnakes turns on its hypodermic-like fangs, its venom, what to do about it if bitten, and what happens to one who is. It's no laughing matter, but an occasion for cautionary tales, warnings, first-aid information, and medical advice. The bite happens so fast that there is nothing to tell, no narrative content really: "a blur hit the back of my hand," is all young Scott Craft knew. People commonly report surprise, shock, sharp pain. Not until high-speed photography broke the strike and bite into stages was it possible to follow the process from lunge to contact to stab of fangs to biting action and withdrawal. Stories of rattlesnake bite almost inevitably draw a listener or reader into an ambience of horror— pain, terrible treatments, lingering effects, swollen limbs, amputations, even death. Some recognition of this affective quality of the bite is incorporated into the specific name of the timber rattlesnake and canebreak rattlesnake, *Crotalus horridus horridus* and *C. horridus atricaudatus.*[4]

If the strike and the sound have been hard to capture, the look of the rattler has not. Pictorial representations of the reptiles have since the earliest times not only accompanied the verbal reports but have in their own right stood as nature reports of great worth. The details of rattles and fangs, of the small teeth, the hemipenis, forked tongue, vertebrae, open mouth, and opened up viscera, for example, add considerably to the twenty-nine-page report on the anatomy of the rattlesnake written for the Royal Society of London's *Philosophical Transactions* in February of 1682–83 by Edward Tyson, M. D. Earlier, rattlesnakes had been depicted for continental natural histories published in 1628, 1635, 1648, and 1735, but so disposed in writhing and decorative poses as to entertain the eye more than feed the mind. With the engraving (fig. 2.1.) of "Vipera Caudisona Americana, The American Rattle-Snake," for his magnificent *Natural History of Carolina* (1731–47), Mark Catesby achieved a wedding of the two dialects, as it were, the matter-of-fact reportage and the iconic presence and impact of the figure.[5]

Catesby originated what became a classic presentation of the rattler, a snake coiled with its head raised on one side and facing outward, its tail on the other side and erect as if ready to rattle. (This is the pose Larson employs for his three rattlesnakes.) The conical helix, or "bedspring" coil, of the don't-tread-on-me snake on Revolutionary War banners achieves essentially the same impact, a simultaneous tension between the gathered body and the extending head and tail, one threatening and the other warning away. The discontinuity expressed by the radical opposition, even the disjunction between head and rattle, is underlined iconographically in Catesby's drawing (1) by his having drawn two extra rattles (one a cutaway view, and both cut from snakes' bodies) and placed them at the bottom of his picture under the tail of the posed snake, and (2) by his having drawn an extracted fang at the bottom on the other side under the head of the snake. Further tension is created as these disjunctions pull against the very strong centripetal draw of the figure and as the continuous body of the reptile connects the symbolically opposite head and tail into one creature again.

Only one other sort of pose is common in the iconography of the rattlesnake in American military and fraternal emblems, the "rampant" rattler. "Rampant" is a little odd as a descriptive term for a legless, clawless creature but I can think of no better characterization of the rather linear, stretched ahead and up, but slightly sinuous rattlesnake on the first Navy Jack. The snake proceeds from lower-right to upper-left across red and white stripes and above the motto, "Don't Tread On Me."[6]

The Catesby-coil has come to carry its own rightness beyond representation, as icons often do, allowing Larson to speak to our right-

2.1. Mark Catesby, "Rattle-Snake. *Vipera Caudisona Americana*," from *The Natural History of Carolina...* (London, 1731–43). Courtesy of the Bancroft Library, University of California, Berkeley.

lobe grasp of rattlesnakeness as well as to our left-lobe understanding. The more one looks at Larson's cartoons in the light of rattlesnake lore, and then looks again at the lore in light of Larson, the richer some of our "readings" of rattlesnake become. The cartoons and the "caudisoniana" fold back on one another, framing and making frames problematic, so that laughter erupts in recognition of the play between silliness and seriousness.

For example, outdoorspeople often harbor the conviction that rattlers like to crawl into one's bedroll at night. The juxtaposition of vulnerability at night out-of-doors in one's bed with resident rattlers creates an exquisitely anxious affect. Larson plays on this bit of common lore in a cartoon that shows an undressed man sleeping under a blanket under the desert stars and moon. One rattlesnake rests coiled on his belly and three more twine around him and under his blanket. "Okay," says the one on his belly, "On the count of three everybody rattles." In another, Larson plays on an old guidebook warning to beware of reaching blindly onto a ledge that rattlers may inhabit: Two men are rock climbing in the desert. We can see what they cannot, that the heap they are scaling is not rock at all but the coils of a monstrous, house-high serpent. The lead man has just paused and said, "Freeze, Earl! Freeze! Something rattled."

And then there are their eyes. Rattlesnakes have no eyelids, no eyebrows, no eyelashes; Larson's do. He pops Ping-Pong-ball-like eyes atop his snake's heads and makes them eloquent of the humor of the snakes—their irony, irritation, evil glee—by the abbreviated lines that stand for lowered eyelids, raised eyebrows, and such. He solves a cartoonist's problem, thereby, but also highlights for us how very much the real rattlesnake's absence of ocular expression disturbs us and leads to inferences of malignant, cold or hot affect projected by rattlesnake staring. The whole matter of the snake's reputed ability to fascinate small creatures, or even people, comes back to its eyes more than to any other feature.

Cartoons invoke an array of contexts the reader shares with the artist. The affective and cognitive exchange between two who laugh together at a shared cartoon is a rich and complex fabric. Three and a half centuries ago this particular fabric did not exist with regard to the rattlesnake; or to be strictly accurate, a different fabric built on experience with European snakes and on experience with travelers (notorious liars) stood instead ready to frame reports of these New

World reptiles and to interpret what they meant, and what their presence in America meant. Folklore collections and indices offer access to this heritage of serpent lore and to some of the adaptations of motifs to American creatures as well as to new lore specific to the peculiarities of *Crotalus* and *Sistrurus* species.[7]

Native Americans had of course constructed cultures over the millenia which made sense of the rattlesnake in one way or another. Except for their "cures," however, very little of the native ethnobiology, much less cosmology or theodicy, made it across into new fabrics the settlers were weaving. Native wisdom has remained essentially untranslated and undigested, though a great deal has been collected and transcribed into English. It would be a mistake to think of native learning as a coherent heritage, wrenched out of context as much of it is, and derived from and tuned to distinctly different cultures as it also is, as different as Hopi and Mohawk, Miwok and Menominee. Any systematic and responsible study of the rattlesnake and its importance among native, pre-Columbian peoples or among post-Columbian Native Americans, requires skills and training outside my competence and will have to await another. Nevertheless, certain well-documented, historical, ritual uses of rattlesnakes by the Hopi, for example, suggest that the culture of those making use of rattlers makes a difference in what the snakes signify and even in how they behave. Much attention has been devoted to descriptions of Hopi rattlesnake handling and to debunking or otherwise "explaining" their spectacular achievements in scientific terms. In any case, the Hopi and other Native Americans accommodated rattlesnakes into systems of meaning different from those carried to America by the first European explorers and settlers.[8]

THE RATTLESNAKE AS WONDER

Among the early writers who mention the rattlesnake or describe it and interpret it briefly are Capt. John Smith (1612), Edward Winslow (1624), Rev. Francis Higginson (1630), William Wood (1634), Thomas Morton (1637), Thomas Lechford (1642), and John Josselyn (1672). Some of the flavor of these early reports can be gathered from the account of rattlesnakes Thomas Glover included in his "Account of Virginia," sent to the Royal Society of London, then just entering its second decade, and published in its *Philosophical Transactions* (1676):

> There are five or six sorts of *Snakes*, amongst which the *Rattle-Snake* is most remarkable, being about the bigness of a mans legg, and for the most part a yard and a half long; he hath a Rattle at the end of his Tail, wherewith he maketh a noise when any one approacheth nigh him, which seemeth to be a peculiar providence of God to warn people to avoid the danger; for this Creature is so venemous, that the bite of it is of most dangerous consequence, unless they speedily make use of the proper antidote; of which I shall take occasion to speak somewhat hereafter.

Three things are worth noting: Glover's largely matter-of-fact tone; his "reading" of God's purpose in this as yet unintegrated New World reptile; and his interest in cures. His invocation of "mans legg" to characterize the girth of the creature conveys a perhaps subliminal thrill in that legs are the handiest and commonest places for a snake to bite.[9]

Glover's essay treats a number of subjects briefly in its thirteen pages—rivers, tides, fish, a "monster," falls, passes, gems and precious metals, minerals, trees, fruits, herbs, beasts, birds, and snakes. He concludes, as many early reporters did, with a separate section on Indians, their ways, and especially their medicine. The Europeans had no taken-for-granted treatment for rattlesnake bite, but the Native Americans did. "Indian cures" for rattlesnake bite continued to excite interest among medical and lay people well into the nineteenth century. In this case Glover can only report that "all *Indians* carry a Powder," that its composition is different in every town, but that each recipe works. Since he fails to say what is in it, it cannot do us or his readers much good. The report nourishes the continuing belief that the Native Americans, because they were native (and so cousin to the snake, as it were), must possess special ways and wisdom that non-natives might learn to use.[10]

Many of the new Americans presumed that Creation was ordered in such a way that snakebite cures would be found growing in the neighborhood of snakes, just as poison-ivy cures ("Touch-me-not," *Impatiens biflora*) did near that weed. If so, such cures could be counted as undeniably American. In fact, however, the majority of cures and treatments they actually used descended instead from ancient European folk and medical sources. Such bizarre cures as split chickens, powdered human teeth, cheese poultices, and snake stones simply shifted from Old World application to New. A wide array of botanics (Klauber lists twenty genera) have been used singly and in combinations, internally and externally. Scarifying, cutting and sucking, tourniquets, cauterization, excision, vinegar, turpentine, ammonia, alcohol, oils and fats, iodine, potassium permanganate, salt, gunpowder, mud, opiates, strychnine, whiskey, ether, and adrenalin have all been adopted at one time and another. Interesting, and even impressive, as this array of inventions is, it tells us more about American medicine, first aid, and home remedies as cultural systems than it does about the rattlesnake; for the rattler as it figures in these therapeutic dramas functions more as a generic viper than as a rattler. Not until the advent of modern antivenins was there a reliably effective specific to rattlesnake bite. In this case finally, then, something specific to the rattlesnake was turned to use in treating its bite.

Between 1676 and the Revolutionary War a number of visiting and resident reporters on the "productions of Nature" in America produced accounts of rattlesnakes and anecdotes about their own or others' encounters with them. These add to but do not materially alter the genre of which Thomas Glover's report is the type. The snake is reported as more-or-less a wonder and the subject of various beliefs, some affirmed and many debunked. Paul Dudley describes them for the English "virtuosi" in a 1723 account sent to the Royal Society of London. He passes on a story he has heard about the snake's powers of fascination, a topic we will return to, and on a tale told by "a Man of Credit" of a snake killed "some Years since," with between seventy and eighty rattles (assuredly a hoax or a lie according to the best herpetological understanding today). He also scotches the notion, however, that the snakes can "traject" their venom and corrects an earlier notion held by "Our People" that the rattling sound came from "hard loose Kernels lodged in their Tails." Throughout these early accounts especially, but all the way down to the most recent books and articles on rattlesnakes as well, a kind of persistent drama of belief and disbelief, of proof and plausibility and credulity, winds through the literature. What it amounts to is an epistemological motif. Can we believe our eyes, our memories, stories told by "A Man of undoubted Probity," as Dudley says, by frontier trappers, and by raconteurs; or "stories told" as it were by woodcuts, engravings, oil paintings, and finally photographs; or "information" conveyed by mounted, skinned rattlers or by long rattles chopped off killed snakes and kept as trophies? Sometimes the answer even to these relics is "No," for sloughed skins stretch and rattles can be assembled by clever piecers. [11]

Several admirable accounts of rattlesnakes, too many and too long to be made much of in the limited space of a chapter such as this, were produced during the century by worthy people who made it their avocation to collect and transmit the news of nature in the New World back to the centers of science abroad, as well as up and down the seaboard. Benjamin Gale of New England, Christopher Witt, John Bartram, and Joseph Breintnall of Philadelphia all contributed pieces to the Royal Society of London's *Philosophical Transactions* or to *Gentleman's Magazine,* the two premier organs of what was called Natural Philosophy or Natural History then. As Tyson had earlier, a number of English "virtuosi" commented upon reports or specimens they had received—people like Sir Hans Sloan, John Ranby, and Peter Collinson. One of the best accounts of that era was penned before the Revolution but did not appear until 1781 in England, when Jonathan Carver finally managed to publish his eventually most popular *Travels Through the Interior Parts of North America, in the Years 1766, 1767, and 1768.*[12]

Carver's description in chapter 18 is as good and sober an early account as exists, but in the narrative portion of his travels he recounts a tale told him by a Frenchman about a Menominee who kept a rattlesnake he took to be a deity. He kept it in a box but let it go for the winter, "telling him, whilst he did it, to be sure and return by the time he himself should come back, which was to be in the month of May following." Next May, after one day's delay and suspense, the snake did return, Carver was told. "The French gentleman," Carver says in conclusion, "vouched for the truth of this story, and from the accounts I have often received of the docility of those creatures, I see no reason to doubt his veracity."[13]

Carver was ridiculed by critics for his credulity in the matter, and he defended himself in "An Address to the Public" prefaced to his second editon. He avows the "undoubted veracity" of his informant and supplies background information about the hibernating of rattlesnakes in special spots and their habit of returning in the spring to their former grounds. While at least one modern account of rattlesnakes suggests that they may be relatively tamed by considerate care (see note 32), no one can say at this remove of more than two centuries whether Carver was taken in by a credible tale told naively, was the victim of a hoax, or was himself putting one over on his readers, telling a tall tale, as travelers do, to amaze and amuse his audience.

What would later be called "science" had its beginnings in the seventeenth and eighteenth century. What inspired much of the study of nature was a conviction that false ideas needed to be junked if new, verifiable knowledge based on experience rather than tradition and ancient prejudice were to thrive. Working hard at just such problems about what snakes really do and do not (like swallow their young to protect them, or hypnotize potential prey by staring) came to preoccupy students of nature in the next two centuries. Superstitions were chased down, cures tested, behavior recorded, field studies accomplished, venoms analyzed, antivenins produced, therapies tried and rejected or recommended. Without any doubt, Laurence M. Klauber's monumental work caps that tradition. But while the snakes are uniquely American, and Klauber and other herpetologists are products of American culture, herpetological study of rattlesnakes contributes to and derives its meaning from that cosmopolitan and elite culture shared by the scientific community, and not from American culture *per se*, that web of everyday values and meanings, of institutions and performances, which underlie and inform the productions of popular, of military, and of literary American culture.

THE RATTLESNAKE AS ICON

"The land was ours before we were the land's," Robert Frost wrote in 1942 in "The Gift Outright." The same might be said about rattlesnakes. The rattlesnake was ours (or the Indian's, or nature's) before we were its. With the Navy Jack of 1775, though, the first "Don't Tread On Me" flag, the rattlesnake became a symbol within and under which colonials found an identity which the rattlesnake helped them to project. How that happened and how it worked, and continues to work, makes a complicated story, but what it amounts to is a whole different mode of making sense of and in the new land from the scientific approach that Glover and Dudley worked out and Klauber perfected.

An alternative epistemology, perhaps really an esthetic, appears to underlie and inform the iconographic enterprise initiated by Catesby but articulated by Franklin and others, executed by insignia makers, and then flaunted by artillery companies or ships of the line during the war. It is as if during the mounting stress of the 1770s Americans confronted their inchoate identity (Britons? Colonials? Americans?) and discovered in the rattlesnake a "pronomial predication" from which they could gain a plausible, potent, native and natural, subjective identity. By identifying their armed branches with the rattlesnake, they made a part of themselves rattlers, and proud of it. They established a facet of American character that would turn out to be long lasting indeed, especially, perhaps, but not exclusively among men.[14]

The process by which an image achieves iconic plausibility involves a community of people coming to credit an emblem with (1) the ability to refer to meanings the people agree are signified by the beast portrayed and (2) the ability to invoke the presence and powers incarnate in it, and in the people themselves as part of creation. In other words, the figured rattlesnake should look like a snake and flourish the parts that matter, that mean—rattles, fangs, helical poise—and the figure should strike the viewer right off as somehow owning the essence and energy of the rattlesnake in its iconic configurations. It should achieve what Robert Plant Armstrong has denominated in a different context as "affecting presence." When the attributive and the analogic come together syndetically, additively, as they do especially in the coiled Don't-Tread-On-Me flags, the result is an icon.[15]

Where do icons come from? They are radically nonverbal and consequently occur to the individual and achieve some refinement outside of the spotlight of verbal consciousness. Luckily in the case of the rattlesnake we have some emblematic and verbal shards that may be pulled together so as to suggest some answers.

Catesby's column of text facing the plate (II: 41—reproduced in fig. 2.1) of the rattlesnake includes in one sentence a description of the snake's character: "They are the most inactive and slow moving Snake of all others, and are never Aggressors, except in what they prey upon, for unless they are disturbed they will not bite, and when provoked, they give Warning by shaking their Rattle." What he took to be the nature of the rattlesnake may well have struck some colonial readers in the 1770s as metaphorical of their own compatriots' character.

In any case, a similar "reading" of the rattlesnake is advanced in 1775 by a correspondent to the *Pennsylvania Journal* (December 27) who works the notion into an extended conceit. This writer sees the snake as an embodiment of courage, courtesy, and deadliness. Signing the long letter "An American Guesser," the correspondent decodes the device of arms he saw on a drum belonging to the marines, with the motto under it: "Don't Tread On Me." He begins to understand the identification of the snake with the colonials because the rattlesnake is "found in no other quarter of the globe than America." Since its eye is brilliant and has no lids, it "may therefore be esteemed an emblem of vigilance." It never begins an attack or ever surrenders, making it magnanimous. "Anxious to prevent all pretentions of quarreling with the weapons with which nature favored her, she conceals them in the roof of her mouth," so that she appears "most defenceless"; and she never wounds until she has generously given notice even to her enemy.[16]

The clincher for the correspondent is the discovery that the snake image has thirteen rattles, "exactly the number of the colonies united in America." "Perhaps it may have been only my fancy, but I conceived the painter had shown a half-formed additional rattle, which I supposed may have been intended to represent the province of Canada," this colonial chauvinist avers. Thus, this elaborate metaphor works out in detail the likeness latent in the thirty-year-earlier Catesby description. One treads on such denizens of the New World at one's peril and out of ignorance or inattention only. And the message is, beware.

Some prior preparation for the seemingly instant and certainly timely selection of the snake for an emblem occurred in 1751 when Benjamin Franklin in his sharply ironic "Exporting of Felons to the Colonies" in the *Pennsylvania Gazette* (May 9) proposed tit for tat. If the British are so benevolent as to send felons to America, he suggested, the colonies might repay them by sending rattlesnakes to England: "*Rattle-Snakes* seem the most *suitable Returns* for the *Human Serpents* sent us by the *Mother* Country." And actually, the English get the better deal, "for the *Rattle-Snake* gives Warning before he attempts his mischief; which the Convict does not." A kind of equivalence, American snake for British convict, is accomplished in this satire that either documents a dawning identification of the colonies with the rattler or documents the invention of the conceit by this prolific American wit.[17]

Three years later, during the French and Indian Wars, Franklin used the snake again to symbolize his message, "Join Or Die." The masthead of the *Gazette* featured a snake cut into eight parts, each labeled with initials to represent a colony. In any case, as the colonial patriots began to hammer out the rhetoric of pamphlets and devices, the rattlesnake lay waiting in the reservoir of native flora and fauna (bison, pine trees, possum, moose, turkey, eagle, beaver) suitable for metaphoric use. Whether some one person started it, or it spontaneously arose in several locations, by 1775 the rattlesnake appeared as a symbol of patriotic solidarity and ominous force on a number of flags.[18]

Rattlesnakes seem to speak to fraternal impulses as well as military and political ends. The campfire tales told about "the biggest rattlesnake ever" or about snake-hunting dogs and hogs that hate rattlers; the never-ending run of stories about rattlesnakes, snake hunts, snake barbecues, and snakebites in periodicals for men such as *Outdoor Life* and *Field and Stream;* the place in Boy Scout camp-life of the game "Step on the Rattler," sometimes called "Stung," "Poison," or "Poison Pit"; the place on the flag and pin and coat of arms of Theta Chi fraternity of a rattler in a theta pose and the name of their magazine (*The Rattle of Theta Chi*); the use of the rattlesnake on naval, Army Air Corps, Air Force, and Marine airplanes and on ship insignia; and even the apparently overwhelming majority of men among the publishing herpetologists—all document the appeal to the fraternity of the rattlesnake. How to account for it is less obvious.[19]

"An American Guesser" gave us a clue to part of the pattern: " 'Tis curious and amazing to observe how distinct and independent of each other the rattles of this animal are, and yet how firmly they are united together so as to be never separated except by breaking them to pieces." "One of these rattles, singly," he goes on, "is incapable of producing sound; but the ringing of thirteen together is sufficient to alarm the boldest man living." The mix of collective effectiveness and individual separateness suits both the heroic men-without-women élan of freelances in revolution and, later, of free men in a *laissez faire* political economy. In any case, the syndetism of the rattle—that is, its being made up out of apposite units abutted one to the next without any very strong sense of climax or development—serves as well to present the esthetic underlying egalitarian social arrangements as it does to present the rattling belligerence of comrades in arms.[20]

Synthetic process has dominated art in the West, celebrating hierarchies of affect, the way one thing culminates in another, the way conclusions derive efficiently and satisfyingly from the opposition and dialectic of themes and counter-themes. Sonatas, sonnets, symphonies, romances, the Mass—all start at a beginning and achieve a necessary climax; proportion counts more than bigness, timing more than duration in synthetic process. Something very different characterizes the sense of pleasure the person got who assembled the seventy to eighty rattle hoax Dudley reported. The power lay in its more-and-moreness, not its finishedness.

People taken by the rattlesnake and its rattles not uncommonly express their interest by accumulating rattles. At Dutch Miller's Yolo Sportsman's Club in Knight's Landing, California, rattles broken off killed snakes decorate the shelf behind the bar, one rattle after another, beneath ranks of bullets, shotgun shells, stuffed ducks, curios, Highway Patrol patches, and gilded statues of horses. At the Buckhorn Curio Store in San Antonio, some of the most extravagant objet d'art assemblages of rattles have been preserved from turn-of-the-century Texas. In one the tails of 847 rattlesnakes have been arranged on a blank field to represent two prickly pears and an eagle with a bundle of arrows in its talons and a rattlesnake in its beak. This bricolage of rattles and union of images of the dry West (cacti) and the emblems of two nations (the eagle and rattlesnake from the Mexican flag and the eagle and arrows from the Seal of the United States) achieves a kind of odd coherence of affect. The dryness of the rattles suits the cacti they make up, and the rattles ending in buttons (pointed in effect) furnish the talon tips, arrow tips, feather tips, and cactus spines of the image. This rather chilling assemblage of bits broken off snakes syndetically realizes the arid presence and mortal meaning of the rattlesnake to many southwesterners.[21]

A sort of de-iconization appears to have infested the production of military insignia during and after World War II. Of the Army, Navy, and Air Force insignia featuring rattlesnakes, none I have seen retains the kind of balance of threat and warning, the tension between nonaggression and preparedness, that the earlier icons realized. The flag of the U.S.S. *Henley* (DD-762) shows a rattler coiled (but in four loops rather than two, or two and a half, as earlier) with its head up and mouth open. Its rattle dangles out the bottom of the coil, however. The motto on the flag featured in the design is "Don't Tread On Me," but the motto along the bottom edge of the circular insignia says "Ready To Strike." The warning half of the emblem has atrophied. The 59th Division (U.S. Army) shoulder patch features a rattler (white) coiled on a gold base against a medium dark blue ground. Again, its head is raised in readiness, but its rattle sticks out parallel to the horizontal line of the base. The Navy's antisubmarine unit (CARAEWRON 88) shows a rattler coiled, a representation of a submarine in the water inset as a section of circle with its apex at the rattler's eye (like Superman's x-ray vision), and two jagged electric bolts emanating from the snake's rattle, indicating that for this unit the rattle functions as a warning to the snake and its allies rather than to its potential enemies, the classic recipients of the warning. The VF-102 Diamondbacks, also Navy, show a rattlesnake wrapping itself two times around the world, head raised at the top and tail dangling out the bottom, a distinctly more imperialistic image, very different from the former flags.[22]

Several insignia convey their threat as much by what the rattlesnake is made to coil about as by the snake's potency itself. The 317th Bombardment Squadron of the World War II Army Air Corps wore a patch of this sort, described officially, thus: "On a yellow disc, thin border red, piped white, a rattlesnake preparing to strike affronte proper, coiled about a green aerial bomb dropping to dexter base." Similarly, the 364th Bombardment Squadron showed a rattler coiled about a falling black bomb. One especially odd, if intriguing, emblem is that used by the 50th Fighter Pursuit Squadron during World War II: "From a bank of clouds argent a winged rattlesnake coiled to strike, . . . head erect, open mouth gules, . . . tail erect showing rattle" spits "four projectiles" up and ahead, in an echo of the myth about rattlesnakes "trajecting their venom" which Dudley debunked more than two centuries earlier. The "Don't Tread On

Me" motif has largely been lost in these bellicose, later images.

The dead end of this military use of the rattlesnake as a natural icon seems surely to have been reached in two Navy insignia, one of the VMFA-323d and the other from the U.S.S. *Hissem* (DER-400). Cartoon iconography has been absorbed and integrated. In each the rattles shake or sound in terms of those little "arcs" or "ripple" lines cartoonists use to indicate sounds emanating from a source or the vibrating back and forth of an object. But that is not the chief index of downfall. The U.S.S. *Hissem*'s coiled rattler, head erect, tail rattling, wears a pert sailor's cap. The motto reads "Early Warning," not "Don't Tread On Me." The figure is not adequately alien to sustain that older motto. The snake has been tamed into a cartoon cliché. In the VMFA-323d emblem a distinctly Disneyized snake coils with its bigger than proportionate head raised on the left and its little rattle wiggling on the right. The big head juvenilizes the image, making it cute instead of scary.[23] Whatever presence and power rattlesnakes seemed to incarnate to early icon makers, these recent images seem to be symbols of the second order as it were, the fabrications of morale merchants bent on making images that refer to images we have of rattlesnakes, in lieu of invoking the rattler itself as earlier images did.

THE RATTLESNAKE AS DISORDER

The psychic distance between taking rattlesnakes as signs of ourselves, our group, vis-à-vis threatening aggressors, and taking the rattler as an embodiment of all that is alien to humankind and ought to be erased is not as great as the words would make it seem. In the first case, men have made the creature a kind of totem, a stand-in for and representative of the awful presences they themselves wish to project in the world. In the second they have made conquering it, killing it, or eating it a sign of their own courage, canniness, and civic responsibility. J. Frank Dobie, the great Texas folklorist, concedes, "I grew up understanding that a man even halfway decent would always shut any gate he had opened to go through and would always kill any rattlesnake he got a chance at." Men return from the woods brandishing dead snakes, or at least snake stories, as proof of their competence, their survival of the wild.[24]

The tone of such tales may vary. The self-deprecating humor of the would-be countryman skunked on a snake hunt meant to impress visiting city folks in "Snake Hunt At Old Hollow," for *Field and Stream,* in no way undercuts the structured meaning, by which the narrator's status and quality get a boost from his ability to exhibit rattlesnakes and rattlesnake stories with equal aplomb, with grace. To be able to encounter a rattler and not get rattled ranks high as a virtue. In "Encounters With Diamondbacks," Archibald Rutledge leads off his piece for *Outdoor Life* with an account of old Henrietta Manigault, who killed an eight-foot-four-inch rattler that had lived under her porch with her for years and only became a problem when her dog got after it. "But Henrietta," Rutledge reports asking, "do you mean to tell me you knew that thing had a den right there in your yard?" "I sure did," she answered, "he often rattled at my baby." Rutledge takes her attitude to be "a classic example of poise and composure."[25]

The granddaddy of mass-mediated rattlesnake lore is surely T. B. Thorpe's long piece for *Harper's New Monthly Magazine* in 1855, "The Rattlesnake and its Congeners." Like many journalists since, Thorpe assumed a tone suited to passing along true encounters, valuable information, and exciting anecdotes about rattlesnakes. He begins his long essay by saying that, "of all animated life, the serpent at first sight, is the most repulsive; and yet, with the species, there is such a combination of the beautiful, the terrible, and the mysterious, that the beholder, in spite of himself, is attracted by their appearance." Disorder draws us even as it affronts us. As is often the case in this genre, the rather matter-of-fact, unruffled tone of Thorpe's prose contrasts with the horrific impact of the illustrations accompanying the text. Writhing rattlesnakes threatening dogs, fascinating a bunny, getting torn apart by wild hogs, being stomped by deer, and being killed by a black snake convey without qualification the message that the timber rattlesnake deserves *horridus horridus* as a name.[26]

In "Once Upon a Time," for *Sports Illustrated,* Bil Gilbert continues the sort of journalism Thorpe began, opening with an allusion to "the classical monsters—harpies, hydras, scaly [*sic*] giants and werewolves"—and making the bridge to "our monster," the rattlesnake. In the body of the piece he passes on recent findings about venom, debunks superstitions, dispenses wisdom about snake behavior, and closes thus: "It is a good thing to have something outside the human line to respect. It gives a man a sense of proportion." Setting aside the moral for the moment, we can notice that again a man has, in talking about rattlesnakes, gained a kind of poise and authority. In mastering the rattler in print, the author imparts to readers eager to attain the same poise in the presence of horror some of his own aplomb. Mastering one's own fears counts for as much as mastering the monsters themselves.

Something of a test of manhood may be involved even in the rattlesnake-bite reports and anecdotes written up by herpetologists and published in professional organs such as *Herpetology,* the *Bulletin* of the Antivenin Institute of America, the Herpetological Information Search System's *HISS News-Journal,* and the *Herpetological Review.* While fortitude under great distress is a common motif in these tales, the keep-calm ethic is the other. Don't panic, don't run, capture the snake if you can, and get it to the hospital with you (so they can be sure it is a rattlesnake, and which species). Young Scott James Craft, thirteen, concludes "Half Hour From Death," an account of being bitten, with advice to stay calm, always carry a good snakebite kit, and learn to use the kit and put a tourniquet on with either hand.[27]

An alternative address to the rattlesnake's radical otherness and its infestation of "our world" is enacted in the rattlesnake roundup. In such affairs people gather to hunt the snakes down, to exterminate as many as possible, and then to eat them. The Sweetwater, Texas, roundup has become the most famous. The Jaycees have taken over and made a pageant out of it, with Rattlesnake Queens and a Rattlesnake Dance, rattlesnake patches for hats and jackets, rattler curios, rattlesnake milking, prizes for the biggest snake, the smallest, and the greatest total weight. Slain snakes are disdained, so bringing them in alive is the rule. They are slaughtered in a plywood enclosure on a chopping block by a butcher with a machete. People stand around and take pictures. The barbecued snake tastes like chicken, diners report. "If you eat more than anyone else you win a prize for *that*" too, a participant told *Esquire.*[28]

"There are lots of cultures where snakes are worshipped and feared," the *Esquire* piece concludes, "but when you get right down to it, eating them is probably the best revenge." The title of this piece, "West of Eden," suggests that a degree at least of striking back at the tempter of Eve informs the slaughter of these New World representatives of the reptile kind. Perhaps. I have been told by a friend that even the Mennonite conscientious objectors working in the Appalachians during World War II never let a rattlesnake escape, though other pacifists clung to a tolerance more attuned to the Peaceable Kingdom. But whatever the slaughter means must be complex, for while all serpents should logically bear any stigma of that first temptation, it is rattlesnakes that are especially rounded up and butchered. Some crossing of biblical and New World lore has produced a hybrid legitimation for exacting a manly and righteous "revenge" on the creature so much like ourselves as Americans in one of its manifestations, and, at the same time, so alien to all that is human in its avatar as a "creeping beast," as Thomas Morton termed it in 1637.[29]

THE RATTLESNAKES OF THE PEACEABLE KINGDOM

"It really does not matter that the snakes symbolize Satan," a member of the snake-handling Jesus Only Church of Micco, West Virginia, told science reporter Michael Watterlond, "I'm just not afraid." Since 1909 certain Christian sects have taken up serpents and interpreted their ability to do so with impunity as a sign they are anointed in the spirit, for the present. The psychology, theology, sociology, and even physiology of this practice has attracted attention in the press and from academia now and again, but since rattlesnakes are no more crucial to this exercise of faith than copperheads (or than strychnine, which they ingest, and fire, which they handle), the cult's interest in rattlesnakes simply confirms the creature's granted horror without adding a dimension to its meaning in American culture. More to the point is the rattlesnake pictured in the lower left corner of Edward Hicks's 1825 painting, *The Falls of Niagara*. In the left foreground with the rattler are three other typical New World creatures, a moose, a beaver, and a bald eagle. In the background is Niagara and three tiny people (Hicks and his companions), one with arms raised, presumably in "astonishment" and awe at this "sublime" and "o'erwhelming work of awful Time, . . . That bids us kneel, and Time's Great God Adore." The words by poet and naturalist Alexander Wilson are made by Hicks into a framing device and gloss on the scene. Clearly this rattler, then, is no stand-in for Satan, but an emblem of the New World if not itself a sign of redemption. America in both its historical and natural reality was for Hicks a ground on which the new order prophesied by Isaiah and led by Christ would be realized. Hicks's unique "ministry" *qua* artist led him to paint more than fifty versions of this Peaceable Kingdom in which a child, a leopard, a wolf, some cattle, a kid, a lion, and bear all lie down together in harmony. In another (*The Peaceable Kingdom of the Branch,* 1825–30), the famous "natural bridge" of Virginia with Quakers and Indians dwarfed by it occupies the background. If the real America and the redeemed world coincide in this way, the rattlesnake as an emblem of America and a sign of the spirit come together in *Niagara.* It presents still a third avatar of *Caudisona,* then, the pacific or tamed rattlesnake, the rattlesnake seen for what it is at the core and not what it seems to be to the uninformed or unenlightened.[30]

"To an unprejudiced eye a rattlesnake," conservationist Fred H. Avery, Jr., writes, "with its gaudy colors and pattern and its graceful movements, is as beautiful a work of nature as any bird or mammal." To another contributor to the *Conservationist,* William S. Brown, "the timber rattlesnake represents a unique symbol of our remaining wild places . . . and should be left undisturbed." While such nature lovers admire and cherish the rattlesnake, they hardly handle them as pets. They would leave them alone in their solitary and potent splendor in the wild rather than bring them home to tame. In fact, to tame one would rob it of its virtue as a "unique symbol" of the wild. So while their rattlesnake may be admirable, it is not lovable, not benign. But there was at least one American to whom rattlers were truly "fellows" for whom she felt "a transport/ Of cordiality," in the words of Emily Dickinson.[31]

Grace Olive Wiley kept rattlesnakes for the Museum of the Minnesota Academy of Science (housed in the Minneapolis Public Library) from 1922 to 1933. She evidently was a more than competent herpetologist, for she became the first to breed captive rattlers, according to Raymond L. Ditmars, Curator of Reptiles at the New York Zoological Park. She describes her way of taming them in her contributions to the *Bulletin* of the Antivenin Institute of America in 1929 and 1930.[32]

To keep them clean and healthy, she bathed them in warm soapy water twice a week and placed them in a box on the radiator to dry while she cleaned their cage. They were frightened at first so she handled them gently, moved slowly, and soon they "came to understand and submitted very good-naturedly." Not many authors have used that adverb to characterize rattlers. When they grew tamer she noticed more about them. They had different temperaments. She named one male "Huckleberry Finn," another "Stanley," and a female "Ethel." "All . . . like to be stroked and petted, some individuals showing their fondness for this attention by arching their backs like cats. Stanley was "exceedingly tame but never arched his back when stroked." Huckleberry Finn did. Stanley liked instead to have his throat scratched, "so this was often done after feeling around for his head, without even looking." Stanley would rest on her lap at night while she sewed, "for he was like a contented old cat." He "was fond of hiding away in an ordinary paper bag to rest." She would open the cage, present a bag, and in he would crawl. She let them loose in her back yard. She put down a bag for him to retreat to and in he went, an incident which calls to mind Carver's Menominee and the tame snake he kept in a box 153 years earlier. When Huckleberry Finn was about to slough his skin and she and a photographer meant to capture it on film, she kept the snake by her at night in an open traveling bag into which she had tossed crumpled bits of paper, so that when the snake began to stir she would hear it and could call a cab, get to the studio, and catch him shedding. This she did, without, she says, telling the cabby what she had in the bag, and the session produced "a wonderful picture, from start to finish."

Some "Cascabel," Mexican West Coast rattlesnakes (*C. basiliscus basiliscus*) arrived in 1927. These she tamed in the same way, first force-feeding one while "patting her great body with my free hand." A second she tamed in five days. He would climb about her shoulders and up around her neck. "For long intervals he would pose with his head held high as if in deep thought." She comments, "truly, this is one of the most thrilling experiences imaginable, to hold one of these huge creatures thus, realizing fully its ability to inflict a deadly bite, but knowing it *will not*." She finds it:

"a joy beyond the telling"—an ecstasy similar to that experience when one beholds a wonderful sunset, views grand scenery, or listens to soul-thrilling music. I have at times wondered if Nature

doesn't sometimes touch a chord in the being of little dumb
creatures, too, so that they come to know that one is a friend!

This, indeed, is "a transport of cordiality." And yet for all her rap-
ture, Wiley was equally a practical and capable keeper and breeder
of rattlesnakes. A kind of matter-of-fact domestic tone pervades her
descriptions of her handling of healthy snakes and nursing of sick
ones.

Whatever may be said about the uses of rattlers for fraternal purposes or the abuse of them by outdoorsmen, the affiliation Wiley
makes the heart of her practice presupposes a rattlesnake of quite a
different nature. She treats them as fellow beings, nervous and need-
ing nurture and reassurance: "It must lose its fear and be made contented and happy," she concludes; "the more nervous and high-
strung the animal, the harder the task and the more patience it requires." Her willingness and ability to empathize, to notice and care
about *their* fear first, pretty well remakes the traditional relationship
between rattler and human in America. While some intuit instantly
the ambiguity of the rattler, or others the horror of it, she knows
right off how to keep them: just like any other creature with a
"chord" that can be touched.

THE RATTLESNAKE AS NEXUS

The several avatars of *Caudisona*—monster, pet, icon, wonder—say
something about the complexity of modern American culture. One
cannot pronounce confidently on the meaning of the rattlesnake in
American culture as one might on the meaning of cows in India or
chrysanthemums in Japan. There is not one system of belief and
value, but a flux of contending contexts within which a phenomenon makes one sort of sense or another. A good example of this is
the often reported "text" of a mother rattlesnake that opens her
mouth to let her little rattlers crawl in when danger threatens. Scientists go to great lengths to debunk the story as mis-observation and
misinterpretation: her mouth is not big enough, the little ones
would be digested, they probably crawled by her open mouth into
the hole behind. Or they remind us that rattlers, being viviparous,

will spill a bunch of little snakes out when slaughtered—but out of the uterus and not the gut.

Other honest and observant outdoorspeople, however, insist they or other reliable witnesses have seen it with their own eyes. What are we to believe? And according to what standards? The experience of those who have collected these accounts and savored them or explained them away suggests that an epistemological gulf, a cultural disjunction never to be healed, separates those who credit the accounts of swallowing from those who discredit them. The "common sense" of eyewitness, or trusted witness, clashes with the uncommon sense fostered by distrust of superstitions and lore among scientists. It represents a clash between two sorts of culture, a face-to-face, oral community rich in shared narratives and a cosmopolitan elite devoted to tested, replicable, published knowledge. Some few, like J. Frank Dobie and Laurence M. Klauber, retain citizenship in both worlds and are the richer reporters and raconteurs for their flexibility.[33]

The Disneyized insignia of World War II, it seems to me, similarly draw our attention to a gulf between two esthetics, one born of face-to-face familiarity with rattlesnakes and the other of popularized presentations of them and other animals in cute drawings for cartoons. And the gulf between the way herpetologist William de Jesus treats snakes and talks to audiences about them at the daily "behind the scenes" tour of the snakehouse at the Sacramento Zoo and the way the Sweetwater Jaycees or roadside "snake farms" make use of rattlers for fun and profit is immense. The Sweetwater promoters once sent de Jesus an invitation to the roundup. For them to invite a herpetologist to their blow-out shows their total incomprehension of the chasm that yawns between that world and theirs. And unlike the rather good-natured dispute about swallowing young or not, this rift cannot be straddled easily. The alienation between these two worlds is many layers deep, made up of an amalgam of values and beliefs fused with regional and class loyalties and washed with genderal and religious affinities. It seems unlikely that the Jaycees of Sweetwater will ever see the light and foreswear the slaughter or that the herpetologists will ever embrace the roundup as rite.[34]

Something like such a shift of feeling, a kind of migration of affect from one context to another, seems to have happened between the Revolution and the Civil War with regard to what was called "fascination" and referred to the often-reported power of a rattler to fix its prey with its stare, immobilizing it at least, or even drawing it into its jaws. Dudley credited accounts he had heard, Peter Kalm believed in it, and the phenomenon remained a live and interesting question among the virtuosi until Benjamin Smith Barton, in 1799, thoroughly demolished its credibility and furnished a counterexplanation of the phenomena reported.

Barton's piece must count as a watershed, at least in one small corner of zoology. In his thirty-nine page review of what had been reported and explained to date, he raises each argument and considers it before passing on to the next. His is a model of thoughtful, systematic, candid consideration of evidence and arguments, and a model for the activity of bringing everyday field and laboratory experiences to bear on a puzzle. His greatest achievement, however, is intellectual and rhetorical. He shifts the focus from the "fascinating faculty" of the snake (its eye, its "mephitic breath," its rattling) to "the farce of fascination" played out in the woods between snake and bird beneath a tree at nesting time. This drama involves the audience (the naturalist) as well as the players. His interactional model recasts the phenomena and opens the way to new answers, ones which partake of the ecological complexities invoked by the reframing. Barton asks, for example, which species of bird most often are reported to act fascinated, where they commonly nest (near the ground or high in trees), what season the reports occur in, etc. He concludes that what people see as fascination and attribute to the agency of the reptile is really the distress and dissembling of mother birds protecting their young from predacious snakes, a genuinely new sort of explanation made possible by reforming the question. He demystifies fascination by naturalizing it.[35]

At the same time, he opens a place in the psyche for the affect that attended fascination in the field. Barton admits his own susceptibility to the "poison" of the snake's "creeping motion," and says in a note that "no man experiences the force and the miseries of this prejudice in greater degree than I do." Miserable or not, he kept his eye on real rattlers, those he saw or those his friend Charles Willson Peale kept.

Meanwhile, the literary rattlesnake had been freed from natural history and soon found a habitat within the gothic sensibility. T. B. Thorpe debunks the naturalists who debunk fascination and dismisses them as city folks who look at pickled snakes or stuffed ones and find no fascination there. Then he launches into his tales of wonder and tells of one Mr. Rowe of Philadelphia who was out riding and met a large rattlesnake. He dismounted to lead his horse out of danger of fascination but soon found himself fixed by the stare and unable to advance or retreat. Thorpe tells of a physician horrified one night to hear "a light sliding noise along the floor" of the room he slept in and of his having to stay there till morning. As if alluding to Barton's "poison" he assures the reader that "if its spiral motions once find a response...in your own mind,...you will be conscious of some terrible danger."[36]

The mystery, the ambiguity, the compound of horror that colonials projected into the objective rattlesnake had, at least for some, become introjected. Writers internalized the serpent, even to the extent of depicting literally internalized snakes. Hawthorne and Thoreau both make use of the swallowed serpent, and Oliver Wendell Holmes made the rattlesnake in one's blood (by prenatal influence) a metaphor for all that is inexplicably untameable and yet fascinatingly attractive in young Elsie Venner. One might ask if these forced fictions have anything to add to our understanding of what goes on between rattlesnakes and some Americans. Does the metaphorical snake within find a resonance to the creature without so that certain mutualities and overlaps of consciousness occur? John Steinbeck confronts a disturbing dissolution of boundary between a rattlesnake and a woman in "The Snake," but leaves the sympathy unexplained, though it is clear that he feels her fascination is out of bounds, somehow, a kind of violation of the snake's integrity perhaps.[37]

Whatever we make of fascination in the narrow sense, there is no disputing that in the wider sense of that word many Americans have been fascinated by rattlesnakes over the years, herpetologists as well as hunters, iconographers as well as authors, conservationists as well as fliers and fraternity men. The ongoing cultural project to "read" the rattler turns out to be, also, a way of making sense of ourselves, of our country, and of the cosmos.

NOTES

1. Since 1980 *The Far Side* has been syndicated by Chronicle Features and carried in a wide range of papers, coast to coast. Larson, himself an amateur herpetologist, uses snakes often in his gags and makes rattlesnakes and their understood qualities and significance the subject of a number of cartoons.

2. Laurence M. Klauber devotes a seventy-page chapter of his monumental work *Rattlesnakes, Their Habits, Life Histories, and Influence on Mankind* (Berkeley: Univ. of California Press, 1956) to the rattle, its uses, origins, functions, and what people have taken it to mean; see also David Scofield Wilson, *In The Presence Of Nature* (Amherst: Univ. of Massachusetts Press, 1978), 39–40, 134, and 148–49, for a fuller discussion of the significance of the rattlesnake in colonial America.

3. See Klauber, ch. 17, "Post-Columbian Knowledge of Rattlesnakes," 1188–1212; while I shall cite Klauber time and again, I wish at the outset to acknowledge the influence of his thought and work on every page I write, more than it would make sense to footnote bit by bit; anyone wishing to follow up on a point is advised to consult Klauber's 72-page, comprehensive index and his 140-page bibliography.

4. Scott James Craft, "Half Hour From Death," *Herpetology* 8 (Dec. 1976): 6–9; Klauber, figures 12:1–4, breaks the strike down; narratives of rattlesnake bite are abundant, but half-a-dozen citations will suggest the variety: W.H. Over, "A Personal Experience with Rattle Snake Bite," *Bulletin* of the Antivenin Institute of America (henceforth *Bull.* AIA) 2 (1928): 8–10; S. Paul Ehrlich, M.D., "A Case Report of Severe Snake-Bite Poisoning," *Bull.* AIA 2 (1928): 65–66; Major D. B. Sanger, "An Adventure With Snakes," *Bull.* AIA 5 (1931): 34–35; Benjamin Smith Barton, "An Account . . . of the bite of the Crotalus Horridus," *Transactions* of the American Philosophical Association 3 (1793): 100–15; Caroline Mol as told to Ben East, "Death Did Not Rattle," *Outdoor Life* 159 (1977): 88–89; Archibald Rutledge, "Encounters With Diamondbacks," *Outdoor Life* 145 (1970): 78–79.

5. Edward Tyson, M.D., Vipera Caudisona Americana, Or the Anatomy of a Rattle-Snake . . . dissected at the Repository of the Royal Society in January 1682/3," 13, 25–58; see figures 17:14, pp, 1191–96, in Klauber for snakes by Hernandez, 1628, Nieremberg, 1635, Piso, 1648, and Seba, 1735; Catesby's rattlesnake is reproduced by Klauber, fig. 17:5, p. 1199, and Wilson, fig. 15, p. 177.

6. Milo Milton Quaife, *The Flag of the United States* (New York:

Grosset & Dunlap, 1942), fig. 27, pl. V.

7. Stith Thompson, *Motif-Index of Folk-Literature* (Bloomington: Indiana Univ. Press, 1958); Ernest W. Baughman, *Type and Motif-Index of the Folktales of England and North America* (The Hague, The Netherlands: Mouton & Co., 1966); Frank C. Brown, *The Frank C. Brown Collection of North Carolina Folklore* (Durham, N. C.: Duke University Press, 1952–64), 7 vols.

8. Klauber, 1084–87, has ordered the ethnographic matter by tribes, disposed much of the material topically, and treated in particularly thorough detail the Hopi rattlesnake dance; Oscar T. Branson and Ethel Branson, *Fetishes and Carvings of the Southwest* (Phoenix, Ariz.: Associated Lithographs, 1976), 42–43, present a number of carvings of rattlers, "not true fetishes," in this case, "but novelty items using the artist's imagination." See also Earle R. Forrest, *The Snake Dance of the Hopi Indians* (Los Angeles: Westernlore Press, 1961) and the review in *Western Folklore* 22 (1963): 64–65, by T. F. McIlwaith.

9. The two best secondary sources of early accounts are Rheua Vaughan Medden, "Tales of the Rattlesnake: From the Works of Early Travelers in America," *Bull.* AIA 3 (1929): 82–87; 3 (1930): 103–10; 4 (1930): 17–23, 43–50, 71–75; 4 (1931): 106–9; 5 (1931): 24–27, 42–46; and Klauber, ch. 17; primary sources: Smith, *A Map of Virginia*; Winslow, *Good Newes from New England*; Higginson, *New-England's Plantation*; Morton, *New English Canaan*; Lechford, *Plain Dealing, or Newes from New-England*; Josselyn, *New-Englands Rarities Discovered*; and Thomas Glover, "Account of Virginia," *Philosophical Transactions* 11 (1676), 631, 634.

10. Klauber not only lists and considers all known treatments and cures (860–972) but quotes from his wide correspondence with game wardens, foresters, rangers, and ranchers; Louise Pound earlier collected numerous cures and beliefs, later published as *Nebraska Folklore* (Lincoln: Univ. of Nebraska Press, 1957), 25–40; Wayland D. Hand, *Magical Medicine* (Berkeley: Univ. of California Press, 1980) reports several cures and beliefs; Brown, vol. 5, nos. 2122–70, on snakebite remedies.

11. "Of the Way of Killing Ratle-Snakes," Royal Society of London *Philosophical Transactions* (hereafter *RSPT*) 1 (1665): 43; Dudley, "An Account of the Rattlesnake;" *RSPT* 32 (1723): 292–95; Capt. Hall, "An Account of Some Experiments on the Effects of the Poison of the Rattle-Snake," *RSPT* 34 (1727): 309–15; James Irving, "The Negro Caesar's Cure for Poison," rep. fr. *Carolina-Gazette* in *Gentleman's Magazine* 20 (1750): 342–43; *Gent. Mag.* 29 (1759): 161–62.

12. John Ranby, "The Anatomy of the Poisonous Apparatus of the

Rattle-Snake," *RSPT* 34 (1728): 377–81; Sir Hans Sloane, "Conjectures on the Charming or Fascinating Power attributed to the Rattle-Snake," *RSPT* 38 (1734): 321-31; Joseph Breintnall to Peter Collinson, "Containing an Account of what he felt being bit by a Rattle-Snake," *RSPT* 44 (1746): 147–50; "J. B.," probably Breintnall, to Collinson, "Remarkable and authentic Instances of fascinating Power of the Rattle-Snake over Men and other Animals," *Gent. Mag.* 35 (1765): 511–14; Dr. Kearsley, ltr. to Collinson, *Gent. Mag* 36 (1766): 73–76; Gale, "Extract of a Letter...concerning the successful Application of Salt to Wounds made by the Biting of Rattle Snakes," *RSPT* 55–56 (1765-66): 244–45; Witt, ltr. to Collinson on rattle-snake bite, *Gent. Mag.* 38 (1768): 10; Jonathan Carver, *Travels*...(London, 1781), 43–45, 479–85.

13. Quoted and discussed in Wilson, ch. 3, pp. 56–57 especially.

14. James Fernandez, "The Mission of Metaphor in Expressive Culture," *Current Anthropology* 15 (1974): 119–33, argues that "the inchoate pronouns of social life—'I,' 'you,' 'he,' 'it,' [and I would add 'we']—gain identity by predicating some sign-image, some metaphor upon themselves" (122).

15. Robert Plant Armstrong, *The Affecting Presence: An Essay in Humanistic Anthropology* (Urbana: Univ. of Illinois Press, 1971) and *The Powers of Presence: Consciousness, Myth, and Affecting Presence* (Philadelphia: Univ. of Pennsylvania Press, 1981), establishes *affecting presence* as distinct from mediating or documentary signification and in *Powers* brings a discussion of the analogic and digital ways of meaning together in his definition of the powers of the icon: "The analogic and the digital may be syndetically joined (as X-crossed boards by the tracks 'mean' a railroad crossing, or as a blue veil on a female statue, in a church, 'means' Blessed Virgin). Such joinings are called 'icons' " (28).

16. "An American Guesser's" letter is reprinted in George Henry Preble, *History of the Flag of the United States of America* (Boston: Houghton, Mifflin and Company, 1894), 214–16, but also in Medden, 3 (1929): 84–85; though listed in Charles Evans, Clifford K. Shipton, and Roger P. Bristol's *American Bibliography* (Chicago: Blakely, Hollister, and Columbia Univ. Presses, 12 vols.; Worcester, Mass: American Antiquarian Society, last two vols, 1903–59) as item 14377, the *Early American Imprints* microfiche card lacks a reproduction; those familiar with Margaret Mead's characterization of American reticence and aggressiveness in "The Chip on the Shoulder" chapter of *And Keep Your Powder Dry* (1942; reprint, New York: William Morrow and Company, 1971), 138–57, will find a considerable match between her World War II portrait of American character and the *Pennsylvania Journal's* earlier one.

17. Medden, 3 (1929): 84; Preble; Franklin, *Benjamin Franklin*, ed. Chester E. Jorgenson and Frank Luther Mott, rev. ed. (New York: Hill and Wang, 1962), 214–16.

18. The motif of the snake in bits which can rejoin itself appears in Baughman, as item B765.7, "Fanciful qualities of snakes." Quaife tells the history of many of these flags and has plates of the First Naval Ensign, the Gadsden Flag, the Navy Jack and several non-rattlesnake flags; David Eggenberger, *Flags of the U.S.A.* (New York: Thomas Y. Crowell Company, 1959), has John Proctor's Flag, the Culpepper Minute Men flag, the First Naval Ensign, Providence Artillery flag; Preble shows the Naval Ensign, the Culpeper [sic] Minute Men flag, the Massachusetts Navy flag, the First Naval Jack, the Beaver flag and several more.

19. On the Boy Scout games, see Jay Mechling, "Sacred and Profane Play in the Boy Scouts of America," in *Play and Culture*, the 1978 Proceedings of The Association for the Anthropological Study of Play, ed. Helen B. Schwartzman (West Point, N. Y.: Leisure Press, 1978), 206–15; on *The Rattle* and the use of the rattler on the pin and arms of Theta Chi, Dale A. Slivinske, Associate Director, allowed in a July 8, 1983, telephone conversation that a gloss on the colonists' meaning I had put in a letter to him ("the snakes are peaceful, slow to anger, give warning and strike only when provoked, but then fatally") pretty well characterized what the fraternity meant their rattlesnake to mean; later in a letter (Aug. 9, 1983), Slivinske quotes President George Kilavos: "...the new society was named Theta Chi at the time of the founding on April 10, 1856 and...the coiled rattlesnake, representing the Theta, appeared immediately....Certain parts of the confidential ritual directly and indirectly make reference to the features and characteristics of the rattlesnake in an effort to symbolically emphasize certain points. The rattlesnake which forms the Theta Chi badge has remained unchanged since 1856 and is unique among fraternities not only as a manner of identity, but also as a reminder of each member's obligations and commitment" (Preble, 216).

20. "Syndetism" is a term and concept developed by Robert Armstrong in *Wellspring: On the Myth and Source of Culture* (Berkeley: Univ. of California Press, 1975), 128–50, and explored further in *Powers*, 13, 21ff, 24, and 69ff.

21. Halftones of the Buckhorn Curio Store assemblages appear in Klauber, 1028, and in the 1982 250-page abridgement done by the Univ. of California Press, a version lacking notes or any substantial bibliography.

22. Modern military insignia can be found in "Insignia of the United States Armed Forces," *The National Geographic Magazine* 83 (1943), plates 25 and 28 (the Army Aircraft 3d Bombardment Squadron patch with the snake wrapped around the bomb falling sinister and the 50th

Fighter Squadron's); Gilbert Grosvenor et al., *Insignia and Decorations for the U. S. Armed Forces* (Washington, D. C.: National Geographical Society, rev., 1944), 86 and 92 (59th Division, Army); the U.S. Air Force, *Combat Squadrons of the Air Force—World War II* (1960), 215–16, 386, 429–30 (50th Fighter Squadron, 317th Fighter Squadron, and 346th Bombardment Squadron); the Navy insignia for the VF102 Diamondbacks, the CARAEWRON 88, and VMFA-323 were supplied by collector Peter Mancus, Riverside, Ca.; the Henley USS *Hissem* insignia were supplied by the Naval Historical Center Photographs, Naval Audiovisual Center, Bldg. 168, Naval Station, Washington, D. C., 20374.

23. Stephen J. Gould discusses just such a "progress" from little- to large-headed in "A Biological Homage to Mickey Mouse," in *The Panda's Thumb: More Reflections in Natural History* (New York: W.W. Norton & Company, 1980), 95–106.

24. Dobie, *Rattlesnakes* (Boston: Little, Brown and Company, 1956), 60.

25. Richard Starnes, "Snake Hunt . . . ," *Field and Stream* 70 (1965): 28ff.; Rutledge, 78.

26. Thorpe, "The Rattlesnake and its Congeners," *Harper's New Monthly Magazine* (1855), 470–83, illus. on 471, 472, 473, 474, and 476; for the descendants of Thorpe in the modern popular press in the last thirty years, see *Farm Journal* 89 (1965): 54; *Field and Stream* 78 (1973): 72–73; 81 (1976): 168–69; 84 (1980): 176–77; *Reader's Digest* 86 (1969): 196–200; *Sports Illustrated* 41 (1974): 98–104; but especially *Outdoor Life* 116 (1955): 66–71; 137 (1966): 40–43; 138 (1966): 42–45; 149 (1972): 88–89; 152 (1973): 56–57; 156 (1975): 76–79; 157 (1975): 78–79; 157 (1976): 76–77; and 168 (1981): 112.

27. See for example the accounts of Over and of Craft (n. 4, above).

28. "West of Eden," *Esquire* 85 (1976): 80–85; B. East, "Rattlesnake Jamboree," *Outdoor Life* 139 (1967): 60–63; and "Rounding Up the Rattlers," *National Wildlife* 13 (1975): 41–45.

29. Klauber, 1197.

30. Michael Watterlond, "In My Name . . . They Shall Take Up Serpents," *Science 83 Magazine*, repr. in *St. Louis Post-Dispatch*, May 22, 1983, p. 3c; Steven M. Kane, "Ritual Possession in a Southern Appalachian Religious Sect," *Journal of American Folklore* 87 (1974): 292–302; Edward Hicks, *A Peaceable Season*, intro. by Eleanore Price Mather (Princeton, N. J.: Pyne Press, 1973); the rattlesnake and Niagara reappeared as "characteristically American" natural features when Charles Leseur, zoologist and scientific illustrator, came from Philadelphia to New Harmony, Indiana, Robert Owens's model community, painted them on a theater drop-curtain, according to Harry B. Weiss and Grace M. Siegler,

Thomas Say, Early American Naturalist (Springfield, Ill.: Charles C. Thomas, 1931), 167–69.

31. "Rattlesnakes: Their Right to Survival," *The Conservationist* 32 (1978): 34–36, 36 (1981): 27–29; Emily Dickinson, poem J. 986, "A narrow fellow in the grass," *The American Tradition in Literature*, 3rd ed. (New York: W. W. Norton & Company, 1967), vol. 2, 189–90.

32. Grace Oliver Wiley, "Notes on the Texas Rattlesnake in Captivity With Special Reference to the Birth of a Litter of Young," *Bull.* AIA 3 (1929): 8–14, and "Notes on the Neotropical Rattlesnake (*Crotalus terrificus basciliscus*) in Captivity," *Bull.* AIA 3 (1930): 100–3; Wiley, who moved to the Brookfield Zoo in Chicago in 1933, died in 1948 at the age of sixty-four from the bite of her "newest pet," a cobra, at a photographic session, *Time*, (Aug. 2, 1948,) p. 15.

33. M. de Beauvois, "Memoir on Amphibia," *Transactions* of the American Philosophical Society (1779), 362–81, reports babies "swallowed" by a mother and disgorged fifteen minutes later (371–72) and mentions that in Europe the viper is known so to act; Klauber debunks the story, 1249; Dobie devotes a whole chapter to it and its plausibility or lack thereof, 152–74; Baughman, motif B751.1, "Fanciful traits of animals."

34. Interview (July 5) by the author and tour (July 9, 1983).

35. Benjamin Barton, "A Memoir concerning the Fascinating Faculty which has been ascribed to the Rattle-Snake, and other American Serpents," *Transactions* of the American Philosophical Society 4 (1799): 74–113; Klauber, 1220–24, and passim.

36. Barton, "A Memoir," 97–98; Thorpe, 478–80.

37. "Egotism; or the Bosom Serpent," *The Complete Short Stories of Nathaniel Hawthorne* (Garden City, N. Y.: Hanover House, 1959); *The Journal of Henry D. Thoreau*, ed. Bradford Torrey and Francis H. Allen, vol. 2 (Boston: Houghton Mifflin 1906), 392–93; Daniel R. Barnes, "The Bosom Serpent, A Legend in American Literature and Culture," *Journal of American Folklore* 85 (1972): 111–22; *The Portable Steinbeck* (New York: Viking, 1971), 26–38.

The Alligator

JAY MECHLING

"Well, one day," begins my wife in one of her stories that always entertain people at dinner parties, "when I was about nine years old, my brother, his friends and I were playing out in the palmetto scrub that grew behind our house in Miami. We really weren't allowed to play back there because my parents said it was much too dangerous. Our dog Tippy always went with us. On this particular day, we were playing kick-the-can. Tippy started barking and we ran to find him. There he was, barking at an alligator. And before we could do anything, that alligator lunged at Tippy and bit him in half! And ate him! We were horrified. We turned and ran back home. And we never played back there again." Invariably the audience for the tellings of the "the day the alligator ate my dog" story react with amused horror. The story is funny in its telling, especially as my wife lapses into her long-gone Southern accent in the performance, but the core of the story apparently strikes at a shared dread of these reptilian creatures that come out of the water to eat dogs and children.

My wife's sad tale about Tippy is only one of a number of "alligator encounter stories" to be found over the years in oral circulation and in the popular press.[1] The most famous of these, the one quoted by almost everyone who writes on the American alligator, *Alligator mississippiensis*, is William Bartram's 1792 account of his canoe excursion on Florida's St. John's River. Bartram suddenly came upon the "subtle greedy alligator":[2]

> Behold him rushing forth from the flags and reeds. His enormous body swells. His plaited tail brandished high, floats upon the lake. The waters like a cataract descend from his opening jaws. Clouds of smoke issue from his dilated nostrils. The earth trembles with his thunder.

Bartram then describes a battle between this alligator and another, so terrifying that he fled; he realized soon, however, that he was being pursued "by several very large ones." Thereafter follows his account of his most direct encounter with the alligator:

> I was attacked on all sides, several endeavoring to overset the canoe. My situation now became precarious to the last degree: two very large ones attacked me closely, at the same instant, rushing up with their heads and part of their bodies above the water, roaring terribly and belching floods of water over me. They struck their jaws together so close to my ears, as almost to stun me, and I expected every moment to be dragged out of the boat and instantly devoured.

Bartram escaped, of course, and later in his account he testified to seeing alligators "twenty feet in length," describing in detail their jaws, teeth, nests, habits, and especially their "incredible loud and terrifying" roar: "It most resembles very heavy distant thunder, not only shaking the air and waters, but causing the earth to tremble; and when hundreds and thousands are roaring at the same time, you can scarcely be persuaded, but that the whole globe is violently and dangerously agitated."

Bartram's words and drawings established the encounter story and the iconography that seem to have influenced just about all subsequent American encounters with alligators, real and imagined.[3] Herpetologist Wilfred T. Neill blames a number of misconceptions about the alligator and other crocodilians on Bartram.[4] But even Neill does not dispute the fact that "alligator predation on man" is a real issue. "Until the late 1940s," confesses Neill, "I shared the general herpetological opinion that the alligator would not deliberately attack man," that reported attacks could be explained by the alligator's instinctive defense of the nest, a response to a distress cry, or self-defense. "But then, around 1949 and the early 1950s ," he continues, "we had to revise our opinions. . . . from Okefinokee Swamp to southern Florida the reptile seemed abruptly to become less afraid of man. At scattered localities within this area, the alligator would attack a person, or would venture into a garden to eat some outdoor goldfish or the family dog." Neill surveys both the early accounts of "man as prey" and modern accounts from 1948 to 1958, concluding with characteristic scientific understatement that "the alligator's reaction toward man can vary with time and with place."[5]

Still rare enough, alligator attacks on humans always make front-page reading, as did the following account of a recent attack with tragic consequences:

> PORT ST. LUCIE, FLA.—A 12-foot, 550-pound alligator grabbed an 11-year-old boy in its huge jaws and drowned him as game officers frantically tried to shoot the reptile, officials said yesterday.
>
> Robert Crespo of Port St. Lucie was attacked Monday as he swam in the St. Lucie River at Rivergate Park, about 120 miles north of Miami.
>
> "It was terrible," said Mitchell Epstein of Port St. Lucie, a 26-year-old boater. "I could see the gator with the boy's hand sticking out of his mouth, and he was swimming with him down the river."[6]

Police finally shot the alligator and pulled the boy from the water, but too late—he had been drowned in the alligator's grasp. According to an official of the Florida Game and Fresh Water Fish Commission, this "was the first fatal alligator attack in Florida since a 14-year-old boy was killed in a lake near Stuart in 1978, and the sixth death since officials began keeping records in 1948."

The earlier fatal and non-fatal encounter accounts are similar, with attention to the jaws, to the suddenness of the attack, to the feelings of horror and helplessness among those witnessing the attack. The disproportionate number of attacks upon dogs and children add to the horror. American humans do not have many predators (perhaps only the alligator, the shark, and the bear), so the popular press accounts of humans being eaten by these creatures seem especially loaded with the language of fascinated horror and revulsion. Even attacks upon pet dogs, such as poor Tippy, conjure up these feelings of dread, given the special status accorded dogs in the American bestiary.[7] Though somewhat comic on the surface, the Tippy story doubtless opens the window, even if just briefly, upon a pre-modern world where one of the disconcerting worries of life was that a creature would eat your child or your dog.

The American audience hearing a the-time-an-alligator-ate-my-dog story or reading a newspaper account of a fatal alligator attack understands the account, the "text" let us call it, within a "context" of stories about and images of alligators. Americans have a sense of "alligatorness," a reservoir of ideas they use to interpret their real and mass-mediated encounters with alligators. There is no "real" alligator for most Americans, only a "symbolic alligator" that is the product of the humans' interpretation of the meeting of an alligator and the humans' ideas of alligatorness.

To be sure, the "real" alligator contributes somewhat to this cultural reservoir of folk ideas. The crocodilians (the reptile group containing alligators, crocodiles, and a few others) are the only surviving representatives of the Mesozoic Era "Ruling Reptiles" that dominated the earth for 100 million years, until a still-mysterious chain of events ended their rule 63 million years ago.[8] The crocodilians are the closest thing we have to dinosaurs, and they may be the prototypical creature for the Chinese dragon.[9]

There are only two species of alligator among the twenty-nine kinds of living crocodilians—the American alligator (*Alligator mississipiensis*) and the Chinese alligator (*Alligator sinensis*)—and the American alligator is limited in its range to the swamps and marshes of the southeastern United States (the American crocodile, an extremely endangered species, is limited strictly to the southern tip of Florida and numbers fewer than six hundred). The name "alligator" came from an Anglicization of the Spanish *el legarto*, "the lizard." When New World explorers came across the American alligator, they already had a set of images, stories, and ideas about the Nile crocodile that they transferred to the American creature. Neill traces a good deal of the "mythology" about the alligator to "the fables originally inspired by the Nilotic species," including stories of "crocodile tears."[10]

The anomalous character of the alligator made it an attractive symbol of the New World for the European explorer. Like the difficult-to-categorize scaly anteater of the Lele pangolin cult analyzed by anthropologist Mary Douglas,[11] the alligator presents anomalies of appearance, habitat, and behavior. It is a reptile that spends as much time in the water as out, appearing to be able to spend long periods of time under water as well. It occupies primarily the border between land and water. It can run fast on land (for a short time in a straight line). It is the largest living reptile, and it eats people.

There are archaeological instances of the alligator as an icon in prehistoric North America,[12] but the first European instances were in the artistic representations of the allegorical figure, "America." Hugh Honour's rich survey of European images of America shows how the armadillo and the alligator vied as suitable icon to accompany the allegorical America and represent her character. "By the mid-eighteenth century," writes Honour, "images of America, as one of the four continents, were diffused throughout Europe in churches and palaces and private houses, painted on walls, ceilings, or canvases, woven into tapestries, carved in marble, molded in stucco or porcelain, embossed on silver, englazed on glass, painted on tablewares, even carved on a sledge. . . .The alligator, appropriate denizen of the watery continent, became her constant companion."[13]

Bartram's encounter narrative is typical of the American verbal and visual imagery of the alligator from the eighteenth century on. Neill does us a great service by collecting from the exploration and naturalists' literature all the early accounts of the alligator, and we can add to those an unsystematic list of more recent uses of the alligator in American symbolic systems. In just about all these instances, the alligator stands for danger, evil, and deception (i.e., "crocodile tears" used to lure unsuspecting prey). Consider the following "texts." Political cartoonists have used weeping alligators and crocodiles to represent insincere politicians. *Chicago Tribune* cartoonists Locher and Oliphant have used alligators to represent the Internal Revenue Service, and Lurie used alligators to represent the press devouring presidential advisor Ed Meese.[14] A Mark Tansey drawing used to illustrate a review of books about war featured an alligator whose back scales gradually transform into missiles.[15] A Nicholas von Hoffman review of eight books about Ronald Reagan refers to "alligator egg hatcheries like the American Enterprise Institute, the Hoover Institute, the Heritage Foundation, and the Georgetown University Center for Strategic and International Affairs."[16] Humorous cartoonist Gary Larson, an amateur herpetologist, has used alligators several times in his single-frame cartoon, *The Far Side*. Larson's cartoons cover the full range of alligator lore, from their penchant for inhabiting the sewers of New York to their having a special taste for children and pet dogs, so his cartoons are a good index of what commonsense notions about alligators Americans must already possess in order to find Larson's cartoons "funny."[17]

Folk speech is full of similar images of alligators. To be "up to your ass in alligators" means to be in a great deal of trouble or, sometimes, to be inundated with work, and to "cry crocodile tears" is to be insincere and treacherous. Tarzan movies and similar jungle films seem always to have the requisite crocodile-wrestling scene, and Eugene O'Neill used a crocodile as a symbol of evil in his expressionist drama, *The Emperor Jones* (1920). The list could go on. It seems that throughout all of American folk, popular, and elite culture, it is only the alligator in Walt Kelly's *Pogo* that is not the incarnation of evil and deception.

Clearly, there is a vast array of American stories and images that make use of the alligator. But the aim of this essay goes beyond merely creating a catalogue of American alligator items. Far more important would be the discovery of a pattern underlying these apparently disparate appearances of the alligator in the American symbolic bestiary. That pattern (or patterns) would constitute, in effect, the *story* (or stories) that Americans use to interpret the alligator and, mutatis mutandis, the human social relations coded in the alligator talk.

I believe that there is at least one pattern that ties together a great many of the alligator texts. It is a pattern with many twists and turns, some elements of which may seem improbable in isolation. The interpretation that follows has the advantage of making sense of a great many alligator texts that otherwise seem unconnected and meaningless.

The unifying motif for crocodilians in American materials is the *vagina dentata,* the toothed female genitalia.[18] One standard folklore reference work notes that the motif is widely distributed in American Indian materials and summarizes the narrative thusly:

> The hero, a male, encounters a woman who invites him to have
> intercourse with her. She has had many men but they have all

died because of her toothed vagina. The hero inserts sticks in the vagina; the first of these are ground up but the teeth cannot chew the harder ones; he then knocks out all of the teeth, or all except one.[19]

No longer limited to Native American materials, the image of a toothed vagina is still powerful in American male folk materials, as we shall see shortly. But first we must establish that the predominant imagery of the alligator in the American consciousness is, indeed, female. One of the running themes in folk materials about alligators is their fecundity. Typical is the following joke:

> This guy in a bar in New York meets a half-drunk guy. The man asks the drunk, "Do you know that an alligator lays 100 eggs?" "No," replies the drunk. "And do you also know that only two of the eggs survive to become an alligator?" continues the first guy. "No," replies the drunk. "And do you know what would happen if they all survived?" asks first guy. "No," answers the drunk. "Why, mister, you'd be up to your ass in alligators!"[20]

Its multitude of offspring is just one item in a complex of folk ideas treating the alligator as female. The use of alligator hides for suitcases, handbags, and shoes signals another version of the fertility idea. Consider this common jump-rope rhyme:

> I had a little brother; his name was Tiny Tim.
> I put him in the bathtub to teach him how to swim.
> He drank up all the water, he ate up all the soap,
> He tried to eat the bathtub but it wouldn't go down his throat.
> My mother called the doctor, the doctor called his nurse,
> The nurse called the lady with the alligator purse.
> "Mumps," said the doctor. "Mumps," said the nurse.
> "Mumps," said the lady with the alligator purse.
> Out went the doctor, out went the nurse,
> Out went the lady with the baby in her purse.[21]

The baby in the alligator purse brings to mind a "sick joke" in circulation when Michael Rockefeller disappeared off the coast of New Guinea while on an anthropological expedition in 1961.[22] According to the joke, Rockefeller purportedly turns up in Macy's department store in New York City—inside an alligator suitcase. And there is good evidence that shoes, marriage, and fertility are linked as folk ideas in a broad range of genres, from nursery rhymes to American wedding customs.[23] So it is appropriate that purses and shoes, especially, are the objects made from alligator hides.

The American symbolic alligator is more than just female, however; a good many texts suggest that the "business end" of the alligator is, indeed, a toothed vagina. This imagery is encoded, for example, even in as innocent a children's story as Kipling's "The Elephant's Child," which appeared originally in the *Ladies' Home Journal* for April, 1900, and which is still in print in editions of *Just So Stories*. The story begins long ago when the elephants had no trunks, only bulgy noses. A certain curious Elephant Child in Africa begins asking his relatives "why?" questions, such that each in turn is annoyed and spanks him for his " 'satiable curiosity." Undaunted, one day he asks them all, "What does the crocodile have for dinner?" As one, they all hush and spank him. Still his curiosity is unsated, and a Kolokolo bird tells him to go to the banks of the Limpopo River to find a crocodile and ask him what it has for dinner. So the Elephant Child takes off, eating melons all the way, until he reaches the river and finds a Bi-Coloured-Python-Rock-Snake. Elephant Child asks the Snake what the crocodile has for dinner, and the Snake spanks the poor Child, who moves on. Presently the Elephant Child steps on a log on the river and the log winks. It is the crocodile. The Elephant Child asks this creature if it has seen the crocodile. The Elephant Child doesn't want to be spanked again, but the crocodile identifies himself and weeps crocodile tears.

The Elephant Child asks the crocodile what he has for dinner, whereupon the crocodile asks the Elephant Child to come closer so he may whisper the answer. When the Elephant Child bends close, crocodile grabs the Elephant Child's nose. Snake warns the Elephant Child to pull away and escape, and Snake winds himself around the Elephant Child to help him pull free. As they pull, the Elephant Child's nose stretches longer. Finally free, the Elephant Child waits three days for his nose to shrink, but it doesn't. In three instances Snake shows Elephant Child how a long nose can be an advantage. The Snake asks the Elephant Child if he wants to be spanked. No. Does he want to spank someone? Yes. On the way home, the Elephant Child practices spanking a Hippopotamus. When he gets home, the family is prepared to spank him, but he turns the tables and spanks them all. Seeing the advantage of such an appendage, the entire elephant family goes off to the river to get new noses from crocodile. "When they came back," concludes the narrator, "nobody spanked anybody any more; and ever since that day, O Best Beloved, all the Elephants you will ever see, besides all that you won't, have trunks precisely like the trunk of the 'satiable Elephant's Child."[24]

Kipling scholars appreciate in this story the child's revenge fantasy of returning to spank the adults who had spanked the merely curious child. But to see this as a simple revenge story is to miss important symbolic details. It takes no remarkable semiotic insight to see that Kipling's story creates symbolic equivalence both between the Elephant's trunk and penis and between the crocodile's mouth and the vagina. Abrahams's and Dundes's interpretation of the elephant joke cycle focuses persuasively upon the elephant's trunk as a phallus, and Kipling's story furnishes the *vagina dentata* that briefly captures, holds, and eventually stretches the male member.[25] It is relevant, too, that it is a snake that is ally to the Elephant in the story.

It should be noted that merely capturing and pulling on the Elephant's nose is not the most important goal of the *vagina dentata*. Biting off the nose—symbolic castration—is the most-feared outcome. Abrahams and Dundes present several of the elephant riddle texts demonstrating this Oedipal aspect of the cycle, including the following:

> No. 24: What did the elephant say when the alligator bit
>   off his trunk?
> Very funny (nasalized).

In fact, mutilation (symbolic castration) of this sort runs throughout folk and mass media texts about alligators. Disney's *Peter Pan* provides the recurring image of the crocodile who, having had a taste of Captain Hook, forever pursues him.[26] Edgar Rice Burroughs's Tarzan, hero of dozens of films, at least four cinema serials, a 1960s television series, and comic books, wrestles crocodiles that are trying to bite off the limbs of innocent victims (a function taken over lately, it seems, by sharks in film, possibly another incarnation of the *vagina dentata*).[27]

We find not only symbolic castration in folk and popular culture texts involving alligators. Here, for example, are two variants of a joke depending upon the castration motif:

There was this strong man in the circus who wanted to
develop a new routine. He spent months preparing. Finally, he
had it. He entered the ring, dropped his pants, and extended his
penis. An alligator waddled up to him and chomped his ferocious
jaws around the strong man's penis. Demonstrating true fortitude,
the strong man exhibited no emotion. Finally, he took a hammer
and thunked the alligator on the head, at which time the alligator
released its grip. The strong man asked the audience for
volunteers: "Would anyone be daring enough to try this?" There
was silence. Finally, a reluctant and timid man raised his hand.
He said, "I'll try it, but you're not going to hit me in the head
with that hammer!"[28]

A guy comes into a bar and the first thing he sees in the
middle of the room is an enormous alligator. He spins around
and is hustling out the door when the bartender says, "Hey, hold
it! Come back in; this alligator's tame. Look, I'll show you."
He comes out from behind the bar, tells the alligator to open
its mouth, unzips his pants and whips it out, and stands there
with his pecker in the alligator's mouth for a full fifteen minutes.
"Pretty amazing, huh?" he says, turning around and zipping
himself up. "You wanna give it a try?"
"Gee, I don't think so," says the first man. "I don't think I
could keep my mouth open for fifteen minutes."[29]

In addition to the explicit connection between the penis and the potentially castrating alligator in these jokes, we should also note that
there is a homosexual theme, hence suggesting a parallel between
the alligator and the feminized male.

A part of the typical *vagina dentata* American Indian tale is that
the male hero breaks the teeth (Motif A1313.3.1. *Vaginal teeth broken*), and alligator teeth seem to have held a fascination through the
centuries. A common "folk fallacy" that zoologist Neill complains
about is the belief that crocodilians continue to replace their teeth
throughout their lives; alligators do have replacement teeth that
move into place as teeth are lost, but this process is finite and there
are old, toothless alligators.[30] "Alligator hunters," write Minton and
Minton,

sometimes take the teeth of their quarry, which are subsequently
sold as charms or souvenirs. In an early (1882) plea for the

conservation of the alligator, it was said that one man in Florida had collected 350 pounds of alligator teeth. In Rome in the first century A.D., the eye tooth of a crocodile filled with frankincense and tied to any part of the body was a cure for periodical fevers.... A tooth from the right side of a crocodile's jaw was bound to the right arm of either sex "to provoke unto carnal lust."[31]

The medical and conjuring uses of crocodile teeth transferred well to the New World alligator, including the use of alligator teeth as treatments for pain, as antidotes for poison, as charms against witches, and more.[32] Alligator teeth are also prized trophies. "The hollow tooth of a very large alligator was prized in pioneer times," notes Neill; "it was made into a charger and used to dip up a measured amount of gunpowder." Neill also attributes to Bartram the tendency of writers to refer to the alligator's large, eighth, canine-like teeth as "ivory tusks," highly polished and kept as curios by some collectors.[33] Whether put to sacred or secular uses, in short, alligator's teeth seem to have been associated with power. They are, in effect, the male hero's trophy, representing the breaking of the vaginal teeth, thus rendering safe the female parts.

Although it is not readily apparent, the castration theme inheres even in a body of crocodilian lore that seems to suggest anality rather than genitality. I mean here the "alligators in the sewers" urban legend that almost every commentator on the alligator, popular and scientific alike, feels obliged to mention. It is among the most widely known urban belief tales, so much so that the two authors of a recent book on American popular beliefs entitled their book *There Are Alligators in Our Sewers and Other American Credos.*[34] The legend involves a core story wherein children from northern cities (usually New York) buy a pet alligator while on vacation in Florida, take the pet home, and eventually flush the creature down the toilet, where it survives and grows in the sewers.[35]

The alligators-in-the-sewers legend is an interesting instance of the dynamic by which a folk idea provides material for popular culture and elite culture narratives. The motif appears often in television scripts (including an episode of *Barney Miller*), and it was the basis for the 1980 theatrical film, *Alligator*, which featured a giant, devastating alligator (Motifs B16.5.2. "Devastating crocodile," and

B875.2. "Giant crocodile"). In elite literature, Thomas Pynchon chose to use the legend for his own artistic purposes in his intricate, first novel, *V*.[36]

Similar in imagery are the variants of the "up to your ass in alligators" texts in folklore and mass-mediated culture. It appears in jokes, such as the one quoted earlier about what would happen if every egg the female laid hatched, and in office Xerox lore, such as the sign: WHEN YOU ARE UP TO YOUR ASS IN ALLIGATORS, IT IS DIFFICULT TO REMIND YOURSELF THAT YOUR INITIAL OBJECTIVE WAS TO DRAIN THE SWAMP.[37]

One folklorist friend reports seeing a chamber pot with an alligator painted on the bottom. And a formulaic postcard in Florida juxtaposes a woman in a bathing suit and an alligator with mouth agape, appearing to be about to bite the woman on her derrière. Untold thousands of visitors to Musa Isle Seminole Village in Miami posed for a picture with their backsides in the mouth of a huge, stuffed alligator (fig.3.1), and most Florida alligator attractions have similarly posed alligator statues.

My point is that the alligator-in-the-toilet can as much be a castration motif as those motifs featuring mutilation. Alligators flushed down toilets *can* theoretically come at undefended privates. Legman cites a few versions of the joke in which an exploding toilet castrates the poor fellow who sits on it,[38] and even the cover illustration (by R.J. Shay) for the *There Are Alligators in Our Sewers* book features a cartoon man vainly trying to restrain and push back down an alligator already halfway emerged from a toilet, poised between the man's legs and snapping at his plunger. All together, the alligators-in-the-sewers texts quite powerfully evoke the castration meaning.

If the target of the crocodilian castration in Kipling's story is the Elephant, then it is worthwhile pushing our interpretation a bit further and asking exactly who is being represented by the threatened pachyderm. Abrahams and Dundes argue persuasively that a good many of the elephant riddles were about blacks, and the details of the Kipling story (such as its setting in Africa) support this interpretation of the Elephant Child. Legman agrees, pointing out that castration humor directed against blacks vacillates between ideas of the sexual superiority of black males group and "frank fantasies of castrating him in revenge for this."[39]

3.1. Author's mother and other tourists at Musa Isle Indian Village, Miami, Florida, 1941.

In fact, a common folk idea among whites is that alligators have a "preference" for blacks as a food source. Neill found an early example of this notion in a white slave trader's 1565 account, confirmed by at least four nineteenth-century sources that claim alligators will attack "Negroes" in preference to whites.[40] Marjorie Kinnan Rawlings's story, "Alligators," offers ten episodes that are a catalogue of folk ideas about alligators, including one episode in which an alligator passes up three white men skinny-dipping in order to bite the single black man.[41]

"The old idea that the alligator is an especial menace to Negroes still exists," remarks Neill, "and visitors to Florida can find it illustrated by a variety of tastelessly conceived postcards sold at roadside shops" (figs. 3.2, 3.3).[42] The motif extends beyond postcards, as was demonstrated by a 1982 exhibit of artifacts, souvenirs, sheet music illustrations, advertising materials, and more demonstrating "Ethnic

A DARKY'S PRAYER.

Oh, Lawdy, please deliber me
From dese 'gaters dats got hold ob me
If I only had de chance
I'd gib dem my pants
If de'd only let de rest of me be.

3.2. Postcard, "A Darky's Prayer," reproduced courtesy of the P.K. Yonge Library of Florida History, the University of Florida.

Free Lunch in the Everglades, Florida.

3.3. Postcard, "Free Lunch in the Everglades, Florida," reproduced courtesy of the P.K. Yonge Library of Florida History, the University of Florida, Gainesville.

Notions: Black Images in the White Mind."[43] One folklorist recalls seeing an alligator-shaped pencil holder, with the black child at the end of the pencil, protruding from the alligator's open mouth.

This folk idea stays alive in the oral transmission of jokes, such as the following:

> (President) Johnson was flying his plane down around Florida and the swamps. And he seen two men in a speed boat pulling a colored man on water skiis [*sic*]. And he thought that was awful nice, you know, with the whites and the black intermingling, in sports you know, like that. So, he lit on the beach there, you know, and he got out and watched them for a while, and finally he said, "Now that's the way it ought to be." Then he got back into his plane and flew off. And one of the white guys looks over at the other and said, "What in hell is the matter with that guy?" Said, "Ain't he ever seen anyone troll for alligators?"[44]

This joke received national publicity when, in May of 1981, a similar intraoffice "joke memo" accidentally was distributed as an official Tennessee Wildlife Resources Agency fishing report. Added to the straight, rather bland fishing report was a final sentence: "Also, alligators are being taken in good numbers trolling colored people on skis."[45]

True to the persistent, dynamic nature of folklore, the folk idea that alligators are especially fond of eating blacks weaves its way through various genres, both oral and visual. Thus, the symbolic story becomes one in which the threatening, castrating *vagina dentata* is turned by white males upon black male victims. The alligator in a sense becomes the agent of the white, castrating the black male and removing him as a formidable sexual competitor.[46]

The folk and popular texts we have scrutinized so far have all treated the alligator from the white point of view. Now would be a good time to inquire what is the black perspective on the alligator. The Afro-American materials, it turns out, confirm this view that the alligator is the white's agent for threatening the black. We find in the Afro-American folk texts the resistance and parody we have come to expect in the expressive culture of relatively powerless people.

Consider, for example, the two Joel Chandler Harris stories that feature alligators. The first is "Why Alligator's Back is Rough," as told by Daddy Jack. A dog is chasing Brer Rabbit, who hides by the creek near Brer 'Gator. Rabbit tells Alligator that "trouble" is chasing him. Alligator would like to see trouble, so Rabbit says that trouble will catch up with Alligator. Alligator becomes drowsy, makes a bed in the tall grass, shuts his eyes, opens his mouth, and falls asleep. Rabbit says that this day Alligator will know trouble, and he sets fire to the grass. Alligator dreams he is in the hot sun, then awakes and hollers "Trouble, trouble, trouble!" Rabbit taunts Alligator, who flees, scattering the fire, and dives into the creek. And that's why the Alligator's back is rough, because he has bumps where the fire burned.[47]

There is considerable scholarly debate about the origins and intertwining of European, Afro-American, and Native American tale types in the Southeastern United States, but Dundes persuades me that "The Bear Meets Trouble" has African origins.[48] This being so, it is interesting that the tale heard by Harris involves a symbolic substitution of the alligator for the bear, both victims of the rabbit, the

typical East African and Afro-American trickster hero (in contrast to
the typical European trickster, the fox).[49] Afro-Americans chose to
have Rabbit take revenge upon Alligator in their transformation of
the African tale, and therein lies my claim that at some level blacks
recognize the alligator as enemy, as agent of the white male.

The second Uncle Remus story featuring an alligator is also told
by the old African, Daddy Jack. In "How the Bear Nursed the Little
Alligator," a large mother bear with two little bears gets hungry and
goes off to fish, warning the little ones not to leave the hollow tree
where they live. The male cub wakes up hungry from a nap and
wanders off to fish, even though his sister reminds him of the mother's warning. The male cub comes down to the water and, mistaking
Alligator for a log, stands on it to fish. Alligator swims away with
the male cub on his back, planning to feed the cub to her seven children for breakfast. The male cub pleads with Alligator to let him
show her what a fine nurse he can be for the baby alligators. She
agrees to let him nurse her babies for one day, then goes off. Soon
the bear cub gets hungry, so he eats one of the baby alligators and
naps. The mother returns, scolds the cub for sleeping, and asks
where her children are. The cub brings her the six babies one at a
time to be washed and brings the first one again as the seventh. This
pattern repeats every day, with the male cub eating a baby alligator
and bringing some of the remaining babies again to convince the
mother there are seven. On the last day the cub eats the last baby
and runs away home.[50]

Again, this story appears in the Aarne-Thompson scheme as Tale
Type 37, "Fox as Nursemaid for Bear," but Dundes suspects (as did
Harris himself) that this is an African, not European, tale type.[51] In
this Afro-American transformation of the tale the male bear cub (the
black trickster of the tale) eats the female alligator's brood, taking a
new form of revenge upon the white's castrating agent. Read in this
way, the tale is a rather ominous one about the black caretakers of
white children, a meaning that whites could not afford to understand.

It is significant that in the second tale the trickster takes revenge
upon the alligator by eating its children. Additional evidence suggests that *eating* and *not being eaten* are main strategies for black
control over the alligator. Eating, we know, is not simply a culinary
matter; foodways are the locus of powerful cultural symbolism, in-

cluding eating as a form of revenge and eating as a way of acquiring the power of the thing eaten. While white chroniclers commented often upon the edibility of the alligator, it is primarily blacks and Native Americans who incorporated alligator meat into their diet. Although some white alligator farmers in Florida are trying to extend the market for alligator meat to restaurants catering to white tastes, there does not seem to be much headway made in getting whites to ask for alligator steak and gumbo.[52]

This "eating" theme gets dramatic display in a touristic performance known as "alligator wrestling." Beginning in the Florida land and tourism boom of the 1920s, alligator wrestling became standard fare at alligator attractions like Musa Isle and the St. Augustine Alligator Farm. The Seminole tribes of Florida had a relationship to the alligator much like that of the Plains Indians to the bison, but alligator wrestling was never a part of Seminole tradition. It was a daredevil show invented apparently for the white tourists.[53] A highlight of the wrestling show is when the American Indian male holds shut the alligator's mouth, either with one hand or with the jaws tucked underneath the wrestler's chin (fig. 3.4). This trick is made possible by the anatomical fact that crocodilians have very strong muscles for closing their mouths, but very weak ones for opening them. So this performance is a variation on the control-by-eating theme—a member of a racial minority controls the alligator (agent of the whites) by holding its mouth closed and preventing the alligator from mutilating the wrestler.

I have woven a twisted web of symbols and patterned meanings, mustering representative texts from folk, popular, and even elite culture in order to show one cultural "story" that Americans use to "make sense of" the alligator. Briefly stated, my argument has been that the central organizing motif of the alligator is as the castrating *vagina dentata*, that white expressive culture deflects the castrating threat and makes the alligator an ally in castrating the black or American Indian male. I am not claiming that this is the only culturally formulaic story for interpreting the alligator, only that it is a pervasive one connecting many alligator texts and images. Moreover, although this analysis at times relies upon a psychoanalytic interpretation of symbols and relationships, the most compelling argument for its plausibility is the fact that it is the "folk" them-

3.4. Seminole Indian wrestling an alligator at Musa Isle Indian Village, Miami, Florida, 1956. Photo by the author.

selves, both black and white, who make these symbolic equations in their stories, jokes, and rituals.[54]

The story linking alligators, toothed vaginas, castration, and blacks is an important one for us to see and understand, so innocent and benign are the surface structures of many of these materials. The tasteless postcards and souvenirs and the racist jokes are plain enough in their offense to liberal sensibilities, but these are only the most blatant expressions of the same ideas that lie behind our understanding of children's stories, jump-rope rhymes, cartoons, and comics. To discover the ways in which these symbols and stories carry anti-female and anti-black meanings is to see the ideology packed into our most taken-for-granted attitudes toward the world. Thinking anew about the symbolic alligator becomes, then, a moral act, perhaps a moral duty, as we resist the power of the "myths that think themselves in our minds."

NOTES

This essay is a revised and extended version of a paper read at the meeting of the American Folklore Society in San Antonio, Texas, October 21–25, 1981. A grant from the Committee on Research of the Academic Senate of the University of California, Davis, supported fieldwork for this project. Folklorists constitute a wonderful network of friends scouring the world for alligator "texts" and artifacts, but I owe special thanks to Marilyn Jorgensen, Sue Samuelson, and David Scofield Wilson. Dr. Steve Kerber of the F.K. Yonge Library of Florida History at the University of Florida provided crucial assistance. Finally, two owners of Florida alligator attractions—Jay "JC" Bowen of Everglades Gatorland in South Bay and Gene Pickren of Ross Allen's Alligatortown USA in Lake City—spoke to me at length and gave me a glimpse at an entrepreneurial tourist institution fading away in the shadow of corporate tourist attractions like Disney World.

1. Characteristic is the following newspaper story, entitled "Alligator Carries Off Large Dog":

> INVERNESS, FLA.—An alligator, estimated to be 10 to 12 feet long, crawled from a canal, snatched a large dog that was apparently trying to protect two young children, and ate it, authorities say. . . . He estimated the 18-month-old dog, a cross between a Labrador retriever and a German shepherd, weighed between 60 and 80 pounds. . . . According to the sheriff's report, the family's dog, named Sadie, "went after" the alligator, distracting it from the children. The alligator attacked the dog and "returned to the canal with the dog in its mouth." (*San Francisco Chronicle*, Sept. 28, 1983, 3)

For other typical encounter stories, see Geoffrey Norman, "Gators," *Esquire* 94 (1980): 112–14, and Jack Rudloe, "Master of My Lake," *Audubon* 84 (1982): 5, 6, 8, 9.

2. William Bartram, *Travels through North and South Carolina, Ga.*

East and West Florida (Savannah, Ga.: The Beehive Press, 1973), 116–27. This is a facsimile reprint of the 1792 London edition.

3. See Joseph Ewan, ed., *William Bartram: Botanical and Zoological Drawings, 1756-1788* (Philadelphia: American Philosophical Society, 1968).

4. Wilfred T. Neill, *The Last of the Ruling Reptiles: Alligators, Crocodiles, and Their Kin* (New York: Columbia Univ. Press, 1971). Neill does for the alligator what Klauber did for the rattlesnake—that is, he surveys the full range of scientific, historical, and folkloristic treatments of the alligator. Neill sees that "much that passes for crocodilian biology reflects little more than human psychology, human nature, human emotions and attitudes" (44). Neill is very critical of what is still sometimes taken as the leading authoritative treatment of the alligator, E.A. McIlhenny's *The Alligator's Life History* (Boston: The Christopher Publishing House, 1935). Of course, it is precisely McIlhenny's culture-bound "reading" of alligators that makes his book so valuable as a cultural text. Valuable for the same reason is Albert M. Reese, *The Alligator and Its Allies* (New York: G.P. Putnam's Sons, 1915).

5. Neill, 250–61.

6. "Big Alligator Kills Florida Boy," *San Francisco Chronicle*, Aug. 8, 1984, pp. 1, 16.

7. On the special status of dogs, see Edmund Leach, "Anthropological Aspects of Language: Animal Categories and Verbal Abuse," in *New Directions in the Study of Language*, ed. Eric H. Lenneberg (Cambridge, Mass.: MIT Press, 1964), 23–63.

8. Neill, 2. There are several new theories explaining the demise of the dinosaurs. See the cover story, "Did Comets Kill the Dinosaurs?" *Time* 125 (May 6, 1985): 72–74, 77–79, 81, 83.

9. Dick Bothwell, *The Great Outdoors Book of Alligators* (St. Petersburg, Fla.: Great Outdoors Publishing Company, 1962).

10. Neill, 18. A remarkable book that does for the African crocodile what I am attempting here for the American alligator is Alistair Graham's *Eyelids of Morning: The Mixed Destinies of Crocodiles and Men* (New York: A&W Visual Library, 1973).

11. Mary Douglas, *Implicit Meanings: Essays in Anthropology* (London: Routledge and Kegan Paul, 1975).

12. An excellent iconographic analysis of crocodilians in Mesoamerican religion is Terry Stocker, Sarah Meltzoff, and Steve Armsey, "Crocodilians and Olmecs: Further Interpretations in Formative Period Iconography." *American Antiquity* 45 (1980): 740–56.

13. Hugh Honour, *The New Golden Land: European Images of Amer-*

ica from the Discoveries to the Present Time (New York: Pantheon Books, 1975), 109.

14. The Locher cartoon appeared in the *San Francisco Chronicle,* April 13, 1981, 48; the Oliphant cartoon in the "This World" section of the *San Francisco Chronicle/Examiner,* Sunday edition, April 15, 1984, 4; and the Lurie cartoon appeared in *U.S. News and World Report,* April 9, 1984, 17.

15. *New York Times Book Review,* March 8, 1981, 10.

16. Nicholas von Hoffman, "Know Thy President," *New York Review of Books,* June 25, 1981, 24–28.

17. See various cartoons in Gary Larson's *The Far Side* (Kansas City, Kans.: Andrews and McMeel, Inc., 1982) and *Beyond the Far Side* (Kansas, City, Kans.: Andrews and McMeel, Inc., 1983); see also the Larson cartoons in the *San Francisco Chronicle* of Oct. 21, 1982; Jan. 3, 1983; and Sept. 26, 1983.

18. See Motifs F547.1. *Toothed private parts*; F547.1.1. *Vagina dentata*; and K1222. *Woman tricks importunate lover with the head of a pike* (thereafter he thinks vagina is toothed). Stith Thompson, *Motif-Index of Folk Literature* (Bloomington: Indiana Univ. Press, 1958), vol. 3, 164.

19. Maria Leach, ed., *Funk and Wagnall's Standard Dictionary of Folklore, Mythology, and Legend* (New York: Funk and Wagnall, 1972), 1152. For evidence of the persistence of the *vagina dentata* motif in modern American folklore, see Monte Gulzow and Carol Mitchell, " 'Vagina Dentata' and 'Incurable Venereal Disease' Legends from the Viet Nam War," *Western Folklore* 39 (1980): 306–16.

20. Collected from white female in her thirties, who heard it from her brother in 1970. A variant collected from white male in his sixties.

21. Mary Knapp and Herbert Knapp, *One Potato, Two Potato: The Folklore of American Children* (New York: Norton, 1976), 113.

22. Sherman A. Minton, Jr., and Madge Rutherford Minton, *Giant Reptiles* (New York: Charles Scribner's Sons, 1973), 57.

23. Alan Dundes, "Projection in Folklore: A Plea for Psychoanalytic Semiotics," *Modern Language Notes* 91 (1976): 1500–33.

24. Rudyard Kipling, *Just So Stories* (1912; rpt. New York: Doubleday, 1950).

25. Roger Abrahams and Alan Dundes, "On Elephantasy and Elephanticide," *Psychoanalytic Quarterly* 56 (1969): 225–41. For other examples of the nose = penis symbolic equation in patterns of folktale variation, see Alan Dundes, "The Symbolic Equivalence of Allomotifs in the Rabbit-Herd (AT 570)," *Scandinavian Yearbook of Folklore* 36 (1982): 91–98. Of course, loss of the penis is not literally castration, which involves loss of the testicles. But loss of the penis is symbolic emasculation.

26. For an interpretation of the mutilation/castration meaning of the

adolescent urban legend, "The Hook," see Alan Dundes, "On the Psychology of Legend," in *American Folk Legend: A Symposium,* ed. Wayland Hand (Berkeley: Univ. of California Press, 1971), 21–36.

27. See Derral Cheatwood, "The Tarzan Films: An Analysis of Determinants of Maintenance and Change in Conventions," *Journal of Popular Culture* 16 (1982): 127–42.

28. Collected from a Canadian female in her late 20s.

29. Blanche Knott, *Truly Tasteless Jokes* (New York: Ballantine, 1982), 97. Reprinted from Matt Freedman and Paul Hoffman, *What Do WASPs Say After Sex?* (New York: St. Martin's Press, 1981).

30. Neill, 34–35.

31. Minton and Minton, 69.

32. Maria Leach, ed., 37. For a sample of folk medical remedies involving alligator oil, teeth, and flesh, see Lyle Saxon, *et al.,* comps., WPA Louisiana Writer's Project, *Gumbo Ya-Ya: A Collection of Louisiana Folk Tales* (Boston: Houghton Mifflin Company, 1945), 247, 534–35.

33. Neill, 9, 34

34. Paul Dickson and Joseph C. Goulden, *There Are Alligators in Our Sewers and Other American Credos* (New York: Dell, 1983).

35. Jan Brunvand surveys this legend, its variants, its core, and the folklore scholarship interpreting the legend in his *The Vanishing Hitchhiker* (New York: Norton, 1981), 90–101.

36. Thomas Pynchon, *V.* (New York: Bantam, 1963). The extended analysis of Pynchon's use of the legend is Kenneth A. Thigpen, "Folklore in Contemporary American Literature: Thomas Pynchon's V and the Alligators-in-the Sewers Legend" *Southern Folklore Quarterly* 43 (1979): 93–105.

37. Cathy M. Orr and Michael J. Preson, eds., "Urban Folklore from Colorado," typescript (Ann Arbor, Mich.: University Microfilms, 1976), 8.

38. G. Legman, *Rationale of the Dirty Joke: An Analysis of Sexual Humor,* Second Series (New York: Breaking Point, Inc., 1975), 443.

39. Ibid., 481.

40. Neill, 253–54; also see Minton and Minton, 59.

41. Marjorie Kinnan Rawlings and Fred Tompkins, "Alligators," *The Saturday Evening Post,* 206 (Sept. 23, 1933): 16–17, 36, 38; reprinted in Marjorie Kinnan Rawlings, *When the Whippoorwill—*(New York: Charles Scribner's Sons, 1940), 217–32.

42. Neill, 254. Some of the "texts" documenting American uses of the symbolic alligator will shock and offend the sensibilities of most readers of this volume. An important stylistic quality to much folklore is its "earthiness," which usually takes the form of obscenity and other sorts of

indelicate subject matter. For one folklorist's approach to this problem, see Rayna Green's "Folk Is A Four-Letter Word: Dealing With Traditional **** in Fieldwork, Analysis, and Presentation," in *Handbook of American Folklore,* ed. Richard M. Dorson (Bloomington: Indiana University Press, 1983), 525–32.

But some of these alligator folk texts offend in a different manner—they offend liberal sensibilities in their racism and sexism. This, too, is a persistent issue for folklorists, as was evident in the responses by some to Alan Dundes's and Thomas Houschild's, "Auschwitz Jokes," *Western Folklore* 42 (1983): 249–60. There are some who believe that it is bad enough that these offensive folk texts exist at all; must we perpetuate the materials by publishing them? The jokes that follow close on the heels of tragedies like the Chernobyl nuclear plant accident and the Challenger Shuttle explosion raise similar questions.

My answer is that scholars have a responsibility to understand the cultural sources and consequences of these offensive folk materials. Folklorists do not invent these materials, the "folk" do, and the "folk" often include very young members of our societies, members whom we like to think of as innocent. Folklorists are not like a network news camera team that may be as much a cause as a reporter of events. Indeed, folklorists often find that informants avoid obscene and otherwise offensive materials in the formal interview setting.

The responsibility I am describing is partly intellectual, that is, as scholars our role is to explain cultural phenomena. But the responsibility is also an ethical one to the extent that the scholar uses the analysis to "unmask" even the most invisible sources of racism and sexism. Ignoring racism, sexism, anti-semitism, and similar prejudices does not make them go away. They are symptoms, not causes.

43. The exhibit, "Ethnic Notions," appeared at the Berkeley Art Center in August of 1982. There is a published catalog.

44. Donald M. Hines, "Some Hoosier Humor from the Maple Grove Neighborhood, Indiana," *Southern Folklore Quarterly* 32 (1968): 64.

45. Anonymous, "Racial Slur 'Joke' in Fishing Report," *San Francisco Chronicle,* Friday, May 8, 1981, p. 24. The spring, 1984, Democratic presidential primary campaign brought its own surprising version of the use of alligators to harass blacks. *San Francisco Chronicle* correspondent Reginald Smith, following the Jesse Jackson campaign in Los Angeles, reported this development (*SF Chronicle,* May 19, 1984, 1):

Jesse Jackson was in a particularly foul mood one recent day while fielding a round of tough questions from reporters about his much-publicized "Hymietown" gaffe.

"I'm sick of allegations," Jackson snapped. "And I'm sick of the alligators."

Since that day, some reporters traveling full time with Jackson have worn small toy alligator clackers around their necks.

Whenever they get annoyed by something the Jackson campaign does, the reporters—often in unison—squeeze the metal alligators so they make an equally annoying click-clack sound.

Chronicle columnist Herb Caen later traced this malapropism to the *Amos 'n Andy* radio and television shows.

46. One form of the emasculation of the black man in this semiotic complex is the transformation of the black's surrogate—the elephant—into a female. Abrahams and Dundes, 234, note this transformation in some of the elephant riddle texts and in Walt Disney's *Fantasia,* specifically the ballet (to Ponchielli's "Dance of the Hours" from *La Gioconda*) in which the prima ballerina is a hippo and her corps de ballet consists of elephants in toe shoes and tutus. What Abrahams and Dundes do not mention is that the male dancer in this ballet is a crocodile. Elephant turned female, *vagina dentata* turned male, the inversion simply reinforces the encoded meanings.

47. Joel Chandler Harris, *Nights with Uncle Remus: Myths and Legends of the Old Plantation* (Boston: Osgood and Company, 1883), 143–49. Another version, "B' Allegetter Sees Trouble" as told by Albert H. Stoddard of Savannah, Georgia, can be heard on the Library of Congress "Folklore of the United States" long-playing record #L44, *Animal Tales Told in the Gullah Dialect* (recorded in 1949).

48. Alan Dundes, "African and Afro-American Tales," in *African Folklore in the New World,* ed. Daniel J. Crowley (Austin: Univ. of Texas Press, 1977), 35–53.

49. Alan Dundes, "African Tales Among the North American Indians," in *Mother Wit from the Laughing Barrel,* ed. Alan Dundes (Englewood Cliffs; N.J.: Prentice-Hall, Inc., 1973), 114–25. Kipling was very familiar with the Harris stories, further complicating the relationship of "The Elephant Child" to the Afro-American materials. See Howard C. Rice, *Rudyard Kipling in New England* (Brattleboro, Vt.: Stephen Dayne Press, 1936).

50. Harris, 353–58.

51. Dundes, "African and Afro-American Tales," 42, and Harris, xix. The central reference for tale types in this debate is Antii Aarne and Stith Thompson, eds., *The Types of the Folktale,* 2nd rev., *Folklore Fellows Communications,* no. 184 (Helsinki, 1961). Anancy, the spider, is another African trickster figure that appears in Afro-American lore and some-

times takes revenge upon the alligator. See Daryl C. Dance, *Folklore from Contemporary Jamaicans* (Knoxville: Univ. of Tennessee Press, 1985), 14–18, 102–103, for Anancy tales closely resembling the two Harris tales.

52. Rick Dower, "Gator-aid for Dull Life," *San Francisco Chronicle,* Sunday, Aug. 2, 1981, p. A4. On the patterns of eating alligator, see Minton and Minton, 69, and Neill, 12–13. I should add that "eat" has sexual connotations as well as gastronomic, so that eating the alligator is not simply a symbolic incorporation of its power.

53. Minton and Minton, 71–72. While the usual alligator wrestler is a Seminole, the St. Augustine Alligator Farm features white and black wrestlers. For descriptions of the role of the alligator in Seminole expressive culture, see Bothwell, 48–50, and Robert F. Greenlee, "Folktales of the Florida Seminole," *Journal of American Folklore* 58 (1945): 138–44.

54. This cultural story may also account for the symbolic uses of the alligator in the "Preppy" (i.e., wealthy preparatory school student) craze of the early 1980s and the subsequent anti-Preppy backlash. The episode revolved around the smiling alligator that is the trademark of Izod shirts by Lacoste. Commercial "hypes" work only when the images and icons of the mass media messages tap into a reservoir of folk ideas the audience uses to interpret the everyday world. As a WASP-ish class, Preppies represent precisely the people who would employ a symbolic proxy—the alligator—to put down both women and blacks. The anti-Preppy backlash tried to free the alligator from its role as emblem of the Preppy class. Among the commercially available items in the backlash were a button with the international red slash across an alligator, signifying "No Preppies Allowed," and a bumper sticker advising, "Save the Alligator—Eat a Preppy." Like the Uncle Remus story, this tactic takes its revenge upon the oppressor by eating it. Sometimes the popular culture texts featured symbolic inversion—an alligator wearing a shirt with a man on it. Political cartoonist Mike Goters of the *Dayton Daily News* used this inversion in a March, 1982, captionless cartoon of an alligator wearing a shirt with discredited Secretary of the Interior, James Watt, on the left breast.

The Armadillo

ANGUS K. GILLESPIE

I want to go home with the Armadillo
Good country music from Amarillo and Abilene
The friendliest people and the prettiest women
you ever seen.
                    —*Gary P. Nunn, 1973*
                    "London Homesick Blues"

From this remarkable chorus of Gary P. Nunn's most popular song we learn a great deal about Texas music. The narrator is a homesick entertainer stuck on an overseas singing tour. In the body of the song, he complains about his reception among the English people, the coldness of the buildings, and his difficulties in finding any women. He longs to go home to a Texas bar where presumably he will find ready solutions for all of his problems. But why is the armadillo used as an emblem, symbol, or token for home? There are obvious reasons for the choice. The initial letter "A" sets up an alliteration with Amarillo and Abilene. Furthermore, in the song itself he pronounces the word as "Armadilla" so that it will rhyme with "Amarilla." While this is very clever, it does not explain the choice of the armadillo as a symbol.[1]

It is up to the scholar to discover why a given animal, a natural object, becomes a symbol. Over time, a natural object may be represented in a variety of artistic forms—including artifacts, works of art, narratives, songs, and festive events. As George Kubler says: "From all these things, a shape in time emerges. A visible portrait of the collective identity, whether tribe, class, or nation comes into being. This self-image reflected in things is a guide and point of reference to the group for the future, and it eventually becomes the portrait given to posterity."[2]

The evidence suggests two distinct phases in the symbology of the armadillo. The first is the age of discovery—the sixteenth and seventeenth centuries—when the early explorers, fascinated by this strange animal, seized upon it in allegorical representations of the New World. The Spanish conquistadors were intrigued by the Indian, the alligator, and the armadillo. Then there came a period of relative neglect. By the eighteenth and nineteenth centuries, the armadillo was just an animal. The fascination ended, and explorers and others took it for granted. Although it was noticed by Charles Darwin, who studied it, and by John James Audubon, who painted it, for them and for a handful of others, it was a curious mammal rather than the symbol it had been for earlier explorers.

The second period and perhaps the most interesting for the armadillo as symbol began in the twentieth century specifically in the late 1960s—and continues, with some modifications, to the present. The armadillo was plucked from obscurity by Texas hippies who took it as a symbol of the counter-culture. As we shall see, it was in many ways a clever and appropriate choice. In fact, it was so effectively brought into public consciousness that in Texas, at least, the armadillo, in its latest symbolic role, is in the process of being absorbed by popular culture.

Fascination with the armadillo began with its appearance. It is an armored mammal about twenty-four to thirty-two inches long, including the ten- to fifteen-inch tail, and it usually weighs ten to twelve pounds. In other words, it is about the size of a ground hog or a large domestic cat. The body is enclosed by a three-sectioned shell. One section in the front protects the shoulders; another section in the rear protects the pelvic region. In the middle section between these two are a number of movable bands. It is this middle section which gives the animal a very distinctive appearance, a little bit like a knight in medieval armor. The tail is protected by fourteen rings of armor, and the top of the head and the distal portions of the legs are also armored. The vulnerable underside is without armor, but it is protected by a tough skin covered with coarse hair.[3]

Everyone agrees that the armadillo presents a strange appearance. A burrowing mammal with a jointed, protective covering of bony plates is so unlikely that the temptation to employ metaphor in its description is almost irresistible. In more recent times, counter-culture artist Jim Franklin described it as a snake underneath a watermelon. It has also been described as the oldest mammal in North America with "a scaled head like a lizard's, ears like a mule's, claws like a bear's, and a tail shaped like a rat's."[4] A magazine article in *Southern Living* described the armadillo as "possum on the half shell."[5]

These bizarre descriptions provide a valuable set of clues for our analysis. Why has the armadillo been an object of fascination for pre-conquest Mexican Indians, Spanish conquistadors, Anglo explorers, South American Indians, and present-day Texans? Why has this animal captured the imagination of human beings across many cultures over a long period of time? It may well be that our fascination stems from the fact that the armadillo cannot be readily classified. It looks like a reptile, but it is really a mammal. In her intriguing book, *Purity and Danger,* Mary Douglas explains that ambiguity enriches our perceptions.[6]

The armadillo is ambiguous because it confounds our classificatory systems. It is an animal that falls on the boundary between two categories. Normally human culture serves individuals by giving us patterns of rules. The armadillo is a creature that breaks the rules. The shattering of the rules is upsetting, but not necessarily unpleasing. Confronting an armadillo is startling in somewhat the same way that reading good poetry is startling.[7]

Although the armadillo is noteworthy because its unusual anatomy renders classification difficult, what is also equally significant is the armadillo's habitat. It is found naturally only in the Western Hemisphere. Collectively, armadillos make up a suborder, *Cinqulata,* of the endentates, distributed throughout South America and north to Texas. Because the early explorers had not seen the animal before in Europe, it was natural for them to identify the "New Animal" with the "New World." Gradually this identification became so fixed that the armadillo took on the nature of a symbol. It was widely used in such symbolic contexts as decorative map cartouches.

Our focus in this study is not on the entire suborder, but rather on a single species—the nine-banded armadillo, which is known formally as *Dasypus novemcinctus mexicanus* or informally as the Texas armadillo.[8] In modern times the nine-banded armadillo has become strongly identified with Texas by the people who live there. This identification is more of a Texan assumption than a national one. For example, the armadillo is probably not as effective in evoking Texas for someone in New Jersey as perhaps the longhorn steer is. Even for Texans, the longhorn evokes pride while the armadillo evokes fondness and familiarity. The armadillo has emerged as an alternative icon for Texans who find the longhorn too crude and too bellicose. Furthermore, this identification is emotional and symbolic rather than strictly factual, since the armadillo is not at all confined to the political boundaries of present-day Texas.

It is a truism that wildlife generally suffers a shrinkage in its habitat as civilization develops land for its own purposes. In fact, many mammals and birds have been driven into wilderness areas in Mexico as the United States has urbanized the desert. Strangely enough, the armadillo is an exception to the rule. It has actually extended its range to the north and east. It was first discovered north of the Mexican border in 1854 by John James Audubon, who attempted to paint it realistically. Observers today almost universally regard the painting as a failure. Perhaps the animal was just too weird for Audubon to handle. Since 1854 the armadillo has extended its range to Oklahoma, Kansas, Arkansas, Louisiana, Mississippi, Alabama, and Florida. This extraordinary proliferation has several possible explanations. Perhaps most important is the fact that farmers and ranchers have worked toward exterminating the coyote, a natural predator. Another favorite explanation is that the armadillo has simply taken advantage of new roads and bridges to extend its range. It is assumed that its spread eastward as far as Florida has been aided by civilization. Apparently people originally brought armadillos to Florida in the early twentieth century as pets, grew tired of them, and set them free. They have thrived and multiplied in Florida ever since.[9]

Even natural boundaries such as rivers and streams do not seriously thwart an armadillo on the move. The explanation for this is truly incredible. Although I have not personally witnessed an armadillo cross a river, there are reliable accounts. For example, journalist Cary McCally soberly reports:

> When confronted with water, armadillos do one of two things: either sink to the bottom and stroll to the other side, or swallow air to inflate their stomachs and intestines, so they can float to the other side. The Mississippi River is a bit wide for a walk-under, so presumably they floated, reaching the other side with a pronounced belch of relief.[10]

With their almost magical ability to cross large bodies of water, armadillos would appear to have an unlimited potential range. They do not. Most mammals have a fixed body temperature, but the armadillo's body temperature fluctuates with that of the environment, perhaps because the protective shell is a poor insulator. In any event, cold weather is deadly for armadillos. Terry Peters reports that "a climate with a maximum of roughly nine freeze-days per year marks the northern limit of the armadillo's expansion."[11]

Although limited, the range is not confined, as it may once have been, to northern Mexico and southern Texas.[12] In spite of this fact, Texans have claimed the armadillo as their own. While Texans may grudgingly concede that armadillos are found elsewhere, they are likely to insist out of Texas chauvinism that there are *more* of them in Texas. Perhaps the last word should go to R. W. Pemberton, who designed an automobile decal back in 1978 picturing a large snarling armadillo superimposed on a map of Texas surrounded by cacti. At the bottom were emblazoned three words: "NOWHERE BUT TEXAS."

The armadillo had been known by pre-conquest Mexican Indians for centuries before the arrival of Europeans. An excellent source on this period is Donald Cordry's handsomely illustrated book, *Mexican Masks*. Cordry writes that because the armadillo is a burrowing animal and can make itself vanish quickly into the earth, it has been associated with the earth by the Indians in Mexico. This identification of the animal with the earth has led to some interesting scholarly speculation. Cordry continues:

> While there is very little information on the armadillo from ancient sources, its name in Nahuatl, *ayo-tochtli,* literally means "tortoise-rabbit" (Robelo 1904, p. 65), implying that the Aztecs

may have held similar beliefs, as the rabbit was closely associated with the moon and thereby the gods of vegetation and harvest, and the tortoise was a water symbol.[13]

The name "tortoise-rabbit" is a straightforward attempt to deal with an animal on the boundary line of the Aztec classification system. The depictions of the armadillo indicate that it must have been of central importance to the native people of Mexico for ages. They revered the armadillo because of its intimate, burrowing connection with the earth and with fertility, and the animal became associated with their religion and their rituals. Then came the discovery of America by the European explorers, who were confronted with what to them were new terrains, new people, new customs, new plants, and new animals. Their accounts gave a prominent place to the armadillo, which was catapulted into a position of importance as a visual icon of the New World. Hugh Honour documents this process in his book *The European Vision of America*. With the discovery of America, artists and cartographers had to deal with not just the three continents of old, but with four. In the latter half of the sixteenth century, there was a brisk demand for allegorical representations of the four continents. Especially challenging to the artist was coming up with an appropriate design for America. Honour writes:

> In creating their allegories of America, artists attempted to
> compress into a single image as many as possible of the
> distinguishing features of the land and its inhabitants. She is thus,
> almost invariably, represented naked with feather ornaments and
> some indication of riches of the continent in gold and silver. A
> parrot and some four-footed beast—armadillo, alligator,
> opossum, or llama—accompany her.[14]

Honour scrupulously traces early references in prose, poetry, and illustration to these American animals. The early maps sometimes presented the fauna of North America in symbolic and decorative ways. The mapmakers were fascinated with American birds— turkeys, parrots, toucans—and with the armadillo. According to Honour, it was mentioned by Martin Fernandez de Enciso as early as 1518 and then described by Roger Barlow in his *Brief Summe of Geographie* in 1540:

> Ther is a kynde of small beastes no bigger than a pigges of a

moneth olde, and the fete the hede and eares be like a horse, and
his bodie and his head is all covered saving his eres with a shell
moche like the shell of a tortuga, but it is the very proportion of
an armed horse for this shelle hangeth downe by his sides and
afore his brest moving as it were hanged by gynowes hinges, or
moche like the lappes of a complete harneis. It is an admiration
to behold it. Hit fedeth like a horse and his taile is like a pigges
tail, saving it is straight.[15]

Barlow must be given credit for a good effort in verbal description, but it would have been difficult for an artist to come up with a
sketch based on these comparisons to horses and pigs. Gradually, as
stuffed specimens became available, things became easier for the artists. The real challenge, as Honour explains, was to create a representation for America comparable to that of Europa on her bull. In
1594 Maarten de Vos devised a conception of "America as a hand-
some nude girl with a very elaborate coiffure riding an outsize
armadillo—sidesaddle of course" (fig. 4.1.).[16]

The next design to enjoy widespread currency was done fifty
years later by Stefano della Bella in 1644 (fig. 4.2.). The new design
removed the Indian maiden from her uncomfortable bareback position mounted atop the armadillo and placed her in a more regal
chariot drawn by a team of two harnessed armadillos. According to
Honour, "This design was widely copied, for instance, on a massive
silver dish made at Augsburg in 1689."[17]

It is, then, a fact that in the 1500s and the 1600s, during the age of
discovery, the armadillo played a large role in the widely copied and
disseminated allegorical representations of America. Given the be-
wildering array of New World fauna, why was the armadillo singled
out for pictorial treatment? Again the clue comes from Honour's research. He quotes a poem written by a Dr. Powis at the end of the
seventeenth century:

> This animal is arm'd with Scale
> As if it wore a Coate of Maile
> In shape and snout he is a swine
> And like to him doth grunt and whine.
> But if you view his scaly skin
> Hees Fish without and Swine within
> A creature of Amphibious nature
> And lives both in and out of water.[18]

4.1. "America, 1594," by Maarten de Vos. Reproduced from Hugh Honour, *The New Golden Land: European Images of America from the Discoveries to the Present Time* (New York: Pantheon, 1975). Courtesy of Random House.

Once again the source of the fascination seems to lie in the ambiguous nature of the armadillo. Dr. Powis sees the animal as straddling the boundary between pig and fish. This fish-swine commands our attention because it is anomalous, abnormal, irregular.

As time went on, the armadillo began to fade from allegorical representations of America. By the eighteenth century, many of the allegorical representations preserved the nearly nude Indian maiden, but her companion was more likely to be the alligator than the armadillo. Perhaps this shift occurred because the armadillo was becoming more familiar. As it did, people began to realize that it was really less than a yard long and less than a foot tall—hardly big enough for a person to ride, let alone big enough to pull a chariot. It was stretching reality too far to picture the animal twenty times larger that it actually was. Not only was the alligator a more suitable size, it was also more suitably ferocious. As more was learned about the armadillo, people began to realize that it was a peaceful animal, mainly interested in looking for bugs. While the alligator might confront an enemy with its powerful jaws, the armadillo was far more likely to avoid a confrontation by burrowing in the earth. The armadillo was simply not large enough or aggressive enough to make an appropriate heroic symbol once the true facts about its size and habits were widely known.

When the country was being settled during the eighteenth and nineteenth centuries, the conquistadors and adventurers passed from the scene. Now the Southwest was traversed by American army explorers, civilian explorers, and scientific investigators. Though there were boundary surveys and railroad surveys through tracts of land that we assume were populated by armadillos, the animals were not the subject of special mention.[19] Most accounts of wild life in the American West mentioned that the buffalo had a commanding position on the Great Plains. Some accounts mentioned the pronghorn antelope in association with the buffalo; others reported finding the American elk in large numbers. Writers who wished to play up the ferocity of the Wild West might dwell on the fierce flesh-eaters like the wolf, mountain lion, and grizzly bear. Those who wanted to present the West as the land of plenty would mention the fur-bearing animals such as the beaver, bobcat, and otter. Dime novelists looking for local color could be counted on to mention coyotes, jack rabbits, and prairie dogs.[20]

4.2. "America, 1644," by Stefano della Bella. Reproduced from Hugh Honour, *The New Golden Land* (New York: Pantheon, 1975). Courtesy of Random House.

But it would be a mistake to say that the armadillo was totally neglected during the nineteenth century. Instead the armadillo became the subject of scientific and objective inquiry rather than of artistic and iconographic celebration. Indeed the armadillo attracted the attention of two of the most important naturalists of the nineteenth century—Darwin and Audubon. When the *HMS. Beagle* explored the coast south of Buenos Aires, Argentina, in the fall of 1833, Darwin found the remains of giant sloth-like and armadillo-like creatures. His observations provoked speculation. One of Darwin's biographers, John Chancellor wrote:

> Littered around him were the relics of bygone sloths, armadillos
> and giant llamas. But he also saw on his land expeditions from
> the *Beagle* live sloths, armadillos, and llamas—smaller but not all
> that different from their prehistoric counterparts.[21]

Darwin began to think, of course, that in some way the living animals on shore must have descended from the fossils he had encountered. In 1836 the *Beagle* returned to Falmouth, and in the 1840s Darwin began to work out the principle of natural selection.

Meanwhile, in the 1840s, John James Audubon and his son John Woodhouse Audubon were collecting specimens for *The Quadrupeds of North America*. Their plan, a book on the same scale and scope as the earlier classic work on ornithology, called for three volumes with 150 folio plates. While in Texas, Audubon and his son received advice on where and how to hunt various animals, the advice coming from such distinguished sources as the Texas Rangers and Sam Houston. The drawing included for the armadillo, in terms of realism, was a considerable improvement over earlier versions by artists like Maarten de Vos and Stefano della Bella; but somehow Audubon's armadillo was still a little stiff and awkward. Like others before him, Audubon found the armadillo to be an anomaly and had to resort to metaphor in his written description:

> This singular production of nature, it might be said, resembles a
> small pig saddled with the shell of a turtle; it is about the size of
> a large opossum; the head is small, and greatly elongated, and
> the neck can be retracted so far as to entirely withdraw the head
> under the shell. . . . the covering of the head may be compared to
> a helmet, and that of the shoulders and on the hind parts to
> breast-plates and thigh-pieces, the whole forming an almost
> impenetrable coat of mail. . . .[22]

Both Audubon and Darwin were men of science. Though both were intrigued by the armadillo, they both saw it as a natural specimen rather than as an allegorical icon. Of course, anatomically the armadillo had not changed; the animal still presented a startling appearance. But the culture had changed. In the nineteenth century, science rather than allegory was the accepted way to deal with the environment and its animals.

But the scientific point of view is really very limiting. Man's fascination with the armadillo goes back to the dawn of time, and cannot be entirely explained away by science. To understand the importance of the armadillo as icon, we must supplement science with mythology. We have to examine the oral narrative tradition, which begins long ago among the primitive tribal cultures of South America. According to the mythology of the Mundurucu Indians of Brazil, the creator god is Karusakaibo whose constant companion and helper is Daiiru, an armadillo. Conflict between Karusakaibo and his sons is a frequent theme in several of the myths. In one story, Karusakaibo becomes angry at one of his sons and stalks him, wounding him with an arrow; but the armadillo saves the son by drawing the arrow from the wound.[23]

Another body of myth comes from the Gran Chaco, which is made up of parts of present-day Argentina, Bolivia, and Paraguay. Natives of this area believed that a big horned armadillo lived under the ground and that it was responsible for the Flood.[24] From the Chiriguano, a tribe living on the eastern slope of the Bolivian Andes, comes another set of myths. The leading characters of this mythology are Armadillo and Fox, whose names are always followed by the descriptive term, "tunpa" (sacred). Alfred Metraux explains, "Armadillo is a wise and powerful character, always well disposed toward mankind. Aguara-tunpa (Fox) is a trickster, although in many cases he also plays the part of a culture hero."[25]

In the 1930s Alfred Metraux made two expeditions to the Argentine Chaco to collect the myths and tales of natives there. For his day, Metraux was unusually scrupulous in his methods of folklore collecting and made a real effort to present entire texts of collectanea. The published results, *Myths of the Toba and Pilaga Indians of the Gran Chaco* (1946), show both Metraux's respect for the narrative gifts of his informants and the central importance of the armadillo to the Chaco inhabitants. In this marvelous body of material, the armadillo appears sometimes as a gigantic creature, with major roles central to the culture. The armadillo is a key figure in three myths—one relating to the origin of women, another relating to the origin of fire, and a third relating to the origin of agriculture. In all three myths the armadillo is presented favorably and sympathetically.

Narratives about the giant armadillo are not all far away and long ago. In recent years, the Lone Star Brewing Company of San Antonio, Texas, has launched an advertising campaign featuring a giant armadillo. This modern-day creature of advertising is found not in Argentina but in Texas, but, like his South American counterpart, this giant armadillo is aggressive; he attacks beer trucks. I was intrigued by this apparent revival of the old Indian tale, and I talked with Lone Star Beer's Vice President for Marketing, Bill Monroe. He explained that the giant armadillo campaign has worked well for them for several reasons. First of all, it's a humorous notion, which makes the ads pleasing. Secondly, the ads never actually portray the giant armadillo, so that the imagination is engaged in an attempt to envision it, and this makes the ads more memorable. Finally, the armadillo is so ubiquitous in Texas that it cuts across regular ethnic and racial lines. The animal is interesting and appealing to everyone in Texas, just as the company hopes that their beer will be. Indeed, this pluralistic approach is reflected in Lone Star's slogan: "The National Beer of Texas."[26] To appreciate the tone and impact of this advertising campaign, let us examine the text of one such ad. The ad is run under a bold headline, "Giant Armadillo Attacks Beer Truck!" The tone of the copy below is an amalgam of news bulletin and tall tale:

> In the third such incident this week, a Lone Star beer truck was sucked dry by a giant armadillo near Georgetown.
> This follows closely on the heels of the trashing of a bar in Fredericksburg and the leveling of a Quicky-Picky Market in McAllen.
> Driver Shorty Briggs voiced everyone's concern when he said, "He went right for the Lone Star sign on my truck. I didn't know those rascals could read."
> Meantime, highly placed sources at Lone Star assure the public that—despite the armadillo attacks—there will be no shortage of Lone Star, the national beer of Texas.[27]

The Lone Star advertising campaign is appealing to a long-standing tradition in Texas of folk interest in the armadillo. The shift from the folklore of the South American Indians to the folklore of Anglo-Texans is a shift from myth to tale. In the South American material, the armadillo is a godlike creature interacting, often benignly, in human affairs. In the Anglo-Texan tale the plot is usually quite simple—the armadillo is eaten for food. Usually, there is some complication: the meat may be poisonous; the diner may be fooled or tricked into eating the armadillo.

Before turning our attention to the narratives themselves, we should establish the fact that the armadillo *is* edible. There are many reports of people in the South shooting and eating armadillos. It was such a common practice during the depression that the armadillo earned the name "Hoover Hog." Here is Robert Lemmo's description of armadillo dining:

> Once caught and killed, an armadillo can simply be turned over and literally be scooped out of his shell. Without the shell, the armadillo is said to look like a skinny chicken. The meat can be broiled, baked, barbequed, or fried; and it is almost universally described as tasting quite good, like high quality, fatty pork. One of the favorite Tex-Mex uses for armadillo meat is in tamales. Wrapped in corn shucks, the tamales are stuffed with beef, pork, and armadillo meat. Other common dishes are pickled 'dillo and 'dillo gumbo, but the meat can be used anywhere one might ordinarily use pork.[28]

Though Lemmo's account is so cheerful and matter-of-fact that we find ourselves almost assenting, still there is a nagging doubt about the suitability of eating armadillos. To understand this doubt, let us turn to the anthropological analysis of taboo offered by Edmund R. Leach. He explains that the edible part of the environment usually falls into three main categories:

> 1. Edible substances that are recognized as food and consumed as part of the normal diet. 2. Edible substances that are recognized as possible food, but that are prohibited or else allowed to be eaten under special (ritual) conditions. These are substances which are *consciously tabooed*. 3. Edible substances that by culture and language are not recognized as food at all. The substances are *unconsciously tabooed*.[29]

Following Leach's analysis, it seems quite clear that the armadillo belongs in category three. Our disposition or prejudice against eating armadillos stems naturally from a linguistic problem. As we have discussed before, the armadillo defies our categories. It is warm blooded like a mammal, but its bony plates make it appear like a reptile. Leach goes on to say that speakers of English basically recognize three food categories—fish, birds, and beasts. There is a large residue of creatures, rated as either *reptiles* or *insects,* but the whole of this ambiguous residue is rated as not food.[30] What could be clearer? It is the armadillo's reptilian appearance that makes it loathsome to us. No matter how palatable or available the armadillo may in fact be, we still feel an unconscious revulsion. In spite of all reassurances to the contrary, we cannot help but include armadillo meat with things to be avoided.

With this theoretical background in mind, let us examine a number of Anglo-Texan narratives. The first is a story called "The Mystery of the Five Graves" collected by John C. Meyers for an anthology of Texana called the *Golden Log.* Meyers reported finding five marked, but unidentified, graves along the highway between Carrizo Springs and Eagle Pass, about one hundred miles northwest of Laredo. He asked around among local residents for an explanation of the unidentified graves. According to one version, the five crosses marked the graves of a family who died during a fever epidemic. According to another version, the family died from eating spoiled venison. Some said the graves belonged to a Mexican family killed in a buggy that collided with a truck which went out of control. Others said the graves belonged to five Indians killed by bandits. But the most interesting version was the one supplied by one Uncle Ed Walton, here in the words of John C. Meyers:

> Among the first arrivals who settled at Eagle Pass in the early
> days was a family by the name of Larkin. In this frontier town,
> misfortune followed misfortune for the Larkins. Finally the family
> decided to give up everything and move to East Texas, where
> relatives lived. The family now included five boys and four girls.
> They started out early one morning traveling in a wagon drawn
> by mules. Mr. Larkin was determined to leave behind forever this
> severe land which had dealt so unkindly with him. But he and
> four of his sons never quite made it. The second day out, while

they were stopping for noonday rest, one of their dogs dragged into camp an armadillo which it had killed. The family decided to clean the animal and take the meat along to be cooked for the evening meal. Only Mr. Larkin and the four oldest boys could stomach the strong meat of the armadillo. About two hours later the five who had partaken of the armadillo meat died in agony. The next morning, passers-by helped bury the dead and assisted Mrs. Larkin in resuming her journey. The crosses that mark the graves are still there by the road for everyone to see.[31]

Meyers, a knowledgeable Texan, objected to this. He said that it made a good story, except that everyone knows that armadillos are not poisonous. His informant defended the accuracy of the story, explaining that the dogs must have somehow ruptured the intestines of the armadillo during the kill, thus contaminating the meat. Of course, it makes a good story. The clue concerning the mode of kill is built into the narrative, so there is a rational explanation for the poisonous meat. But the story is also effective because it somehow confirms our irrational fear: armadillos are not for eating.

Other narratives on the subject that have come to my attention do not result in the death of the diner. The plots are built around the element of surprise. Only after consuming the armadillo with gusto does the diner realize what he has eaten. One such story, probably a piece of fakelore, is based on linguistic confusion. The story concerns an old Indian Scout who is leading a group of surveyors when they confront a Comanche camp:

> Quickly encircled by the Indians, the old Scout shouted in Comanche tongue to the Chief. The Chief recognized the scout and quickly embraced him. The Scout and his party were invited to the Indian camp. After a long Pow Wow, the chief ordered food for his guest. When the food arrived, the surveyors hesitated, not knowing what they would be eating. The chief seeing doubt on their faces, attempted to put the men at ease. Not speaking good Texan, he said, "Etah, Tejas Tookay!" The men attempting to understand the chief, understood him to say, "Eat, Texas Turkey." The Old Scout grinned, he knew what the chief meant to say, "Armadillo." A Comanche delicacy. Some of the men said it tasted like Pork, others said Beef.[32]

This, too, makes a good story, even if it is apocryphal and without a known basis in oral circulation. The story of the Comanche chief is

4.3. Contestant urges on armadillo during the races at the Lukenbach World's Fair, Lukenbach, Texas, 1981. Photo by Angus K. Gillespie.

based on a legitimate linguistic confusion. Another such story, equally of doubtful authorship and authenticity, is based on deliberate misrepresentation:

> . . . a stranger traveling thru the Great Beautiful and Bountiful
> State of Texas, came upon a Cowboy. The stranger noticed
> something cooking over the campfire. He asked, "What's for
> dinner? Sure smells good!" "A Texas Turkey," the drover replied.
> The stranger laughed, as he related the story to his friends—what
> he actually shared with the stranger, was an Armadillo.[33]

Before leaving the subject of armadillo consumption, we should at least mention a phenomenon on the contemporary Texas social scene, the chili cook-off. Ostensibly, the chili cook-off is a contest in

4.4. Sam Lewis of San Angelo, Texas, erects the fence for Armadillo Races at London, Texas, 1981. Photo by Angus K. Gillespie.

which the contestant cooks pay a registration fee to assemble with other cooks at a given location, usually at some kind of public park, on a given day, usually on a summer weekend. The cooks arrive before noon (often much earlier) in order to prepare their chili to perfection for the judging in the late afternoon at a set time, perhaps 5:00 P.M. Though the event is advertised as a contest and though Texans discuss it as if it were, it really is not a competition at all. To be sure, the chili is cooked and the prizes are awarded, but the event is actually an excuse for Texas foolishness and gregariousness. The contestant doesn't come to cook, he comes to have a good time. The contestant, almost invariably an adult white male, will bring a recreational vehicle and his whole family as well as his cooking supplies. While the chili cooks, he passes the time sitting in an aluminum

4.5. Bumper sticker designed by Cecile Hollyfield of Buda, Texas, 1980. Photo by Angus K. Gillespie.

folding chair underneath a canvas awning tied to his RV drinking Lone Star or Shiner or Pearl. If he gets bored sitting around talking with his family and friends, there are a number of nonsense events to wile away the afternoon—mechanical bull riding, buffalo chip tossing, horseshoe pitching, and lemon rolling. Amidst such amusements there may also be beer-chugging contests and jalapeño-eating contests (figs. 4.3, 4.4, 4.5).

While the cook-off is an interesting event in itself and certainly worthy of study, what is of special interest to us is the food itself. What exactly gets cooked? A survey of the *Goat Gap Gazette* published in Houston for cook-off devotees, indicates that standard categories include beef, sausage, pork, poultry, wild game, mutton, goat, seafood, and sauce. But what about armadillo? As I went about to such events in 1981, my informants almost invariably told me that, although they themselves didn't serve it, armadillo used to be a popular chili cook-off ingredient. However, it turned out that they had a perfectly logical reason to avoid serving armadillo. It seems that some medical researchers had discovered a link between armadillos and leprosy. The low body temperature of the armadillo makes it an ideal host for the leprosy bacillus.[34] Even so, my suspicion is that the leprosy scare simply gave Texans a conscious excuse which let them off the hook of their unconscious fears.

In the rural South, there is a widespread belief that not only do people eat armadillos, but sometimes armadillos eat people. It is said that armadillos are "gravediggers" poking about the fresh earth on new graves to eat the people buried there.[35] This ghoulish belief is discounted by Robert Lemmo, who writes, "This came about because it is true that the animals will root through the soil above a fresh grave—just as they will root through any loosely packed soil looking for nice fresh bugs."[36] Again, Lemmo's soothing words are comforting, but it is difficult to dispel the fear once it has been lodged in the brain.

Perhaps the final word on armadillos and food should be taken from a bit of Texas ephemera—a postcard for "Texas Cowboy Chili." The card pictures a cowboy sitting on two cases of beer watching two armadillos, with a map of Texas in the background. The card begins with the recipe: "4 lbs. chili meat (lean, ground chuck), 1 large onion, chopped, 2 cloves garlic, 1 tsp. oregano, 1 tsp. ground cummin seed, 8 tsp. chili powder (or more), 2 (16 oz.) cans tomatoes, salt to suit you, 2 cups hot water, 4 cases (24 pack) cold beer, 2 grown armadillos." The card then continues with the directions: Place meat, onion, garlic in a large skillet and sear until brown. Add rest of ingredients. Bring to boil. Lower heat and simmer at least 2 hours. Let chili cool for 30 minutes. Feed chili to armadillos. Sit back, relax, and enjoy the beer. Serves 4" (fig. 4.6).[37]

The postcard, of course, reduces the armadillo as ingredient to a joke, perhaps signaling its furthest remove from the dignity accorded it in Native American myth and in the early European iconography of the New World. Somehow, as we discussed, during the Age of Settlement the armadillo lost its symbolic associations. To be sure, Darwin noticed it and Audubon painted it, but gradually the armadillo lost its grip on the popular imagination—with the possible exception of its mention as food in a few folktales.

This period of neglect lasted throughout the nineteenth century and the first half of the twentieth century. For example, a field guide to mammals issued in 1952 simply mentions the armadillo as just another animal. It is shown on a plate in the company of the possum, beaver, porcupine, muskrat, and others.[38] In a 1951 encyclopedia, the armadillo is described simply as:

> A small animal with an armor-like covering. It usually comes out only at night. The armadillo, as found in the Southwest, lives on insects, worms, reptiles, and dead animals. Despite his short legs he can run fast, and often tries to escape by burrowing into the ground. He is harmless and does not put up a fight when captured.[39]

The nature of the armadillo as described here provides the source for its re-emergence as a symbol. In fact, of course, the armadillo had never lost its basic power to command attention because of its unusual anatomy and its place on the boundary of classification. Its "affecting presence" had simply been there all along, lying dormant. But in recent years it was, on the conscious level at least, the armadillo's behavior that made it an effective symbol. It was the armadillo's peaceful nature, the fact that it "does not put up a fight," that invited its use by hippies as a symbol.

The counter-culture of the late 1960s was identified as an antiwar movement. Although the movement was associated with many things—drugs, long hair, sexual freedom, and so on—opposition to the Vietnam War was at its heart. This opposition took many forms—protests in the streets, marches, demonstrations, and draft-card burning. One of the most universal expressions of this youth revolution took place in music. In the East, there was Woodstock; but in Texas the music was a little different. It was rock music with a regional flavor. Archie Green described it this way:

> Young cedar choppers/cowboys/goat ropers had regularly enjoyed country music and Western swing, often blaring it from pickup truck radios. Their antagonists had lived on rock and roll and revival folksong. Yet, in time, some Austin rock freaks borrowed elements of kicker style and perceived themselves as cowboys.... The meeting of partisans from Austin's two separate sectors created new performers and audiences. Native

Texans and strangers drawn to the open Austin community experimented by integrating the sounds of Bob Wills and Mick Jagger. This mix crossed lines of race, residency, and status.... Finally, Texas regionalism (and chauvinism) shored up moves toward independent creativity.[40]

The new music needed a visual identity, and in 1968 hippie artist Jim Franklin met that need with his first armadillo drawing. Asked to come up with a design for a poster for a free concert in a park in Austin, he drew an armadillo smoking a marijuana cigarette. Franklin explained, "I wanted to do something that kind of dealt with the event, symbolizing the people that were there.... I remembered my first encounter with them on a hunting trip with my father. I finally got away from his stalking deer, and I went stalking armadillos. Because you could actually get close to them, you know."[41]

Jim Franklin as a boy out hunting with his father was already developing an aversion to violence. Growing up in East Texas, in La Marque near Galveston, he had plenty of opportunity to take up hunting, but he never acquired a taste for it.[42] Others have remarked on the association of armadillos with pacificism. I talked for a long time with Cecile Hollyfield of Buda, Texas, an artist and street vendor, specializing in armadillo-decorated items including T-shirts, notepaper, and bumper stickers. She explained the genesis and diffusion of the icon:

> I first became aware of the armadillo as a symbol about 10 or 12 years ago. It was sort of a subculture symbol of people with long hair and antiwar sentiments, and all those shaggy folks. Used it as a sort of symbol of their ideas. And now it's become more widely adopted and, I guess, appeals to a broader audience.... Well, it was a real quiet, peaceful little critter that doesn't do anyone any harm. Doesn't mess up anything. And many people in Texas at that time felt the same way about armadillos as they did about freaks. If you saw one across your yard, you picked up your gun and shot it. And so the long-haired people sort of identified with the little harmless animal.[43]

It is difficult to pinpoint with precision the earliest uses of the armadillo-as-symbol in Austin in the late 1960s. It was a time of great turbulence in politics and innovation in music. Many of the

4.6. Ceramic Armadillo with Bottle of Lone Star Beer, Lukenbach, Texas, 1981. Photo by Angus K. Gillespie.

early drawings appeared in ephemeral publications, but Robert Lemmo has assembled a credible account of those early days:

> The earliest armadillo-hippy link was probably in the fall of 1968 when the *Texas Ranger,* a student humor magazine at the University of Texas in Austin ran a photograph on its cover of an armadillo decked out on a platter like the traditional Thanksgiving turkey. Then an underground cartoonist named Jim Franklin catapulted to countercultural fame when his obsessively detailed and surrealistic armadillos began to fill the pages of an underground weekly called *The Rag.* The armadillo became a folk hero the likes of which hadn't been seen in Texas since Davy Crockett days.[44]

4.7. Hippie Artist Jim Franklin proudly points to himself as rendered in his own mural, where he is portrayed as the Master of

It is beyond the scope of this chapter to present the musical history of Austin during this time,[45] a scene already chronicled by Jan Reid in his informal and readable book, *The Improbable Rise of Redneck Rock*.[46] Suffice it to say that the first serious rock'n'roll club in Austin was a place called the Vulcan Gas Company. The resident artist and guru there was Jim Franklin, who often presided over concerts as a regal emcee dressed as high priest of country rock, wrapped in a Texas flag as robe and wearing an armadillo helmet as miter (fig. 4.7). The Vulcan Gas Company may have been a success musically, but it failed financially by 1970. About this time an associate of Jim Franklin's named Eddie Wilson got a lease on an abandoned armory in south Austin. By now it was clear that the name of the new place would have to be Armadillo something-or-other.

They played around with several possibilities and finally decided on the grandiloquent: "Armadillo World Headquarters." Almost in spite of themselves, these young counter-culture businessmen started to make a success of the place. Prominent bands wanted to be booked there because it became known as an important place to play. There was a large group of Austin residents, many of the University of Texas students or hangers-on, who were willing to pay to get in. Why did the new place catch on? For a variety of reasons, of course. "But most of all, the new rock & roll joint had that name," explained Jan Reid. Trying to explain the power of the name, Reid went on:

> The strangest animal this side of Australia, the armadillo was a curious little rodent easily victimized by highway traffic. It had ears like those of a rhinoceros, a tail like that of an opossum, a proboscis somewhat like that of an anteater and a hard protective shell around its vitals that scraped against the rocks as it waddled along. It looked like a meek, miniature version of one of those reptilian, prehistoric monsters that Tarzan used to ride into the Lost Valley. An armadillo was either too stupid or too smart to domesticate, and if startled in a roadside ditch it was apt to jump straight up in the air and run headlong into a hubcap, knocking itself out. An armadillo tried to avoid getting too far away from a hole in the roots of a brushy tree, and if it established a handhold on those roots, Hercules himself would have had a hard time breaking its grip. Yet if an armadillo was captured it would sit in total uncomprehending silence in a corner and would not fight for its life.[47]

Reid's discussion of the armadillo presents us with a now-familiar litany. There is the description by comparison to other animals, which stresses the difficulty of classifying the armadillo. And then there is mention of the armadillo's peaceful nature, which makes it such an appropriate icon for the counter-culture. But it took more than good music and a good club and a good name to lift the armadillo into popular consciousness. It also required a visual image. It started with Jim Franklin, but soon there were a number of artists in Austin making posters. They included Gilbert Shelton, Guy Juke, Michael Priest, Kerry Owen, and Bill Narum. One of them, Bill Narum, later tried to describe the work of this group: "An attempt to bring credibility to an art form shunned by the 'art community'—turning walls, phone poles, and the streets into art galleries—music from pen and ink—images of a local history—focus of an energy—characterization of a society—suffering in solitude while bringing joy to a mass. . ."[48]

Out of the hundreds of images produced during this period of graphic florescence, let us briefly examine the official logo for the Armadillo World Headquarters, designed by Jim Franklin. We begin with the globe which is in the center of the design, with the oceans rendered in blue and the continents rendered in green. Since the armadillo always have four offspring, four are shown by Franklin. The two atop the globe are joined in the middle; the two beneath the globe are joined by their tails. The world globe is divided by two red bands into four quarters, hence Headquarters. Putting it altogether you get Armadillo World Headquarters. Soon the design began to appear everywhere.

The popularity of the new music in Austin catapulted the armadillo into high status at the University of Texas. The armadillo began to be rendered in orange and white, the University's colors. In 1971 the student senate voted to change the school's mascot from the longhorn to the armadillo. The change was never made official, although the counter-mascot made an occasional appearance at football games. Up until this point, the armadillo craze was mostly a local phenomenon, confined to Austin and central Texas.

But in late 1971 the *New York Times* picked up the story of the University of Texas student senate resolution. The story came to the attention of the *New Yorker,* which ran a lengthy and informative interview with Jim Franklin under the title "Armadillo Man." This was the first time that Franklin's posters, handbills, and underground comics received serious national attention. Some artists have difficulty talking about their own work, but Franklin never seemed to suffer from this problem. It was as if Franklin, brilliant and verbal, knew that the *New Yorker* was a splendid platform for his ideas. Among other things, Franklin discussed the origins of one of his most popular cartoons:

> ...I had this concept that they should remodel the capitol in Austin and make it look like an armadillo. You'd go in through the mouth, with the tongue like a big red carpet, and walk into the rotunda, which would be a big oval shape, like an armadillo shell. Then you'd walk out through the tail, which would be a tapering hallway. The tip end of it would be the height of the door. That thought was still on my mind about the time I did my next drawing for *The Rag*. I was still playing with this notion of a giant armadillo wandering around Austin, completely oblivious of the city. I thought, if it sees the capitol, it's so nearsighted that it may mistake it for a mate and start something. So that's what I drew.[49]

About this time, the word was out that Austin had a hot musical scene. Austin was the home of the Armadillo World Headquarters. It was the epicenter for an entirely new musical taste, an alternative to the bland, schlock Nashville sound. Instead of mellow female back-up choruses coupled with smooth strings, you had the raw sounds of West Texas fiddles. The story was that the Austin musicians had broken away from the country music establishment; they were "outlaws." This outlaw band included Jerry Jeff Walker, Steve Fromholtz, Kinky Friedman, and Willie Nelson. The emblem for these outlaws was not the skull-and-crossbones; it was the armadillo (fig. 4.8).

As Armadillo Consciousness permeated this musical subculture, it was inevitable that a body of armadillo folklore began to enter oral circulation. In Texas I collected some of this material, most of it in joke format. Since most Texans encounter armadillos along the highways, it is not surprising that most of the jokes refer to armadillos being struck by cars. (Remember that they have the counterproductive habit of leaping up when they are startled.) Let us consider a couple of examples collected in Austin. The first comes from Flynn Wright, who was careful to set the joke up in such a way that even someone from New Jersey like myself could follow it:

> Well, our jokes down here, instead of being racist, we make our jokes about the Aggies, because they're from Texas A. & M. And that's a military school. It used to be all male, and they're supposed to be the—kind of—nerds of the state, you know? . . . So our jokes go like, "How many Aggies does it take to eat an armadillo? It takes three. Two to eat it, and one to watch out for traffic."[50]

One more example will have to suffice. This one is told by Ken Wilson, also of Austin, and depends on role reversal:

> So there were four armadillos driving down the road in a Volkswagen convertible, and they're out in the middle of the West Texas desert and up ahead of them, just at the edge of the road is a naked man. And he's starting on his hands and knees across the road. And the one armadillo that's driving, just turns to the other ones and says: "Ohh! I just hate that sound they make when you hit 'em."[51]

We have now examined the identification of the armadillo as a symbol of the counter-culture and how it further came to stand for the Austin Sound, a blend of country and rock. The armadillo became familiar in Austin through the musical scene and was reinforced aurally by stories and jokes. I have tried here to unravel the meanings which many different people over a long period of time have attached to the armadillo. In the song "London Homesick Blues" of 1973 Gary P. Nunn said: "I want to go home with the Armadillo." If what he meant was to the Armadillo World Headquarters, then we can only say that he cannot go home again. The last concert was on December 31, 1980. Kaye Northcott was there and described the experience, movingly, in an article in *Mother Jones* called "The Life and Death of the Cosmic Cowboy":

> It was three hours into 1981 at the Armadillo World Headquarters in Austin, Texas, but nobody wanted to go home. . . . To the front of the stage floated ethereal Maria Muldaur, who belted out a gospel number about little children walking through this world of troubles, trying to love one another. It was a feast of nostalgia

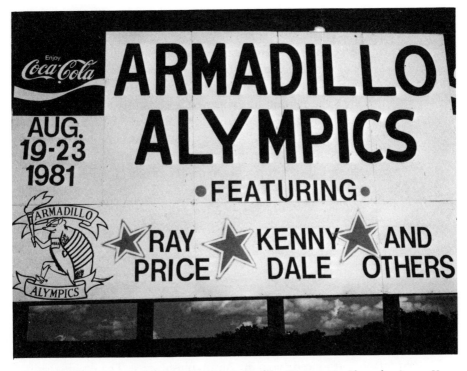

4.8. "Armadillo Alympics" billboard, New Braunfels, Texas, 1981. Photo by Angus K. Gillespie.

and good vibes. Out in the audience, a dancing hippie in frayed Adidas spilled one final pitcher of Lone Star on the malodorous, crusty carpeting. The show finally ended at 4:10 A.M. with everyone linking arms and singing an old Leadbelly tune, "Goodnight, Irene."[52]

Certainly it was the end of an era, the end of ten years of good music and good companionship. It had been a place for both redneck and hippie. It was a meeting ground for the blending of the sincerity of country music with the energy of rock. There is a temptation to interpret the destruction of the old armory to make way for a huge hotel-and-office complex in political terms: Capitalism again crushes creativity. But as usual, the reality is a little more complicated.

Over time, musical styles change. By 1980 already redneck rock was giving way to New Wave. By 1980 armadillomania had been fueled by Texas pride and chauvinism and had spilled over the boundary of the counter-culture into increasingly trivial popular culture expressions. Aesthetic fatigue had set in. No one can predict the future, of course, but as the armadillo craze sputters out, we must remember that the animal has survived and endured for a long time. The armadillo as an icon may once again enter a period of quiescence, but given its unusual anatomy it will never completely lose its affecting presence. Austin musician John Raymond Reed in 1980 wrote a song called prophetically: "The 'Dillo Shall Rise Again." The armadillo's time as a regional pop-music symbol may indeed be fading fast, but its potential as an icon will always be with us.

NOTES

The research for this study was conducted during my tenure as a National Endowment for the Humanities Fellow in the Summer Seminar for College Teachers taught by John Vlach at the Center for Intercultural Studies in Folklore and Ethnomusicology at the University of Texas at Austin during the summer of 1981. My thanks to Archie Green who warmly and hospitably introduced me to the Austin music scene. Thanks also to John Vlach, Jan Harold Brunvand, Barre Toelken, Michael Rockland, Leslie Fishbein, Mary Ann James, and Louise Duus for numerous helpful suggestions. A shorter version of this chapter was read at the annual meeting of the American Folklore Society in Minneapolis in October, 1981.

    1. References to the armadillo in recorded music are sometimes aural (in the song lyrics) and sometimes visual (on the album cover). An example of the former may be found on the New Riders of the Purple Sage, Brujo, Columbia Records PC 33145 "Instant Armadillo Blues" (ASCAP). An example of the latter may be found on Leo Kottke, 6- *and 12-String Guitar,* Takoma Records C-1024. The Kottke album is strictly instrumental, hence there are no lyrics mentioning armadillos or anything else; but the cover features an armadillo drawn by Anne C. Elliott. For a brief Austin discography, see Kaye Northcott's "The Life and Death of the Cosmic Cowboy" in *Mother Jones* (June 1981): 20. For a bibliography, see the unpublished manuscript "Hill Country Music: Popular Music and Musicians in and near Austin, Texas, 1968–1974" by Patricia Gayle Tyler, a selective bibliographical guide to holdings in the Austin-Travis County Collection and Central Branch of the Austin Public Library.

2. George Kubler, *The Shape of Time: Remarks on the History of Things* (New Haven: Yale Univ. Press, 1962), 9.

3. Robin Doughty and Larry L. Smith, "Nine-Banded Armadillo," *Journal of Cultural Geography* 2 (1981): 120–30.

4. Terry Peters, *Armadillo* (Austin: The Stevenson Press, 1978), 2.

5. Gary McCalla, "The Great Armadillo Invasion," *Southern Living* (Sept. 1981): 40.

6. Mary Tew Douglas, *Purity and Danger* (New York: Frederick A. Praeger, 1966), 36.

7. Ibid., 7.

8. Peters, 1.

9. Peter Farb, *The Land and Wildlife of North America* (New York: Time, Inc., 1964), 56.

10. McCalla, 40.

11. Peters, 28.

12. A discussion of the distribution of the armadillo may be found in the article "Fauna of Middle America" by L.C. Stuart in the *Handbook of Middle American Indians*, vol. I, *Natural Environment and Early Cultures*, general ed. Robert Wauchope (Austin: Univ. of Texas Press, 1964).

13. Donald Cordry, *Mexican Masks* (Austin: Univ. of Texas Press, 1980), 187.

14. Hugh Honour, *The New Golden Land* (New York: Pantheon Books, 1975), 112.

15. Ibid., 39.

16. Ibid., 89.

17. Ibid.

18. Ibid., 40.

19. For more on the exploration of the West, see William H. Goetzmann, *Army Explorations in the American West* (New Haven: Yale Univ. Press, 1959); Edward S. Wallace, *The Great Reconnaissance* (Boston: Little, Brown, 1955); Richard N. Ellis, *General Pope and the U.S. Indian Policy* (Albuquerque: Univ. of New Mexico Press, 1970); and Richard A. Bartlett, *Great Surveys of the American West* (Norman: Univ. of Oklahoma Press, 1962).

20. My discussion of wildlife is based on the account given in Howard R. Lamar, ed., *The Reader's Encyclopedia of the American West* (New York: Harper and Row, 1977).

21. John Chancellor, *Charles Darwin* (London: Weidenfeld and Nicolson, 1973), 88–90.

22. John James Audubon and John Bachman, *The Imperial Collection of Audubon Animals* (New York: Bonanza Books, 1967), 20.

23. Donald Horton, "The Mundurucu," in *Handbook of South American Indians,* vol. 3, *The Tropical Forest Tribes* (Washington, D.C.: Smithsonian Institution, Bureau of American Ethnology, 1948), 281.

24. Juan Belaieff, "The Present-Day Indians of the Gran Chaco," in *Handbook of South American Indians,* vol. I, *The Marginal Tribes* (Washington, D.C.: Smithsonian Institution, Bureau of American Ethnology, 1946), 379.

25. Alfred Metraux, "Tribes of the Eastern Slopes of the Bolivian Andes (Chiriguano)" in *Handbook of South American Indians,* vol. 3, 484.

26. Interview with Bill Monroe, San Antonio, Texas, July 22, 1981.

27. *Goat Gap Gazette* 7, no. 6 (July 1981): 16.

28. Robert Lemmo, "The Life and Times of An Armadillo," *Honky Tonk* 1, no. 2 (Feb. 1981): 46.

29. Edmund R. Leach, "Anthropological Aspects of Language: Animal Categories and Verbal Abuse," in *New Directions in the Study of Language,* ed. Eric H. Lenneberg (Cambridge, Mass.: M.I.T. Press, 1964), 209.

30. Ibid., 210–12.

31. John C. Meyers, "The Mystery of the Five Graves," in *The Golden Log,* ed. Mody C. Boatright and Wilson H. Hudson (Dallas, Texas: Southern Methodist Univ. Press, 1962), 53–57.

32. Package Insert, Comanche Pottery, Route 1, Comanche, Texas 76442, 1979.

33. Ibid.

34. Eleanor E. Storrs, "The Astonishing Armadillo," *National Geographic,* no. 34 (June 1982): 820–30.

35. Peters, 2.

36. Lemmo, 46.

37. "Happy Traveler Post Card," collected in Austin, Texas, 1981. The card itself gave no publisher's location.

38. William Henry Burt, *A Field Guide to the Mammals* (Boston: Houghton Mifflin Company, 1952), 36.

39. Bruce Grant, *The Cowboy Encyclopedia* (Chicago: Rand McNally, 1951), 12.

40. Archie Green, "Austin's Cosmic Cowboys: Words in Collision," in *"And Other Neighborly Names": Social Process and Cultural Image in Texas Folklore,* ed. Richard Bauman and Roger D. Abrahams (Austin: Univ. of Texas Press, 1981), 164–65.

41. Interview with Jim Franklin, July 25, 1981.

42. I have in progress a study of Jim Franklin, whose work has attracted some attention. For example, see the 1974 "Groover's Paradise" in

Time (Sept. 9): 70; Stephen Harrigan, "The Drawing of the Age of the Armadillo," *Rolling Stone* 105 (March 30, 1972): 20 ff.; Russell Middleton and O'Neil Provost, "Armadillos Come From Daydreams: A Closer Look at Jim Franklin," *Austin People Today* (Nov., 1974): 18; Chet Flippo, "Texas Music Halls: Uncle Zeke's Rock Emporium," *Rolling Stone* (Oct. 12, 1972): 18; and Jeff Nightbyrd, "Jim Franklin's Odyssey: Doo-dah to Dada," *Austin Sun* (May 29–June 11, 1975): 1.

43. Interview with Cecile Hollyfield, July 7, 1981.

44. Lemmo, 46.

45. Though Jan Reid has probably put together the best and most accessible single account of the Austin music scene in general and of the Armadillo World Headquarters (AWHQ) in particular, one might also consult Frye Gaillard, *Watermelon Wine: The Spirit of Country Music* (New York: St. Martin's, 1977), especially ch. 9, "Putting the Audience Back Together: Willie Nelson and the Austin Sound," 128–46. See also John T. Davis, "Armadillo World Headquarters Making History for 10 Years!" *Performance* 10, no. 12, 4–28; Chet Flippo, "Armadillo Progress Report: Further Texas Observations," *Place Magazine* (Feb. 1971): 90; Jeff Nightbyrd, "We Weave Bullet Holes and Knife Cuts," *Crawdaddy Magazine* (Dec. 1972): 26; Jan Reid and Don Roth, "The Coming of Redneck Hip," *Texas Monthly* 1 (Nov. 1973): 72; and Bill Williams, "Texas Native Musical Songs Returning: They are Helping Build an Industry," *Billboard*, Sept. 8, 1973, T–2. In addition, the vertical file on the AWHQ at the Travis County Collection of the Austin Public Library has much information, including stories from *The Austin American Statesman, The Daily Texan, Rolling Stone, The Texas Observer, The Austin Sun,* and *The Dallas Morning News.* Besides such published sources, the Travis County Collection has a number of manuscripts, including transcripts of two interviews with Eddie Wilson of the AWHQ—one by Robert Heard of the Associated Press (June 26, 1974) and one by Tom Park and Dave Mason for the KLBJ radio show News Magazine (Aug. 14, 1977).

46. Jan Reid, *The Improbable Rise of Redneck Rock* (New York: Da-Capo Press, 1977).

47. Ibid., 53–54.

48. Guy Juke, *Visual Thrills,* vol. 1 (Austin: Void of Course Publishing Company, 1980).

49. "Armadillo Man," *New Yorker,* Dec. 11, 1971, 41–42.

50. Interview with Flynn Wright, July 7, 1981.

51. Interview with Ken Wilson, July 7, 1981.

52. Kaye Northcott, "The Life and Death of the Cosmic Cowboy," *Mother Jones* (June 1981): 14–48.

The Bear

DANIEL J. GELO

The season for bear hunting, stranger, is all the
year round, and the hunt takes place about
as regular.
> —*The Big Bear of Arkansas*[1]

Symbolically, the American bear has been an animal for all seasons;
images of the mighty creature have been employed in a wide variety
of traditions and contexts. Yet when the diverse images of bears in
American folk and popular culture are viewed in the aggregate, a
definite historical sequence emerges. First, the history of Native
American lore provides an image of an animal with extraordinary
physical and spiritual power, an image perpetuated by contemporary
Indians. The earliest European explorers, in contrast, were not interested in the bear as symbol, and considered it only for its negli-
gible economic value. After the Revolution, however, as Americans
were charged with taming the western wilderness and building a
new nation, the bear took on a potent symbolic characterization,
becoming all that was terrifying and ferocious on the frontier, all
that must be overcome in the realization of Manifest Destiny. This
fierce image continued until the closing years of the nineteenth century, as American influence expanded to the Pacific and beyond.
Then, suddenly, there was a proliferation of gentle bears—bear toys,

bear stories for children. In the twentieth century, the bear image is multivocal, with several subcultures and special interest groups making use of either the fierce or gentle characterization.[2]

All animals of symbolic interest exhibit remarkable characteristics that become the focus of or basis for their representations in folklore and popular works. Bears are, of course, big, strong, and potentially dangerous; but, more significantly, bears look and act like human beings. More than any other North American mammal, the bear approximates a human style of locomotion. Bears are not truly bipedal, for they only occasionally rise up to browse or survey their surroundings, but in figurative terms, they "walk on two feet." Further, bears are plantigrade animals; like humans they walk on the flat part of the foot. The hind-foot track of a bear—longish, with five toes—looks very much like a man's footprint, especially when the short hind claws fail to imprint.

The bear's feeding habits also reinforce the bear/human parallel, for bears are omnivorous and have a seasonal foraging strategy. Typically, bears feed on grass and roots, ants in the spring and early summer, berries in midsummer, corn and fruit in August, and acorns in the fall. Western bears will also capitalize on the spawning runs of salmon, and they congregate at streamside like fly-fisherman on opening day.

Bears appear to be, like humans, tailless; their flat, broad, fur-covered tails are hardly noticeable. Several kinds of yelping and grunting noises made by bears resemble human crying or hollering. And it is not outlandish to suggest that bears have individual personalities. Ranger David A. Haskell, who supervises the bear program in Virginia's Shenandoah National Park, put it to me this way in a March 22, 1983, interview: "Bears are as different from one another as people are. You have aggressive bears, you have timid bears, smart bears."

Bear cubs are especially humanlike. Paul Schullery, former Park Historian at Yellowstone, writes: "There is no way to write about bear cubs that does not reflect their playful rambunctious attitude.... The naturalist who dreads anthropomorphism.... will become hopelessly entangled in his own language, for the similarities between child rearing and cub-rearing are too great to be ignored."[3] Like human babies, newborn bears arrive weak and helpless; virtually hairless, blind, and toothless, they depend on the sow's strong nurturing instincts. Cubs undergo a relatively long stage of infantile dependency—up to three years. The cubs play and explore while their mother stands by, at once indulgent and overprotective. Long dependency periods afford both bear cubs and children ample time to develop motor coordination and basic survival skills.

A few more bear traits and habits may have seemed humanlike to Indians and pioneers, but would not appear relevant at first glance. Bears stay home during the winter, so to speak. Also, the male bear is more likely than the female to travel any significant distance from the den site. And bears prefer to hunt alone or with one companion, in the manner of Leatherstocking. As the Big Bear of Arkansas explained: "You see it ain't in the nature of a b'ar to go in droves. But the way they squander around in pairs and single is edifying."[4]

These similarities between bears and humans, or rather the composite picture of similarity, does not always explain why the bear has been chosen as a symbol in a given myth or pictorial representation. In one case, a myth may actually explain the similarity between bears and humans, while another myth may make no mention of the similarity; in the latter instance, similarity may still be invoked as the mythmaker's point of departure, the spark of interest for symbolic creativity.

But some more zoological information is crucial to an understanding of American bear symbology. Bears in the contiguous forty-eight states comprise two species, black bears (*Ursus Americanus*) and grizzly bears (*Ursus arctos*). The species have different ranges, and although the basic traits discussed above apply to both, the two kinds of bears contrast in size and temperament.

Black bears were once found throughout the continental United States but have been wholly eliminated from twelve states: Rhode Island, Delaware, and the prairie-plains states.[5] In the East, these bears generally are black, but west of the Great Plains they are often brown (regional name: "cinnamon bear") or even yellowish ("sun bear"). Even litter mates may wear different shades. Black individuals may have light chest patches. *Ursus Americanus* is shy and retiring: any bear is potentially dangerous, but almost always black bears will avoid confrontation. They are best adapted to an arboreal environment, and trees are their favorite refuge. The average black bear stands two and a half feet at the shoulder, is five feet long, and weighs two hundred and fifty pounds, although many larger specimens have been taken. In most circumstances, black bears appear more clumsy and comical than threatening.

The grizzly bear is a different animal entirely. Grizzlies weigh upwards of three hundred pounds and occasional individuals top the half-ton mark. Correspondingly, the grizzly's head and musculature are more massive than the black's, and his front claws are longer. Grizzlies are also more aggressive for reasons that are not fully understood; one circular explanation holds that, since grizzlies range in more open environments such as prairies and mountain meadows, their extra mass and orneriness are evolutionary alternatives to the black bear's tree-climbing strategy.[6] Originally, the range of the "silvertip" extended from the Black Hills to the Pacific, from Alaska into Mexico. Now only Alaska has significant numbers; remnant grizzly populations survive in Yellowstone and Glacier national parks and adjacent wilderness areas.

The physical characteristics and dispositions that so markedly distinguish blacks from grizzlies in real life tend to be confused by the general public. Very often the two species are assimilated into the popular conception of "bear," one with the symbolic potential of both the comical black and the aggressive grizzly.

The history of American bear symbology begins with Native American attitudes about the bear. Bears were ubiquitous in the myths, ceremonies, and everyday lifeways of virtually all Indian culture groups. The Indian-bear relationship was conceived of ideally as one of mutual cooperation: bears seemed to offer themselves to Indian hunters as a resource, and in turn were propitiated, and their future numbers guaranteed, by the Indian's fulfillment of ritual obligations. Among many tribes, the bones of slain bears were hung neatly in trees, away from the gnawing of camp dogs, as a gesture of respect and gratitude.

Respect and thankfulness found expression also in Native American artwork. Bear representations are everywhere in Indian decoration and material culture—painted on buffalo robes, tipis, and Pueblo ollas, carved on the red stone bowls of calumets. Silhouettes of bear tracks adorned war shields. Necklaces were made from strings of bear claws; knife handles were made from bear jawbones. In this connection, Indian art authority John C. Ewers raises an important point: "Probably no other animal in [the Indian's] environment could be unmistakably identified by a representation of any one of several distinctive parts. Ingenious Indians repeatedly produced bear symbols from the skin, claws, jaws or paws of the bear. The animal could be symbolized in the graphic arts as well as drawings of its paw or distinctive track alone.[7]

One common motif in Indian painting is the depiction of a bear with a line or cloud flowing from inside the animal through its mouth. This motif, popular today in Pueblo pottery and Navajo sandpaintings crafted for the tourist trade, conveys the idea that the bear's invulnerability is a kind of supernatural power with its source in the animal's heart (fig.5.1).

The bear's vitality and strength could be transferred to humans by means of medicines derived from the bear, and the native pharmacopoeia is filled with bear salves and tonics. Early settlers in Virginia found the Indians using bear oil combined with crushed wild angelica root or golden seal as a skin toner and insect repellent. Mixed with tobacco, bear oil was taken to expel worms from the intestinal tract. Unrendered bear grease would relieve general aches and swelling, and was sometimes applied over the entire body, Channel-swimmer fashion, as insulation.[8] Among the Yokuts of California, bear hair was the main ingredient in a drink to ease childbirth.[9] Bear spleen was applied to cure toothache by the tribes of the Great Lakes region.[10] The Navajos used bear gall mixed with ground corn as a ready cure for the "corpse poison" said to be dispensed by witches; cautious Navajos carried gall medicine wherever witches were thought to be operating.[11]

Native Americans could also receive bear power through dreams, visions (actively sought through sensory deprivation or hallucinogens), or they might purchase the power from someone who had extra. In any event, bear power was desirable as war medicine and for curing. Within some tribes, dream societies were formed, composed of those tribesmen with bear power. Members of the Oglala Sioux *mato ihanblapi* ('they dream of bears') ceremonially "paraded around the camp dressed in bearskins, growling like a bear and chasing people."[12]

Bear shamanism was one of the most dramatic forms of animal symbolism in Indian culture. Several accounts of bear shamanism were collected from California tribes by the distinguished anthropologist Alfred Kroeber.[13] Bear doctors were considered almost invul-

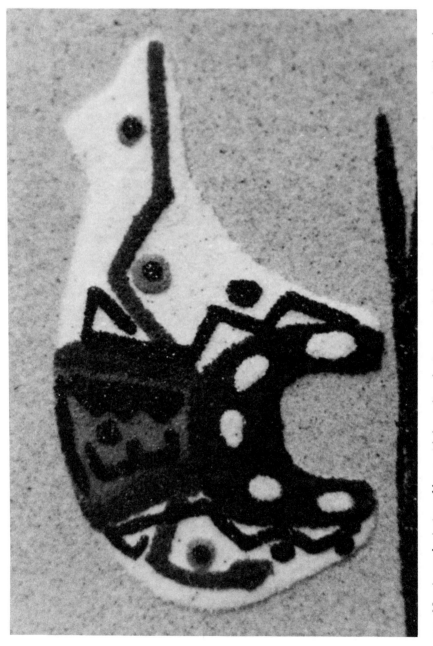

5.1. Navajo sandpainting of bear with heart line, by Bernice Todicheenie; figure approximately 3 × 2 inches. Photo by M. Gabrielle Gelo.

nerable; they might even return from the dead. The vocation came in a dream, or the novice would wallow in the pool formed by an uprooted tree, as bears did. He would stay alone in the woods for perhaps an entire season, living and eating with bears. The novice would *become* a bear, and old Indians could recount the transformation in great detail, including a description of the sensation of the fur growing out of the skin. Upon his return to the human world, the novice would be tutored by older bear doctors in singing and curing, then after passing a further series of hardships, he was considered a bear shaman.

It was the bear shaman's responsibility to cure bear bites, which he did by extracting a bear's tongue from the wound. Such feats, though performed with sleight of hand, were not necessarily intended to be deceptive; they were metaphorical representations of the curing process. The main function of the bear shamans, however, was to act as tribal avengers, to kill members of their own or another tribe against whom they held a grudge. The shamans supposedly turned into bears to do the killing, but again the metaphorical nature of these acts was acknowledged, and some of Kroeber's informants stated that the shamans just wore hardened bear skins. Upon engaging their enemies, the shamans would pretend to bite and claw but actually stab their victims with a knife held close to the mouth. Victims were dismembered and gutted, their entrails scattered around, simulating a bear's kill.

Kroeber was skeptical about some of his informants' reports, and he notes that it was hardly more possible for a shaman to fight efficiently in a heavy bear costume that it was for him to turn into a real bear. Yet even when the sensational aspects of bear shamanism are discounted, a powerful institution for social control remains. The shaman's "grudge" was in reality the tribe's dissatisfaction with an antisocial member. Stories about bear shaman vengeance were circulated to keep people in line, and the shaman complex functioned as ghost belief or witchcraft does in some other cultures.

Bear curing continues among the Shoshonis and Utes of the Great Basin, and elsewhere the bear continues to figure in matters of social control. Among the Chippewa of Michigan's Upper Peninsula, folklorist Richard M. Dorson found belief in the "bearwalk," a witch or evil spirit that may take the form of a fire-breathing bear.[14] The bearwalk stalks at night, bringing a strange illness which kills its victim in sixteen days. On the fourth night after the victim's death, the bearwalk visits the grave and steals a finger, the tongue, or an eyeball from the corpse. Some people said that if the bearwalk fails to make off with a ghastly souvenir, he will die in four months.

Bearwalk tales are reminiscent of the French-Canadian *loup-garou* or werewolf tradition, but they maintain a decidedly Indian quality, with the recurring Indian sacred number four (also sixteen—four fours), emphasis on dreams (the witch transforms into a bear while dreaming), and power (fire) emanating from the bear. Only an Indian can be killed by a bearwalk; it is fitting that the bear, so prominent in protohistorical Indian belief, continues to help define Indian ethnicity.

Many origin myths attest to the importance of bears in the Native American cosmos. Some stories tell how man was endowed with the virtues of the bear when he was created. In a Miwok myth from California, all the animals argue as they advise Creator about the making of man. Each wants man to exhibit his own most notable characteristic. The grizzly proclaims that man should have great strength, great enough to be able to knock his prey senseless with one blow.[15] The Cheyennes and Arapahos of the northern Plains believed that bears were their ancestors and that bears were capable of having sexual intercourse with humans.[16] Conversely, the Cherokees of the southeast woodlands maintained that bears originated from men.

According to a Cherokee tale collected by anthropologist James Mooney, there was a boy of the Ani-Tsaguhi clan who disappeared every day into the forests of the Great Smoky Mountains. His parents were dismayed and they scolded him, but to no avail. Pretty soon they noticed that long brown hair was sprouting all over his body, and they demanded an explanation. The boy replied that he always found enough food in the woods, and the food was better than corn and beans, and soon he would live in the forest permanently. He was beginning to feel different; he could not stay in the village any longer. But he invited his clan mates to go with him, telling them that if they decided to do so they must first fast for seven days.

The clan members held a council and, tempted by the prospect of a steady food supply, they decided to go with the boy. They fasted as he had instructed them, and after seven days they followed him into the mountains.

Some messengers from the other Cherokee clans went after the Ani-Tsaguhi and pleaded with them to turn back, but already the messengers could see that the Ani-Tsaguhi were becoming hairy. The Ani-Tsaguhi would not relent, saying: "We are going where there is plenty to eat. Hereafter we shall be called *yanu* [bears], and when you yourselves are hungry, come into the woods and call on us and we shall come to give you our own flesh. You need not be afraid to kill us, for we shall live always." They paused just long enough to teach the messengers the songs that the Cherokees would need to hunt bears. Then the Ani-Tsaguhi headed out again for the wilderness, and as they disappeared from view, the messengers could see that they were bears.

This haunting tale explains why Cherokee bear hunters had to fast before the hunt, and also the origin of bear hunting songs:

> He-e! The Ani-Tsaguhi, the Ani-Tsaguhi,
> I want to lay them low on the ground.
> And now surely we and the good black things,
> the best of all, shall see each other.[17]

In contrast with the Indians' sacramental attitude toward bears, the earliest European explorers showed indifference to the animals; they were concerned only with the bear's utility as a source of food and fur. This lack of interest is understandable, since bears were not a new animal, and the New World offered many bizarre life forms that captured the European symbolic imagination. Besides, the American black bear which the early explorers encountered was unimpressive compared to the giant Eurasian brown bear. (Thus Captain John Smith of Pocahontas fame noted: "their Beares are very little in comparison to those of Muscovia and Tartaria."[18]) The English explorer Robert Hore killed some bears off the coast of Newfoundland in 1536 and "tooke them for no bad foode"; Frenchman Jacques Cartier compared the taste of bear flesh to that of "a calf of two yeres old."[19] But except as an occasional source of fresh meat for vitamin-deficient seamen, the American bear was held in low esteem. Bear pelts were only moderately important in the fur trade, much less desirable than beaver, otter, or muskrat. Indifference to bears was therefore consistent with the colonial philosophy that the

New World was foremost a trove of resources. The black bear was not fabulous or grotesque and it was not important to commerce, so it stood little chance of being adopted as a symbol during colonial days.

After the American Revolution, however, and particularly with the Louisiana Purchase in 1803, a new brand of colonialism was instated. Americans faced the task of taming the newly acquired wilderness, and as a result of this activity, they were furnished with a new image of the bear, as reports trickled East about a ferocious silver-haired giant.

The time was ripe for a big bear. About 1785, Thomas Jefferson became involved in a debate with the prominent French naturalist Count de Buffon concerning the size and ferocity of American quadrupeds. During and after the Revolution, Buffon and his European colleagues labored feverishly to convince their kings that America would remain forever a backwater. They claimed that America was a barren environment; the animals of America were less robust than those of Europe, and by implication so were the men. Jefferson was a rank amateur compared to Buffon, but he took up the gauntlet and in *Notes on the State of Virginia*[20] published a table of comparative weights for European and American quadrupeds. Jefferson scored for America with a bear specimen weighing 410 pounds; Buffon's European contender weighed only 153.7 pounds.

Lewis and Clark were among the first white men to encounter the grizzly, and the first to provide a detailed description. Lewis had been skeptical of the Mandan Indians' reports of a monstrous bear, thinking that they overestimated the animal's power because their bows and arrows were relatively ineffectual weapons. Imagine his surprise and terror when, as the expedition rounded a bend on the Upper Missouri, an enraged grizzly charged from the bush! Shot after point-blank shot staggered the creature only momentarily. At the last possible moment, the bear collapsed, dead. This scene was played out again and again as the party moved upriver, until grizzlies became a major source of anxiety. One bear took ten balls before it succumbed. Lewis was no longer a skeptic: "I must confess that I do not like the gentlemen and had reather fight two Indians than one bear."[21]

Paul Wilhelm, Duke of Wurttemberg, also provided early information on the grizzly. Wilhelm was an adventurer who became a

captain in the army of his native state at the age of nine (his uncle
was the king); he retired from the military while still a young man
and devoted himself to the study of natural science. Accompanied by
his body servant, Wilhelm traveled up the Mississippi and Missouri
in the early 1820s, recording an extensive collection of flora and
fauna along the way. Out in the wilderness Wilhelm developed a
taste for bear meat, which he found more appealing than the cold
cornbread of the settlements. Historian Savoie Lottinville even suggests that this taste for bear meat marked Wilhelm's transformation
from European blue blood to red-blooded frontiersman. The Duke's
most lively confrontation with a bear took place when his companion Louis was bleating like a fawn to attract deer. He attracted a
hungry bear instead, and the animal was brought down just in the
nick of time.[22]

Meriwether Lewis and the naturalists who followed him were motivated by the spirit of scientific investigation, but they tended to observe bears that were in an enraged, not wholly typical state. The
scientists' descriptions were further distorted by exaggerators among
the lay public, who were as common on the frontier as bears. Soon
the grizzly had a reputation as a hunter of men, a demonic brute
with a thirst for human blood.[23]

In fact, it is difficult to distinguish between the interests of science
and commercialism even during this early era of bear awareness. A
case in point is that of Charles Willson Peale, the painter best known
for his portrait of George Washington, who operated a museum and
small zoo at Independence Hall in Philadelphia. Outside, Peale displayed two large grizzlies which had been captured by Zebulon Pike,
until one of the bears escaped one night and both had to be destroyed. Afterwards a stuffed specimen, obtained from the Lewis
and Clark Expedition and labeled "long clawed grizly [sic] from the
Missouri," was mounted in the museum. It is speculated that this
stuffed bear was eventually purchased by P.T. Barnum for his New
York hall of wonders; for a time, Barnum also showed the enormous
"Samson," shipped alive from California by the legendary Grizzly
Adams.[24] Another artist, George Catlin, shipped live grizzlies to
London as part of his "Indian Gallery" exhibit in Egyptian Hall.
Catlin's slice of the wild and wooly was an extremely popular attrac-
tion in the 1840s.

Taxonomists did not pretend to be dispassionate when it came time to give the grizzly a scientific name. In 1815 George Ord used the Latin binomial *Ursus horribilus*, "terrifying bear." Edward Harris, who accompanied John James Audubon on a western trip in 1843, called the grizzly *Ursus ferox*, *ferox* meaning "wild" or "defiant" but used here as "ferocious." Eventually the grizzly was classified along with the brown bear of the northern latitudes as *Ursus arctos*. The silvertip's common name has also been disputed at times. Theodore Roosevelt argued for "grisly" rather than "grizzly," horrifying rather than hoary.[25]

Pioneers, the popular masses, and the scientific community alike were awed by the ferocity of the western bear. For all segments of American society, the bear was a ready symbol for the evils and dangers encountered during westward expansion. Every time a bear was blasted into oblivion, the wilderness became slightly more tame. Bears, like Indians, were only good when dead.

The bears of nineteenth-century folklore and fakelore loomed larger and more numerous as the struggle became more intense. The abundant Boone and Crockett literature provides some evidence of this pattern.

Probably the most remarkable record of Daniel Boone's adventures is *The Mountain Muse*, by Boone's nephew from Rockingham County, Virginia, Daniel Bryan.[26] This homespun Miltonic epic has a "Hero who no terrors can appal" (Boone) scaling "the Alleganean Mount." Among the frontier dangers enumerated by Bryan is the "surly Bear"; however, it is the panther and not the bear which provokes the most dread. Even deer and buffalo are mentioned more often than the bear. *The Mountain Muse* was published in 1813, seven years before Boone's death, and before the image of bear-as-sinister-giant was firmly established in the American consciousness.

This is not to suggest that Boone was indifferent to bears. A beech stood along a tributary of the Watanga River in East Tennessee until the 1890s, upon which was carved: "D Boon cilled A BAR on this tree year 1760." It was one of several such bear hunt memorials that Boone left to mark the extent of his wanderings. But the overwhelming association between Boone and bears we know today seems to have developed in the mid-nineteenth century, after the fierce bear-frontier symbol crystallized. By 1862, when F.L. Hawks's *The Ad-*

ventures of Daniel Boone, The Kentucky Rifleman appeared, the following scene was typical: Boone stumbles upon an immense she-bear guarding her cubs. His usual steady aim fails, the bear charges, and it is impossible for Boone to reload in time. As the bear draws Boone to its chest in a death hug, the stalwart frontiersman draws his knife and plunges it into the bear's heart.[27]

Davy Crockett writes in his autobiography of being in a similar situation: "I got back in all sorts of a hurry, for I know'd that if he got hold of me he would hug me altogether too close for comfort."[28] Crockett made an art out of bear slaying, and parlayed his reputation as a bear hunter into a congressional career. At election time he appealed to the common man by characterizing himself as an "ignorant back-woods bear hunter." Almanac stories from the period 1835–56 play on this connection; in one almanac tale, Crockett says "I turned round my head and thar was two big black bears looking over the top of my raccoon cap, as gravitatious as the Speaker of the House when he gives his casting vote." In another almanac story Davy grins a grizzly into submission, and the bear is described as "big as Kongress Hall."[29]

Of course, these almanac adventures—published after Crockett died—were exaggerated or fabricated, in the best frontier tradition. According to Crockett's autobiography, bears did become more plentiful as he realized his political ambitions. Recalling his days as a young newlywed in Lincoln County, Tennessee, Crockett wrote: "The bear had been much hunted in those parts before, and were not so plentiful as I could have wished." Ten years later, after a stint in the Tennessee state legislature: "I made corn enough to do me, and in the spring I killed ten bears." About the time that Davy fixes his aim on Washington, he slays "The biggest bear that was ever seen in America," one weighing six hundred pounds, and he kills another one with only his knife: ". . . I just took out my butcher, and went up and slap'd it into him." Near the end of his autobiography, and corresponding to his election to Congress, Crockett kills bears almost continuously. No sooner does he shoot one bear than his lead dog has another treed! During 1825, Crockett slays 17 bears in one week, 47 in one month, 105 for the year. Bear killing was the allegorical measure of Davy Crockett's progress on the frontier, and by pushing westward he somehow arrived in Washington, D.C.

Several humorous tales concerning bears appear in the mid-1800s. The bears in these stories are never themselves funny; they are cantankerous or purely evil. The stories are comical because of the diction and contorted logic of the bumpkins who have to deal with the troublesome animals. Such tales have folklore precedents, but they come to our attention via the almanacs and magazines directed at parlor-bound easterners.

Thomas Bang Thorpe's "The Big Bear of Arkansas" is the most notable example of this kind of story. The Big Bear is an extroverted bear hunter from Arkansas who spins yarns for some travelers on a Mississippi riverboat. He boasts: "[T]hat gun of mine is a perfect epidemic among b'ar." As for his dog, "if he should suddenly learn how much he is acknowledged to be ahead of all other dogs in the universe, he would be astonished to death in two minutes. I never could tell whether he was made expressly to hunt b'ar or whether bear was made expressly for him to hunt." The Big Bear speculates that some day he will run a fat Arkansas bear so long that it will just melt into a skin full of bear grease—"Much onlikelier things have happened."[30]

When bear motifs from nineteenth-century black oral tradition were popularized, humor again depended upon language and stereotype, but the resulting texts were often blatantly racist in tone. And an undercurrent of brutality runs through the texts even though they are ostensibly comic. (Joel Chandler Harris, the white "cornfield journalist" who collected the Uncle Remus stories, would not allow them to be read to his own children.)[31] The following example was based on information gathered from "a Negro huckster" in Durham, North Carolina, for the Federal Writers' Project.[32]

A black man is driving home through the woods with a wagon load of fresh pork. A bear leaps out onto the road behind the wagon, gives chase, and in no time at all is just about over the tailgate. Says the driver: "I know he's a smellin' that fresh meat in the back of the car'yall, and I know som'thin' else—that a bear know the smell of cullud pusson and all bear like to eat cullud folks." The wagoner then throws a hog's head overboard to distract the bear, but the animal gobbles it up and resumes pursuit; the driver throws more meat and the bear swallows it as fast as it comes flying. When the pork runs out, the bear springs for the driver but overshoots the wagon and lands on the horse's back. The bear devours the entire horse, and in doing so he works his way into the harness. "That were pie to me, and I drove him right on home as slick as you please, and lock him in the stable." The wagoner shoots the bear, eats bear meat instead of pork all winter, and trades the bearskin for a new horse!

References to race abound in white traditions too. The black wagoner states that all bears like to eat "cullud folks," but in one almanac story, a grizzly sniffs Davy Crockett's slave boy and runs away in disgust.[33] Elsewhere, Crockett may be reiterating a commonly held association between black bears and black men when he writes about an omen foretelling his greatest bear fight: "I had a dream the night before of having a hard fight with a big black nigger, and I knowed it was a sign that I was to have a battle with a bear, for in bear country, I never know'd such a dream to fail."[34] References like these are reminders that the doctrine of Manifest Destiny was a doctrine of white supremacy. The ferocious and gluttonous bears that represented the hardships of frontier life also evoke the injustice of minority life in the nineteenth century.

Another persistent, if not so invidious theme in bear tall tales is the association between bears and pigs. One widespread story tells of a farmer who notices that his corn and pigs have been disappearing. At the far edge of his cornfield he finds a bear trail leading deep into the woods. The trail leads to a hog pen, where the bear is fattening the stolen pigs on stolen corn. This theme has a factual basis, for bears are especially fond of pork. The rangers in Shenandoah National Park bait their bear traps with Virginia ham. Black bears have been known to scare a pregnant sow into aborting, and then to eat the fetal pigs. Some coincidental similarities also reinforce the bear-pig association. Adult male bears are known as boars, adult females as sows. Frontiersmen referred to bear meat as "bear bacon." And bears, like pigs, may be carriers of trichinae, the parasitic worms that cause trichinosis.

In the late nineteenth century we meet the most successful manipulator of the symbolic bear, Theodore Roosevelt. The Roosevelt era marked the apex of American expansionism, and Roosevelt was, metaphorically and in real terms, the consummate bear hunter.

A look at T.R.'s early autobiographical writings reveals that he was skillfully forging a public image, based in part on an idealization of the American frontiersman.[35] Roosevelt believed Daniel Boone to be the "archetype of the American hunter. . . leading his bands of tall backwoods riflemen" to Caintuck. He praised "quaint, honest, fearless Davy Crockett," whose career was representative of those constituting the "masterful race" of adventurers and "hard, dogged border-farmers." Roosevelt even perused George Washington's journals and private letters and discovered that the first president "found both a Bear and a Fox, but got neither" on a winter foray near Mount Vernon.

Washington, Boone, and Crockett were hard acts to follow, but T.R. set about establishing his pedigree with the great bear hunters in American history. The bespectacled New York dude headed for the Badlands of South Dakota, and grizzly hunting became his obsession. Roosevelt killed his first bear by tracking it from the carcass of a bull elk that he had shot earlier. When the bear stood its ground, T.R. took aim "between his two sinister-looking eyes" and placed the bullet "exactly between his eyes as if I had measured the distance with a carpenter's rule." This was just the excitement Roosevelt craved; he was disappointed, however, that his guide was no more awed by grizzlies than by jack rabbits, and wished to torment the bear by breaking its leg with a bullet, just to see what it would do. In a letter to his sister, Roosevelt related: "After I had begun bear-killing, other sports seemed tame. . . unless I was bear hunting all the time I am afraid I should soon get as restless with this life as with the life at home." But home he eventually went, to the world of mugwumps and trusts, armed with the Boone and Crockett mystique.

Political cartoons from the period attest to the effectiveness of Roosevelt's bear-hunter image. Albert Shaw's *A Cartoon History of Roosevelt's Career* contains several sketches in which bears are employed as allegorical devices.[36] The symbolic bears in these drawings can be organized roughly into three categories. The first type includes Russian bears—one of the cartoons deals with Roosevelt's involvement in the settling of the Russo-Japanese War, and another with his denouncement of the Czar's persecution of Jews. The Russian-bear metaphor is not an American invention, but rather dates back to the Middle Ages of Europe, where the bear stood for China and later Muscovy. The second type of cartoon bear represents the thorny issues in Roosevelt's political career. For example, a cartoon entitled "The Fight of His Life" shows Teddy wielding a knife labeled "railroad regulation" as a giant bear labeled "railroad interests" charges from a railroad tunnel den. In some cartoons the predator-prey relationship is reversed, as when Teddy is stalked by a bear labeled "third term," this referring to the controversial movement to nominate Roosevelt for a third term in 1908. The third and most prevalent type of bear appears in jocular and satirical cartoons. Here the bear is just an animal, the hapless victim of Roosevelt's legendary enthusiasm. These bears cower wide-eyed in the recesses of their caves as Teddy charges in; they climb down from the trees and rejoice as Teddy heads back to Washington.

This last symbolic use of the bear signals a turning point in bear symbology. Bears could be depicted as submissive or harried. One might even pity a bear. Concurrently, the nation could breathe a collective sigh of relief as the turmoil of annexation and settlement moved off the continent and into the Pacific and Caribbean. The spirit of the Monroe Doctrine might even be brought into question, now that it was being exercised in far-off places like Panama and the Philippines.

Given that the advent of the gentle symbolic bear coincided with the Roosevelt era, it is fitting that Teddy himself provided the inspiration for two of the earliest bear toys. The development of these toys is discussed in the book *Toys in America*, by Inez and Marshall McClintock, who work on the premise that "toys might give some insight into our entire society: that the... nature of toys might reveal a great deal about any state of our history."[37]

During the late 1800s, the J & E Stevens Company of Cromwell, Connecticut, manufactured a line of cast-metal banks. Some were inspired by current events, like the Tammany Bank and the Spanish-American War Artillery Bank. Others featured various animals that gulped down nickels and dimes. One favorite, the Bear Hunt Bank, featured a crouched Indian who shot coins from a spring-loaded rifle into the jaws of a bear. A spin-off of the Bear Hunt Bank had a figure of Teddy Roosevelt instead of the Indian, and a bear head popped out a tree stump when the coin was shot (fig.5.2). The Teddy and the Bear Bank was rife with subtle symbolism. Roosevelt the frontiersman replaced the Indian, and the bear coin depository was like the frontier, frightening yet full of resources.

5.2. Teddy and the Bear bank. Photo by Dennis Sutton.

During the same period, a few manufacturers were making stuffed bears, "although no one had looked upon these particularly ferocious beasts as the ideal model for snuggly toys."[38] Things changed in November, 1902, when Roosevelt visited Mississippi, intent on settling a boundary dispute between that state and Louisiana. The president took time out for a bear hunt, and when he refused to shoot a black bear in unsportsmanlike circumstances (it had been bayed and tied by his guides), the press had a field day. Cartoonist C.K. Berryman commemorated the incident in the *Washington Star* with a sketch entitled "Drawing the Line in Mississippi"; Teddy went south to draw the line between the states, and he drew the line at slaying a defenseless animal.

Inspired by the Berryman cartoon, a Brooklyn toy store owner named Morris Michtom dubbed the stuffed bear cub in his window "Teddy's Bear." Soon the demand for these toys outpaced Mrs. Michtom's ability to sew them. Michtom wrote to the president and obtained permission to use his name, then increased production. The Michtom family founded the Ideal Toy Company, eventually one of the world's largest.

Teddy Bears enjoyed a surge of popularity at the Jersey Shore in 1906, then swept the nation. European firms began to export Teddies; this prompted an editorial in an American trade journal which argued, in the best Jeffersonian tradition, that America could make bears as well as anybody. A no-nonsense ad in the 1907 Sears, Roebuck catalog proclaimed that Sears Teddy Bears were "the most sensible and serviceable toys ever put before the public."

The gentle bear was here to stay. And just as black bears had been previously invested with undue ferocity to lend consistency to the fierce bear image, so grizzly bears were portrayed as peace-loving creatures once the notion of gentle bears was fashionable.

Ernest Thompson Seton was instrumental in popularizing a semi-tough grizzly. A nature writer, artist, and founder of the Scouting movement in the United States, Seton offered his readers a curious blend of romanticism and expert natural history. Seton believed that bears evoked vestigial memories of cave bears and other giant beasts that preyed upon our ancestors in paleolithic times. But, almost apologetically, he added: "The giant has become inoffensive now. He is shy, indeed, and seeks only to be let mind his own business. . . . Man with a club is one thing—a joke, an easy meal maybe. But man with a modern rifle is a very different creature."[39]

These sentiments are developed in Seton's *Biography of a Grizzly*, published in 1900.[40] Wahb, the grizzly in question, starts life as an innocent, harmless creature (fig.5.3). "His Mother was just an ordinary silvertip, living the quiet life that all Bears prefer, minding her own business and doing her duty by her family, asking no favors of any one excepting to let her alone." Wahb leads a carefree life until his mother and four siblings are shot by a rancher. The cub is brutalized in encounters with other animals (including a black bear) and a steel trap. As Wahb grows and becomes more aware of his size and

5.3. Impromptu sketch of Wahb by Ernest Thompson Seton, from an autographed copy of *Biography of a Grizzly*. Photo by Daniel J. Gelo.

strength, he seeks revenge, first upon a coyote ("Oh, but it was good to feel the hot, bloody juices oozing between his teeth!") and then upon a stalking Indian. "Thus he learned that one must fight for peace...."

In order to convey the idea that there is logic to the grizzly's instinctive behavior, Seton has his bears speak their thoughts, although occasionally he does remind his readers that animal thoughts exist unexpressed. Thus, "their Mother said in Grizzly, 'Let me show you how' " to lick up ants. The orphaned Wahb whimpers, "Oh Mother, where are you?" Seton even employs synesthesia when Wahb *hears* the odor of an appetizing succulent root. Seton's grizzlies are merely wild animals, instinctive yet somehow sensible, and not provocative, bloodthirsty monsters. This kind of thoughtful and sympathetic treatment of the grizzly bear would not have been acceptable fifty years before.

More and more, bears inhabited the dreamy domain of childhood fantasy. In Albert Bigelow Paine's *The Arkansas Bear*, a variation on the Arkansas Traveler theme, a lost and hungry little boy comes upon a fiddling bear.[41] The boy, Bosephus, and Horatio the bear become fast friends and share many adventures. A.A. Milne, the British writer whose Winnie-the-Pooh was and is hugely popular in America, stated that his bear was wholly a creature of the nursery; he never conceived of the bear as anything but a stuffed plaything.[42]

Bears have also been emblematic of the problems inherent in a boy's transition to manhood. Both fierce and gentle bears have appeared in coming-of-age stories, though fierce ones seem more appropriate for the genre. Faulkner's novella *The Bear* and the "Slewfoot" sequences in Marjorie Kinnan Rawlings's *The Yearling* offer fierce bears which are symbolic of the responsibilities of the "real world." Walt Morey's Gentle Ben was a grizzly in the book and potentially truculent, but the television series featured a benign black bear. An episode of *The Waltons* has John-Boy overcome his reluctance to take life (and so become a man) by having to shoot a bear that is attacking his father.

A less dramatic introduction to responsibility was for years offered to Cub Scouts of the Bear rank. The introduction to the 1954 edition of the *Bear Cub Scout Book* admonishes: "The bear cub in this book gets into a little trouble every once in a while. That's the way he learns things. You may see him stick his nose into a beehive, but you won't see him do it twice. You may see him stick his paw into a hollow tree where the squirrels have hidden their winter supply of nuts. He will bring it out quickly when the squirrel bites his paw—but the bear cub won't do that twice, either. You will be just like the bear cub as you follow him down the Cub Scout Trail."[43]

Things are not so simple when hunters and environmentalists square off, both promoting their ideologies with the bear image. The cover of *Outdoor Life* magazine blares "Bear Attacks" with bright blue lettering over the drawing of a toothy black bear clawing the boots of a treed hiker. Inside, "The Killer Bears" by John O. Cartier recounts half a dozen maulings, then concludes that "some bears simply regard us as defenseless prey, far easier to catch and kill than rabbits."[44] Afterwards, the reader can turn to the "Where to go" advertisements in back to find out how to arrange his or her own bear hunt.

Blair and Ketchum's Country Journal appeals to a different readership. This publication offers sage Yankee advice about woodburning stoves and other small-is-beautiful technology. The ads in the back are for heirloom reproductions and Down East recipes. The bear pictured on a recent cover of *Country Journal* looks rather dignified, like a setter pointing out a bird. Inside, "In Pursuit of Bears" by Nathaniel Tripp chronicles the combined efforts of a wildlife biologist and an old bear hunter.[45] The men tree the bears, erect a net under them, and shoot them with a tranquilizer, causing them to fall into the net. The bear's weight, age, and sex are recorded, they get an ear tag and lip tattoo, and are released unharmed. The writer's style is not sanctimonious: the trappers he travels with have killed bears on occasion. But he argues that "[n]obody has yet been killed by a bear in New England, at least not in modern times. . . still the myth persists. Bears come close to men in both appetite and weight, and by imagining them as ferocious competitors we put life on more simple terms." There is no passionate slay-the-bears or save-the-bears rhetoric in *Country Journal*, just a pleasant, informative article for the fireside reader.

Audubon Society members, on the other hand, are urged to lobby and donate money to "save the griz"; bears are juxtaposed with acid rain, shrinking wetlands, and solar energy on the Audubon list of pressing issues. An article in Audubon Action Newsletter by Amos Enos reports that the Society recently filed suit to close certain dumps in Montana that were attracting grizzlies and encouraging man-bear encounters. Enos begins by noting that "Africa has the lion and India her tiger. In America, the grizzly bear is the ultimate symbol of nature uncontrolled by people."[46]

It is true that those who live in the wilderness today, or those who perceive themselves as doing so, may feel a special affinity with bears. This identification is celebrated in song, tall tales, traditional bear hunting, even in the bear bric-a-brac sold in mountain regions (and at virtually every tourist spot, whether or not bears live nearby). The bear is especially symbolic of the Appalachian and Ozark mountaineer. The Mid-West Crafts Company of Whitley City, Kentucky, manufactures a bear statuette out of molded coal dust and resin; it would be difficult to find a more condensed icon for the Cumberland Mountain region (fig.5.4). In the bluegrass song "Ole Slew Foot," the mountaineer likens himself to a marauding bear:

> He's big around the middle and he's broad across the rump
> Runnin' ninety miles an hour takin' thirty feet a jump
> Ain't never been caught, he ain't never been treed
> Some folks say he's a lot like me
>
> (Copyright © 1959 by LITTLE HURRY MUSIC INC., c/o Mietus Copyright Management, P.O. Box 432, Union, N.J. 07083. Used by permission.)

Appalachian chronicler Eliot Wigginton reports that bear hunting is still a popular pastime for men of the southeastern states, although they are likely to travel to Michigan where bears are more plentiful.[47] Bear hunt tale-telling is a time-honored tradition, and bears are still individualized and given personalities. Wigginton's researchers collected references to notable bears with missing toes and eyes, recalling Marjorie Rawlings's Slew Foot: "[F]rom the print of the right front paw, as big as the crown of a hat, one toe was missing."[48]

Modern mythology holds that in the old days people hunted bears for meat, not for sport. Today, hunters may eat the bear they kill as a matter of morality, authenticity, necessity, or because they

5.4. Bear statuette made from coal dust and resin by Mid-West Crafts Company, Whitley City, Kentucky. Photo by Dennis Sutton.

enjoy the taste of the bear meat. The meat is not marbled, so the standard way of preparing bear is to marinate it for a day or two, then roast it.

The non-edible parts of the bear also have practical, aesthetic, and symbolic appeal. Muzzle-loading rifle enthusiasts have found that bear oil is a superior patch lube; they will pay top dollar for a quart of bear oil, if they are lucky enough to find someone who can obtain bear oil and knows how to render it. Bear oil is an extremely fine all-around lubricant, rustproofer, and leather preservative. The colonial history buffs indulge in frontier hyperbole when they claim that bear oil will permeate anything, even a gun barrel.

There is currently a great deal of black market activity in bear parts, especially claws. Ranger Haskell notes that "a lot more men are wearing stuff around their necks now, especially among the, you might say, macho group. . . There's still kind of mystical power associated with bears, sort of a holdover." A single black bear claw, polished, with a silver cap, will fetch upwards of fifty dollars, and grizzly claws cost considerably more. Poachers who supply bear parts find a ready market in the Asian communities of California. Bear paws are an Oriental delicacy, and the slimy green gallbladder, called *ungdam* by the Koreans, is valued as medicine.[49]

Bear parts and bears in general are prominent in American sexual imagery. The connection is actually a very old one—the notion that bears are unusually lustful was recorded by Pliny and repeated in medieval bestiaries. In America, the bearskin rug that lay enticingly in front of so many Victorian fireplaces has come to represent spontaneous, passionate sexuality. Here the bear more specifically suggests the aggressive aspect of female sexuality; the temptress lying on the rug is a devourer, the rug itself a representation of the *vagina dentata*. Akin to this image are the formulaic accounts of frontier combat with *she-bears* that *hug* their victims to death, accounts which also make the unlikely connection between ferocity and femininity. Complementing the aggressive female image is the ultimate gesture of debilitation customarily practiced on male bears by hunters: removal and display of the animal's *os penis*. The four-inch bone is used as a swizzle stick, and it may be gold plated (fig.5.5). One Pennsylvania hunter I spoke with tanned a bear's scrotal sac to make a change purse for his fiancée.

The gender of human victims is of consequence in some modern

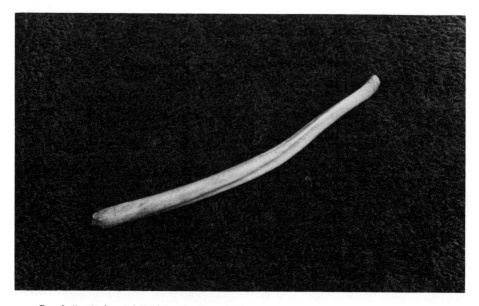

5.5. Bear's "swizzle stick." Photo by Dennis Sutton.

popular beliefs about bear behavior. Biologists have been accumulating evidence that the presence of a menstruating woman in the area around a grizzly den will enrage the mother bear. This is a highly plausible theory, and even without absolute proof, it circulates among backpackers as a folk-scientific explanation for bear aggression. Yet other beliefs from oral tradition have it that the presence of a woman will mollify a bear. According to a Cleveland policeman interviewed by folklorists in 1960: "When berry picking with a group of people and a bear crosses in front of the group, have one of the women lift her dress to show the bear that she is a female, and the bear will leave."[50]

Madison Avenue admen have been adept at manipulating both the fierce and gentle bear images. A recent television commercial for the Parke-Davis hemorrhoid remedy Anusol begins with a grumpy man dressed in a fur coat, entering his house. His wife faces the camera and complains, "When my husband has a hemorrhoid flare-up, you'd think he was a bear!"

Andrew Neisser, account representative for the J. Walter Thompson ad agency, explained the logic behind the "Bear" commercial: "By describing a hemorrhoid sufferer as a 'bear,' we hoped to set up the problem that Anusol could solve. Since bears are often considered ill-tempered and are known for growling, we felt the metaphor offered a subtle and effective means of describing a hemorrhoid sufferer's discomfort. The 'Bear' TV commercial was proven successful in both copy testing and real-world situations. Anusol's market share has grown steadily since this commercial aired."[51]

The most successful bear in advertising history is a gentle one. According to the Advertising Council, Smokey the Bear is one of the two most recognizable symbols in American advertising, second only to the Coca-Cola trademark.[52] Since the cartoon character was originated on January 10, 1945, he has appeared in innumerable Forest Service posters and television commercials. One of the more poignant posters shows the bear without his ranger hat, praying, ". . . and please make people more careful, amen." Since the 1950s, the National Zoo in Washington has displayed a living counterpart to the cartoon Smokey. The original zoo Smokey was orphaned during a forest fire in Lincoln National Forest in New Mexico; he died in 1976. His replacement, Smokey Junior, was also rescued in a New Mexican fire. Smokey the Bear's stern but friendly reminder that "only you can prevent forest fires" has evidently been taken to heart by the American public, for in the past forty years the incidence of forest fires has been reduced by 50 percent.

Bears represent individuals and places as well as products and concepts. The late University of Alabama football coach Paul Bryant was called "Bear" not because he had a surly manner in the locker room, but because as a teenager he wrestled a bear. The animal and its owner were on stage in the theatre in Bryant's home town of Fordyce, Arkansas. All comers were challenged to grapple with the bear for an entire minute. Tempted by the prize money (one dollar) and the chance to impress his sweetheart, Bryant stepped up. He lasted the one minute, but not without being badly scratched and bitten on the ear. Somehow the showman skipped town without paying the prize money, and Bryant was left with nothing but a new nickname.[53]

The famous coach's home state was in fact known as "The Bear State" until 1923, when a resolution by the Arkansas Legislature substituted "The Wonder State." Next door in Missouri, the state flag still depicts two standing bears. New Mexico adopted the black bear as its state animal in 1963. The grizzly is the state animal of California, having been designated in 1953, though unfortunately the grizzly has been extinct in California for many years. The grizzly that has adorned the California state flag since 1911 survives from the so-called Bear Flag, which was flown by Anglo-American settlers in California during their short-lived revolt against the Mexican government on June 14, 1846. Again we find the legacy of Manifest Destiny, which endures beyond the existence of real grizzly bears in California. Thus four states have used the bear symbol to elicit some image of natural or political history.

There are other American symbolic bears too numerous to investigate: team mascots, Indian names, Wall Street bears, Disney characters, more television and Hollywood bears. In tracing the development of the symbolic bear, it becomes evident that the symbol has all the power and resilience of its natural prototype. It is expected that bears will continue to be emblematic of American attitudes, places and products for a long time to come. Perhaps space exploration will result in a transformation of the frontier bear metaphor; already, the bruin-like Ewoks and Chewbacca of *Star Wars* seem to suggest this possibility. As the Big Bear of Arkansas would say, "Much onlikelier things have happened."

NOTES

1. T.B. Thorpe, "The Big Bear of Arkansas," *Spirit of the Times* 11 (March 27, 1841): 43.

2. Paul Shepard and Barry Sanders provide an excellent, cross-cultural survey of bear symbolism in their recent book, *The Sacred Paw: The Bear in Nature, Myth, and Literature* (New York: Viking, 1985). Their work provides a useful background for my more detailed inquiry into bear symbolism across the whole range of American folk, popular, and elite cultures.

3. Paul Schullery, *The Bears of Yellowstone* (Wyoming: Yellowstone Library and Museum Assoc., 1980), 20.

4. Thorpe, 43.

5. Ben East, *Bears* (New York: Crown, 1977), 55–62.

6. Schullery, 53.

7. "The Awesome Bear in Plains Indian Art," *American Indian Art* 7, No. 3 (Summer 1982): 44–45.

8. Virgil J. Vogel, *American Indian Medicine* (Norman: Univ. of Oklahoma Press, 1970), 38–39, 208.

9. A. L. Kroeber, *Handbook of the Indians of California* (New York: Dover, 1976), 516.

10. Vogel, 248.

11. Clyde Kluckhohn, *Navajo Witchcraft* (Boston: Beacon, 1967), 47.

12. William K. Powers, *Oglala Religion* (Lincoln: Univ. of Nebraska Press, 1977), 58.

13. Kroeber, 200–1.

14. Richard M. Dorson, *Bloodstoppers and Bearwalkers* (Cambridge, Mass.: Harvard Univ. Press, 1952), 26–37.

15. Stephen Powell, "The Tribes of California," *Contributions to North American Ethnology*, vol. 3, ed. J. W. Powell (Washington, D.C.: U.S. Dept. of the Interior, 1877), 358–60.

16. Alice Marriott and Carol K. Rachlin, *American Indian Mythology* (New York: Mentor, 1968), 159.

17. James Mooney, "Myths of the Cherokee," *Nineteenth Annual Report of the Bureau of American Ethnology*, pt. 1 (Washington, D.C.: Government Printing Office, 1900), 325–27.

18. John Smith, *The Generall Historie of Virginia, New England and the Summer Isles*, vol. 1 (1624; Glasgow: MacLehose, 1907), 56.

19. Henry S. Burrage, ed., *Early English and French Voyages* (New York: Scribner's, 1930), 6, 107.

20. Thomas Jefferson, *Notes on the State of Virginia* (1787; Chapel Hill: Univ. of North Carolina Press, 1955), 50.

21. Paul Russel Cutright, *Lewis and Clark: Pioneering Naturalists* (Urbana: Univ. of Illinois Press, 1964), 140–41.

22. Paul Wilhelm, Duke of Wurttemberg, *Travels in North America 1822–1824*, ed. Savoie Lottinville (Norman: Univ. of Oklahoma Press, 1973), xv, xvii, 225, 272.

23. Cutright, 141.

24. Ibid., 352–53.

25. Ibid., 142.

26. Daniel Bryan, *The Mountain Muse* (Harrisonburg, Va.: Davidson and Bourne, 1813).

27. F.L. Hawk, *The Adventures of Daniel Boone, The Kentucky Rifleman* (New York: D. Appleton, 1862), 48.

28. *Narrative of the Life of David Crockett of the State of Tennessee* (New York: Nafis and Cornish, 1845), 164.

29. Richard M. Dorson, ed., *Davy Crockett: American Comic Legend* (New York: Rockland, 1939), 103, 113.

30. Thorpe, 43–44.

31. Bob Brinkmeyer, "A Return Visit: Joel Chandler Harris," *Southern Exposure* 5, nos. 2–3 (1977): 214–15.

32. Robert B. Downs, ed., *The Bear Went Over the Mountain* (New York: Macmillan, 1964), 37–39.

33. Dorson, *Davy Crockett*, 113.

34. Crockett, *Narrative*, 161.

35. Theodore Roosevelt, *The Wilderness Hunter* (New York: Collier, 1893), 14–18, 270–71, 282–83.

36. Albert Shaw, *A Cartoon History of Roosevelt's Career* (New York: Review of Reviews Co., 1910).

37. Inez and Marshall McClintock, *Toys in America* (Washington, D.C.: Public Affairs Press, 1961), 5, 278–81, 353–59.

38. Ibid., 353.

39. John G. Sampson, ed. *The World of Ernest Thompson Seton* (New York: Knopf, 1976), 55–56.

40. Ernest Seton, *Biography of a Grizzly* (New York: Century, 1900).

41. Albert Bigelow Paine, *The Arkansas Bear* (Philadelphia: Henry Altemus, 1902).

42. A.A. Milne, *Autobiography* (New York: Dutton, 1939), 285.

43. *Bear Cub Scout Book* (New Brunswick, N.J.: The Boy Scouts of America), 5.

44. John O. Cartier, "The Killer Bears," *Outdoor Life* 171, no. 1 (Jan. 1983): 37–38, 82.

45. Nathaniel Tripp, "In Pursuit of Bears," *Country Journal* 9, no. 11 (Nov. 1982): 57–67.

46. Amos Enos, "Symbol of Wild America," *Audubon Action Newsletter* 1, no. 2 (Feb. 1983): 11.

47. Eliot Wigginton, *Foxfire 5* (Garden City, N.Y.: Anchor/Doubleday, 1979), 435–94.

48. Marjorie Kinnan Rawlings, *The Yearling* (New York: Scribner's, 1938), 25.

49. Dennis G. Hanson, "Poaching: Oriental Demand for Ungdam and Paws Decimates California Bears," *Audubon* 85, no. 4 (July 1983): 127–28.

50. W.D. Hand, Anna Casetta, and S.B. Theiderman, eds., *Popular Beliefs and Superstitions*, vol. 2 (Boston: G. K. Hall, 1981), 1287.

51. Letter to author, April 18, 1983.

52. Eleanor Hangley, spokeswoman, the Advertising Council, Inc., pers. comm.

53. Paul W. Bryant and John Underwood, *Bear* (New York: Bantam, 1974), 26.

The Fox

MARY HUFFORD

Beautiful, repugnant, exasperating, mysterious, the fox straddles numerous boundaries. Its cunning evokes our admiration. Its barnyard raids provoke our outrage. The smell of this noxious beast disgusts us. In its eleventh hour it stirs our pity. For centuries we have invaded the fox's realm in search of its fur, expelling it from our own when it covets our chickens. Yet, long after foxes have ceased to threaten our poultry, and apart from any desire for their pelts, we chase them.

The longstanding relationship between people and foxes has not only enriched our vocabulary of pursuit and avoidance, but it has made the fox what it is, according to zoologist Ernest P. Walker: "As a result of contact with man [red foxes] have developed a cunning that now connotes the name fox with the acme of cleverness."[1]

If foxes could talk they might protest that Walker's words are a trifle homocentric, that it is actually people who have become fox-like. Walker has touched upon a certain dialectical tension between the beast as it occurs in nature and its image as it resonates through culture. At the interstices of the natural fox and the cultural fox are the interactions of foxes with farmers, trappers, and hunters. Farmers interact with foxes to keep them out of the cultural realm, trappers to entice them into it. In their perennial pursuit of foxes, foxhunters construct a parallel universe that mirrors the social order while exploring the natural world and exploiting their knowledge of it.

All three groups have shaped our image of the fox by reporting on its behavior. Most people first encounter the fox in an allegorical world, in which the image leads a life of its own, recasting facets of the social order in terms of classic fox behaviors, which we might distill into two fox paradigms. In the first—"the fox on the prowl"— the fox often invades our world. In the second—"the fox on the run"—we invade the fox's. It is difficult, after all these centuries, to know which came first, though we are probably correct to suspect that the fox started it.

The paradigms, of course, begin in descriptions of fox behavior, descriptions in which fox and human attributes are so thoroughly blended that, after several millenia of anthropomorphic foxes and vulpine humans, the natural fox is hard to see.

THE NATURAL FOX

Though biologists have identified eighteen species and scores of sub-species of these small canids through the world, the generic fox most firmly implanted in the popular imagination derives from the Euro-pean red fox (*vulpes vulpes*).

It is difficult even for the naturalist to extricate the red fox from his cultural milieu. One zoologist lamented: "Accounts of the cun-ning and extraordinary reasoning ability of red foxes have become so firmly entrenched in our folklore that one has difficulty conduct-ing an objective study of the animal."[2] For centuries the recitation of fox traits has featured certain obligatory elements, including the ani-mal's barnyard pillages, performance before the hounds, methods of luring birds in the wild, odor, and love of grapes. Nineteenth-century naturalists imposed moral judgments on the fox in descrip-tions like the following by Richard Harlan:

> This dextrous and cunning animal lives in the woods near the
> dwellings of man; during the night committing depredations
> upon poultry; first killing all within his reach, then carrying them
> to his hole, or burying them beneath the leaves; he also destroys
> rabbits, birds, and robs the snares of the hunter, is fond of eggs,
> milk, and fruit, particularly of grapes. . . . The fox emits a

disagreeable odour. In cases of extreme danger and surprise these animals have been known to simulate death.[3]

These themes, rooted in classical authorities like Physiologus, Aesop, and the Bible, are probably here to stay. Konrad Lorenz, impatient with such notions, tried to correct them in 1952:

> Strange what blind faith is placed in proverbs, even when what they say is false or misleading. The fox is not more cunning than other beasts of prey and is much more stupid than wolf or dog, the dove is certainly not peaceful, and of the fish, rumour spreads only untruth; it is neither so cold-blooded as one says of dull people, nor is the "fish in water" nearly so happily situated as the converse saying would imply.[4]

It appears impossible *not* to mention the fox's cunning, which is alway referred to by naturalists, at least obliquely. In a volume published in 1979 we read: "The red fox scarcely needs description. . . . Best known for its sagacity and cunning, the red fox continues to maintain itself and even increase in spite of constant persecution."[5] Walker notes: "These animals. . . have a keen sense of sight, smell, and hearing; and, at times, they exhibit what almost seems to be a sense of humor."[6] Foxhunters often say that the fox seems to be laughing at them, as Nunn Balew does in Harriet Arnow's classic *Hunter's Horn*: "He knew King Devil stood there less than twenty feet away;. . . looking him over, laughing at him, weighing the worth of the pups."[7]

Scientists cannot seem to agree on whether there are four or six species of fox in North America. The six species recognized by some scientists include the old world red fox (*vulpes vulpes*), the smaller, new world red fox, (*vulpes fulva*), the kit fox (*vulpes macrotis*), the swift fox (*vulpes velox*), the gray fox (*urocyon cinereoargenteus*), and the arctic fox (*alopex lagopus*). Other authorities argue that *vulpes vulpes* and *vulpes fulva* are actually the same species, as are the kit fox and swift fox, found in mutually exclusive sections of the Southwest. The arctic (white) fox is found in the northernmost regions of the continent, the gray primarily on the eastern half (fig. 6.1), and the red throughout the entire continent (fig. 6.2).[8]

Some naturalists believe that the red fox in America is a post-contact phenomenon, introduced to this continent by fur-traders and foxhunters.[9] If so, then the American red fox is literally an Old

Gray Fox

6.1. "Gray American Fox," drawing by Mark Catesby, from *The Natural History of Carolina,* (London, 1731–47), vol. 2, plate 78. Also published in Peter Kalm's *Travels Into North America* (Barre, Mass.: The Imprint Society, 1972).

World legacy laden with cultural baggage from England and from antiquity. Americans have increased this cargo.

We know that in the eighteenth century red foxes were introduced at both ends of the North American continent. While Russian fur traders were training the Aleuts to trap introduced foxes in Alaska,[10] the British were importing red foxes for sport in the Middle Atlantic region, having found the gray fox wholly unsatisfactory:

> The fox of Carolina is gray but smells not as the foxes in Great Britain and elsewhere. They have reddish hair about their ears and are generally very fat; yet I never saw anyone eat them. When hunted they make a sorry chace because they run up trees when pursued.[11]

The sight of a red fox caused a stir in the thirteen colonies. In 1789, in Perry County, Pennsylvania, a group of sportsmen stood gaping in astonishment at the carcass of a creature their hounds had run down. A boy who witnessed the kill recalled years later:

> Not a person present, or any one who saw it for some days had ever seen or heard of an animal of the kind. At last it was shown to a Mr. Lenarton, an old Jerseyman, who pronounced it an *English* fox. He said the red fox was imported into New York from England by one of the first English governors, who was said to be a great sportsman.[12]

The red fox was allegedly introduced in a number of places. J.S. Skinner, editor of *The American Turf Register,* noted that in 1729 a group of foxhunters on Maryland's eastern shore imported red foxes from England to improve their fox chases. He speculated that they made their way across the frozen Chesapeake during the hard winter of 1779.[13] In 1748, Peter Kalm observed the occurrence of red and gray foxes in the English colonies, the gray being "less nimble than the red." He also reported the story that foxhunters were the cause:

> The red foxes are very scarce here: they are entirely the same with the European sort. Mr. Bartram and several others assured me, that, according to the unanimous testimony of the Indians, this kind of foxes never was in the country, before the Europeans settled in it. . . . Mr. Evans, and some others, assured me that the following account was still known by the people. A gentleman of fortune in New England, who had a great

6.2. "Red Fox," lithograph by Thomas Doughty, from *The Cabinet of Natural History and Rural American Sports* (with illustrations), ed. Gail Stewart (Barre, Mass.: The Imprint Society, 1973).

inclination for hunting, brought over a great number of foxes from Europe, and let them loose in his territories, that he might be able to indulge his passion for hunting.[14]

Since the red fox is at least partly an English legacy, embodying at various levels our ties with Great Britain, it is important to understand its significance in English culture.

For Englishmen the fox is so important that anthropologist Edmund Leach assigns it to its own class among the six classes of British animals, which include: 1) wild animals, 2) foxes, 3) game, 4) farm animals, 5) pets, and 6) vermin. The categories progress from those animals most removed from culture to those that are most incorporated—with vermin being too close. Leach links the very specialized vocabulary for foxes with the fox's ambiguity in English minds—its borderline status between edible field and inedible wild animals.[15] Following this line of thinking, Leach also assigns hound dogs, bred as working animals for pursuing game, a borderline status, somewhere between farm animals and pets. For example, unlike farm animals, they have names and are not eaten, but unlike pets they are working animals, not permitted in the house.

The dogs, wedged between nature and culture themselves, serve as crowbars for prying open the worlds of nature. Exploring the natural world by means of hunting dogs and then trading observations about it has long been an important traditional activity. One topic intriguing to foxhunters, trappers, and biologists is the liminal status of foxes, lodged as they are somewhere between dogs and cats. The relationship between red and gray foxes is a particularly compelling subtopic.

The Case of the Feline Fox

As a canid, the fox is anomalous. There is something disturbingly undoglike about it. In strong light it displays elliptical, catlike pupils, in contrast with the round eyes of its canine cousins. A solitary hunter, it stalks its prey like a cat, unlike canids who hunt openly in large, sociable packs. Its omnivorous diet features insects and berries as well as rabbits, mice, and chickens. Subcaudal glands at the base of its round bushy tail, which comprises half of its body length, account for a distinctive "foxy" odor not possessed by wolves or dogs.

The gray fox has semiretractile claws, enabling it to climb trees. A fox's canine teeth are actually feline—long and thin, for dispatching its prey the way cats do.

Because classification automatically freezes the constantly evolving world of nature, all schemes invite criticism. Journalists and scientists alike raise the issue with some frequency. The fox, with its doglike skeleton and catlike behavior, seems to be caught in a crack between categories. Although the Linnaean category has been changed from *canis vulpes* to *vulpes vulpes,* the issue refuses to die.

"This canid hunts like a cat," wrote naturalist J. David Henry.[16] J.N.P. Watson, a chronicler of formal foxhunting, suggests that "The vulpine surely provides the link between the worlds of the canine and feline."[17] In a 1955 issue of the *London Illustrated News,* an article appeared entitled "Dog-Fox and Cats." Its author, Maurice Burton wonders why we accept the traditional classification so passively:

> ...a fox is, in fact, very catlike. It has contractile pupils and scent glands, both catlike characters.... It can climb trees, and there are a number of instances on record of vixens having had their litters in the tops of old pollards.... the young fox is known as a cub, a name it shares with the young of lions, tigers, leopards, and other cats. The fact that the name is also given to young bears, which are classified in the family Ursidae of the Carnivora, is merely another of the anomalies already mentioned.

He concludes that "whenever Nature draws a straight line, she smudges it."[18]

In America, where the gray fox introduces a new variable, the debate shifts. Foxhunters marvel at the differences between red and gray foxes, resolving the dilemma by reclassification. They concur that Linnaeus erred, but only in part. By their reckoning, the red fox is a member of the dog family, and the gray fox is a member of the cat family. The evidence, they say, speaks for itself. The track of a red fox is large and doglike, while the gray fox leaves a small catlike print. A gray fox can climb straight up a telephone pole, in contrast to red foxes that only climb leaning trees. A gray fox has smaller litters than a red fox, just as cats have smaller litters than dogs.

One hunter reports that a red fox he reared in captivity ran rabbits alongside his beagles. Another claims that a gray fox can be trained to use a litter box in captivity, and that a cat will nurse a young gray fox more readily than it will a red one. He also suggested that a cat and a gray fox would mate, and that a red fox and a dog would mate, but that a gray fox and a red fox would never mate.[19]

Red and gray foxes occur in complementary distribution, according to foxhunters, who are not in total agreement over whether the red drives the gray away or vice versa. One foxhunter, writing in to the *American Turf Register* in 1829, argued that the red fox is the superior animal, drawing a chilling racial parallel:

> It proves, I think, a mortal antipathy between the two species, and that the red fox possesses the same superiority over the grey, which has been assigned to the white man over the red or black. Another fact in corroboration of their hatred is, that they never copulate—dogs and foxes, dogs and wolves, copulate; every species of the dog copulates with every other species; but it is certain from all I have heard or observed, that the red and the grey never do.... The red fox is spreading over all Virginia, and it will soon be said of the grey, that "the places which once knew them, know them no longer." The revolution is not to be regretted. The red is greatly the nobler animal, of larger size, higher form, greater foot and bottom, and incomparably superior beauty.[20]

On a similar note, Spencer Fullerton Baird, the Assistant Secretary of the Smithsonian Institution in 1859, reported that while the gray fox was well represented among fossils found in Eastern America, archaeologists had not encountered any fossil records of the red fox. He concluded that the American red foxes could well be descended from imported English foxes. He compared the difference between American and English red foxes to the difference between Anglo-Americans and the English:

> Nor is there any difficulty to be met with in the different characteristics of the American animal as the finer fur, brighter color, narrower and more delicate head, sharper muzzle, &c., as it is in precisely such osteological peculiarities that the Anglo-American race differs from its English stock.[21]

The red fox continues to be the preferred quarry, although in urbanizing areas the gray fox is favored, because it travels in circles, confining the chase within a smaller territory. In general, the gray fox is regarded as the weaker species. It seems to tire quickly and does not dazzle the hunter with tricks as the red fox does. Frank Pope Wilder, a South Georgian foxhunter observed:

> Now a gray fox, he is a little on the dumb side, but you know what I mean, he doesn't know how to move like that red fox. You can't catch many red foxes, not with hounds; they are just smart.[22]

At the surface level the argument represents an effort to reclassify the fox, placing it on an equal taxonomic footing with dogs and cats. However, unless scientists create a new category, "vulpidae," to stand alongside "canidae," "felidae," and "ursidae," the fox's discrepancies will probably continue to baffle and fascinate its audience. The American debate is more complex. Foxhunters evaluate the suitability of the gray fox—which is not even a vulpid according to its latin binomial—as quarry. What consequence would the designation of gray foxes as cats have? One can imagine the controversies inspired by this doglike cat.

At another level, we see the red fox emerging as the embodiment of ties with England, even as it begins to co-evolve with the Anglo-American who is emerging as a distinctive social and cultural entity. It also embodies the limits of that evolution, being made to symbolize the racial superiority of the Anglo-Americans who identify with it, and who would no sooner merge with Blacks and American Indians than the red fox would with the gray fox.

The Natural Fox As Trickster

> ". . . they play grinning, entrap soothing, and kill smiling. That is the nature of a fox." (*Reynard The Fox*)

Stories from far-flung sources in time and space suggest that the fox has developed quite a stockpile of tricks over the centuries. The famed method of flea-divesting (Motif K921, fox rids himself of fleas) has been reported on by various naturalists:

> One man reported seeing a fox carrying a piece of bark in its mouth. The fox waded into a creek, completely immersing itself, leaving the barest portion of nostrils and the bark above water. The fox was only briefly submerged: emerging it dropped the

bark, shook off the water and trotted away. The observer went down to examine the bark. It was crawling with hen fleas.[23]

The fox, who in fables deceives his victims, particularly birds both wild and domestic, with flattery, has been observed luring birds in the wild by several means. An Athabaskan trapper reported hearing a red fox mimic loons in order to entice one to the shore.[24] Noting a similar behavior in Arctic foxes, Reverend Wood writes: "It is found that this animal possesses the power of imitating the cries of the birds on which it loves to feed, and it is probable that it employs this gift for the purpose of decoying its prey to their destruction."[25] Foxes have been observed "tolling" (i.e., summoning them, the way that church bells summon people) for birds, exciting their curiosity by running in circles, and leaping about:

> The mode in which some species entrap water fowl is also extremely ingenious. They advance a little way into the water and afterwards retire, playing a thousand antic tricks on the banks. The fowl approach, and as they come near, the animal ceases, that he may not alarm them, moving only his tail about, and that very gently, till the birds approach so near that he is enabled to seize one or more.[26]

Native Americans were allegedly the first to exploit the fox's bird-luring abilities:

> Observing this foxy method of duck hunting, American Indians copied the ruse. They attached a fox skin to long lines and jerked it across a bit of open beach between two blinds in which the hunters lay with bows and arrows. When the ducks were lured close enough by the cavorting fox skin, the hunters potted them on the water.[27]

The early French, according to the story, took the technique a step further, training their dogs to play at being foxes, wolves in foxskins, so to speak. Centuries later the Nova Scotia duck tolling retriever emerged:

> Like the fox, a tolling dog has a long reddish outer coat laid over an extremely thick, wool-like undercoat. Smallish dogs were favored because they were quicker in their movements, more foxlike in the way they played and dashed about on the beach when tolling waterfowl. . . . Then there is the tail. Part of the

6.3. A Nova Scotia Duck Tolling Retriever, from Harbor Light Kennels. Courtesy of Avery and Erna Nickerson.

allure of a cavorting fox is the dashing way in which it flags and gestures with its thick-furred, white-tipped brush.

Today's tolling dog carries a similar tail (fig. 6.3). Gerald Parsons, a folklorist and wildfowler himself, adds that it is not actually necessary that the dogs resemble the foxes, only that they emulate this behavior, so that "foxiness" is truly a folkloric feature.[28]

Trappers, public enemy number one to foxes, must be more deceptive when preying on the fox than the fox is when preying on birds. Many trappers claim without hesitation that the fox is the most challenging furbearer of all. "You have to remove all suspicion and put down a big attraction," says Tom Brown, who for sixty years has trapped for fox in South Jersey. Such advice might have been given by a fox itself.

Deceiving the fox, itself the grand deceiver, is difficult. The traps cannot smell like themselves, nor can the trappers, who must wash their hands in "fox suspicion eraser" when setting for fox. Trapping authority Pat Sedlak writes that "fox suspicion eraser is usually made by blending the anal, ear and foot glands of foxes with fox urine. Fox droppings mixed with water have also been used." "That's where you get the saying 'The old trapper doesn't die, he just smells that way,' " said Tom Brown.[29]

The sets have to be varied, because foxes may quickly learn to avoid one kind of set (Motif J655.2, fox jeers at fox-trap). "The fox is smart," goes the saying, "Because he is old, not because he is a fox."

Curiosity kills the fox. The large and varied repertoire of sets for fox include "curiosity sets" that act on the fox's inquisitive nature and on all of its senses. "Flag sets" invite the fox to investigate the whipping sound produced by a white banner hung near the set. In "candle-light" sets a burning candle in a mason jar augments a dirt-hole set. The wind whistling over the bottle placed in a "wine jug" set produces a jug band effect, and a "clock" set, combining a clock with a "blind set," tantalizes a fox with its ticking.[30] In the "water set" the bait is placed in the water, close to the shore. Between the shore and the bait the trap is covered with a piece of sod. The fox, in an effort to keep its feet dry, steps onto the sod and is trapped. "They're like cats," said Tom Brown. "They hate to get their feet wet."[31]

In a sense, trappers themselves are becoming an endangered species, their livelihood threatened by a sentimental view of wildlife conservation that fails to recognize the utility of human beings as predators with a role to play in the ecosystem. Lydia Black notes that, ironically, two centuries after Russian fur-traders introduced foxes and trapping methods to the Aleuts, environmentalists lobbied successfully to restrict trapping:

> . . .with the result that the increased fox population demolished
> nests, eggs, and young of various protected species of birds,
> before the foxes starved. Recently, the Polar foxes on Attu had to
> be poisoned by Fish and Game personnel, as they were
> endangering the emperor geese there.[32]

Several years ago the "antis" (as trappers call their opposition) were themselves tricked by an antithetical fox. Most trappers are acquainted with the rare "Polish blue fox," a fabulous beast that chews off three of its feet but is still caught in the trap. Folklorist Paula Johnson reported on a Maryland trapper who, on his way to the fur buyer, spied a road-killed gray fox by the roadside. He helped himself to the fox's tail, which he then sewed to the pelt of an albino muskrat. He presented the pelt to the fur buyer, who, greatly amused, displayed it publicly with the sign: "The Rare Polish Blue Fox." Going along with the gag, a journalist reported the "find" in the newspaper.

Months later a group of trappers attended a hearing at the Maryland House of Delegates, at which anti-trappers were testifying. One of the antis waved the newspaper article before the legislators, lamenting that the trappers were cold-bloodedly destroying the rare Polish blue fox, to the astonishment and delight of the assembled fur-takers.[33]

The Natural Fox in the Domestic Realm

Several senses of the word "fox" suggest that it is hard to get the best of this creature. To "fox" someone is to trick or to baffle him by ingenuity or cunning. To be "foxed," as in books that are discolored, or wine that has soured, is to be spoiled. The fox was for centuries regarded as a verminous, noxious beast with no respect for cultural boundaries. Those who strike back at the fox may find it exacts a post-mortem penalty. Wood recalls:

> I remember an instance when a fox was captured by an old
> laborer, in revenge for killing his fowls, and which he exhibited in
> an outhouse for a short time. The animal could not have been in
> the shed for more than twenty minutes, and yet the odor which it
> evolved was so pertinaciously adherent to everything which had
> been touched by the animal that the shed was not free from the
> tell-tale scent for many weeks.[34]

In the popular mind, the fox is still the bane of the henhouse, despite the efforts of foxhunters to temper this image that has been centuries in the making. The fox lives at the edges of the civilized world. From infamous outposts in coverts and thickets he violates the cultural order, capturing cocks and geese, throwing barnyards into confusion, drawing his pursuers behind him when he escapes back into the world of nature, as Chaucer tells us:

> And out at dores stirten they anon
> And syen the fox toward the grove gon,

And bar upon his bak the cok away,
And cryden, "Out, harrow, and weylaway!
Haha, the fox!" and after him they ran,
And eek with staves, many another man
ran Colle oure dogge, and Talbot and Gerland;
And Malkin with a dystaff in her hand,
Ran cow and calf and eek the verray hogges.
So fered for the berkyng of the dogges
And shoutyng of the men and women eke;[35]

An Americanized portrait of this barnyard marauder emerges in a song that is also popular in Great Britain:

He grabbed a gray goose by the neck,
Throwed a duck across his back,
He didn't mind the "quack, quack, quack,"
Or the legs all dangling down-o.

Old lady Flipper-Flapper jumped out of bed,
Out of the window she popped her head,
Crying, "John! John! The gray goose is gone,
And the fox is out on the town-o."

Old John he ran to the top of the hill,
Blowed his horn both loud and shrill,
The fox, he said, "I better flee with my kill,
Or they'll soon be on my trail-o."[36]

These thefts have sometimes provided an excuse for foxhunting and, by extension, for the destruction of property that accompanied the hunt. The history of foxhunting is peppered with lawsuits filed by aggrieved property owners. In a famous nineteenth-century case before the New York State Supreme Court the counsel for the fox-hunter declared that "the interests of our husbandmen, the most useful of men in any community, will be advanced by the destruction of a beast so pernicious and incorrigible."[37] In another lawsuit of that era the plaintiff declared that "the destruction of a noxious beast was not the real reason for the trespass."[38] That foxhunters import foxes for their chases when foxes are scarce lends an air of truth to this complaint.

Where foxes are limited, foxhunters now maintain that foxes rarely invade the chicken coop, and only then if spurred by the need to feed their young. Foxes, they argue, eat berries, and help to control rodent and snake populations. Furthermore, they suggest, trappers not only decimate the fox population, but endanger fox hounds, and should be more strictly regulated. As they see it, then, the fox chase has evolved from a system of chicken protection into something the foxes enjoy as much as the hunters do.

The Fox on the Run

> "Now, the red fox, he likes to be run by the hounds. I think he enjoys it as much as the hounds." (Frank Pope Wilder)

Foxhunters themselves dwell in a cultural twilight zone—pursuing a crepuscular creature who conducts his business hours on the threshold between night and day. Oscar Wilde called hunters "the unspeakable in full pursuit of the uneatable."[39] And in the *Burlington Almanac* in 1789 Timothy Truman, an early American chronicler, observed "There are three kinds of people: thinkers, writers, and foxhunters."[40]

Nunn Ballew, the hilltopper in Harriet Arnow's classic *Hunter's Horn,* felt himself hounded by King Devil, a fox who preyed upon farm animals in the Cumberland Mountains:

> . . . The damned red fox had put a wall between him and the rest of the world; other men did what they pleased; he chased a fox because he had to; King Devil ran because he had to—he couldn't stop—he had to run; he was bewitched, Nunn was bewitched; they couldn't die, they couldn't stop; they lived in some God-damned bewitched world that other people didn't know about. King Devil had to run, and he had to follow—had to—had to—[41]

Two traditions of foxhunting persist in this country: English-style, or "formal" foxhunting, and an informal equivalent known as hilltopping, ridge-running, "one-gallus" hunting, fox chasing, and foxhunting. The former hunters "ride to the hounds" on horseback, while the latter "listen to the hounds" around campfires or in their pick-up trucks. The former are sometimes disdainfully called "tally-hos" by hilltoppers. The tally-hos, for their part, have some pride: "We say 'tally-ho,' not 'there goes the son-of-a-bitch!' "[42]

The two styles of foxhunting cast into relief the different ways in which Americans and the English formulate the relationship between nature and culture. While the English impose civilization onto nature, the Americans, bewitched by wilderness, maintain a frontier in which they immerse themselves via their sports, and in which social differences are often subsumed.[43]

The English style of foxhunting encodes social hierarchy into every aspect of language, costume, and procession. As Leach points out, the specialized language dramatizes the elevated nature of the chase. The fox's head is a "mask," his tail a "brush," his feet are "pads," and his excreta "billets." "Charley," not Reynard, is his generic nickname. He resides not in a den, but in an "earth," somewhere in a "covert," which is any thicket capable of supporting a fox. A "bob-tailed" fox is one with no brush, or a very short one. His trail is his "line." If he runs in circles, close to the home covert, he is a "ringing" fox. If his birth occurred above ground he is "stubbred." When he tires toward the end of a chase, he is "sinking." Young foxes are called "cubs" until November 1, when they become foxes. Male foxes are "dog foxes" and females are "vixen." The now obsolete term for a group of foxes is "skulk."[44]

Hilltopping, truly an American sport, de-emphasizes hierarchy. The hilltopper's vocabulary is specialized, but not standardized, varying from region to region. As horses are seldom used, there is no contest in horsemanship. There is no formal dress code, and no master or mistress of the hunt, for the social order displayed is egalitarian rather than hierarchical. There is no division of labor in pursuing the fox—no whippers-in or master of hounds. Most importantly, the hounds are individually rather than communally owned. Each hunter may conduct his own chase with his hounds, though he would rather show off their strengths in competition with another man's dogs. The chases highlight achievement by merit rather than by birth; dogs, which are often not registered, are valued more for their performances than for their pedigrees. Dogs that are good only for show may be disparaged as "parlor boys."[45]

In each chase the same themes are transposed and reconfigured. Through their dogs the hilltoppers aspire to a united effort—the production of a rich, orchestral sound. However, individual notes have to be discernible. The hunters also compete with one another through their dogs. The dogs enact social conflicts: the collective versus the individual, music versus din, fair versus foul play, domestic order versus the wild unknown, or merit versus chance. A fox chase is like a book on a shelf, and each time the hunters open it up, a new story on the old theme emerges.[46]

Fox chasing has practically institutionalized the bag of tricks played by the fox on the hounds, standard mysteries that foxhunters enjoy solving. As Frank Pope Wilder described it:

> The old man red fox, he's sly. You've heard of the sly red fox.
> Well, he is too. I mean he'll play every trick in the book.
> Sometimes they get away from him, just like how they'll hit a
> paved road and run two or three hundred yards, and then turn
> off the road. When they do that, a fox can't leave a scent on a
> road. . . . . In the woods they leave their scent on the bushes and
> leaves but when they go down a paved highway there is nothing
> there to scent.[47]

Hunters report that the fox plays tricks by running the hounds away from water to make them thirsty, or into traffic to kill them. It will also lose them by obscuring its scent in automobile fumes or by running through livestock, riding for a time on the back of a sheep. It also doubles back on its trail, and hunters have also reported that a fox will fling itself to the ground allowing the frenzied pack to rush over it, picking itself up and walking away at its leisure.

Any hilltopper will say that the most important aspect of a fox chase is the "music" of the hounds:

> The music is what the fox hunter loves! And if you don't love the
> music of the hounds, you wouldn't be a foxhunter. You've got to
> love hearing the hounds run! The music of it! When I hear a
> pack of hounds run, to me, it's just like Wayne King or some
> band playing. I could just listen to it all night![48]

Each hound has its own "note," whereby it transmits information about the fox to his owner: what kind of fox it is, what kind of terrain they are in, which dogs are in the lead, or whether the fox has tricked them yet again. The fox is like the conductor of a symphony. On the trail of the fox, each hound unleashes his own "notes." Hounds can be, for example, "chop-mouthed," "horn-mouthed," "parrot-mouthed," or "turkey-mouthed." A very few have the coveted "bugle note."[49]

There is a strong musical tradition on both sides of the Atlantic based on this music of the hounds. "The Fox Chase," a virtuoso instrumental piece that mimics the sound of the hounds, has been recorded on uillean pipes, fiddle, harmonica, and banjo. Curley Ray Cline, that "Old Kentucky Foxhunter," featured himself on the fiddle accompanied by his hounds in a recording of "Mountain Fox Chase." String bands like the Red Fox Chasers and the Roan Mountain Hilltoppers have named themselves for the practice, which is also alluded to in lyrics like those of the bluegrass standard "Fox on the Run."[50]

The fox, as he is structured into the fox chase, is a prolific symbolic resource. The chase itself is a highly concentrated enactment of pursuit and avoidance, in which the referents are ambiguous. Like poetry and Scripture, the chase bears multiple reading, yielding up homilies as readily as bluegrass songs. One subscriber to *The Hunter's Horn,* a contemporary foxhunter's magazine, reported that in one chase he watched with his companion as the fox, in no apparent hurry, trotted to the mouth of his den, where he proceeded to groom himself, pricking up his ears at intervals, to listen for the approaching pack:

> Finally as the dogs got close, he trotted unhurriedly into the dark
> cavern behind him, and as I imagine, sat there relaxed and
> unafraid as he listened to the furor of the hounds as they
> surrounded the entrance to his home. Mr. McDaniel laid his
> hand over on my saddle and with deep emotion said, "Roy,
> there's a great lesson. When you have a safe refuge to which you
> can go in the times of trouble, the hounds of life don't worry you
> much."[51]

Thus the fox chase, in formalizing relationships among men and wild and domestic canids, provides one framework for hunters and their audiences to explore and interpret foxes, natural law, and the social contract.

THE ALLEGORICAL FOX

The Fox on the Prowl

The fox on the prowl is an opportunist, ready to turn everything to its advantage. A Wall Street brokerage firm recently exploited this image in order to lure prospective investors. "There's a fox on Wall

There's a fox on Wall Street.

Instinct. Nurtured by experience. It's part of Advest's special nature. Cautious as a rule. Alert and quick when required. Like a fox.

Since 1898, Advest has been involved with investments and investors. Our success has come from offering investment vehicles as diversified as stocks and mutual funds for potential capital gains; tax free income; retirement plans *you* control; real estate for income and tax relief, and more.

Call Advest. Let's talk about the business of investing the same way you approach your own business.

Carefully. Intelligently. Like a fox.

Advest

Members of New York, American and other Principal Stock Exchanges.

Corporate Headquarters: Six Central Row, Hartford, Connecticut 06103. / 1-800-243-8115 or in Connecticut 1-800-842-3807

SIPC

6.4. "There's a Fox on Wall Street," advertisement from Advest.

Street," is the slogan, which plays against the bulls, bears, and lions used by larger financial institutions. "Alert, smart, fast," the advertisement reads, "Ready to seize today's investment opportunities as they develop." (fig. 6.4) The fox can be a powerful ally for those whose interests are the same as his. However, the fox on the prowl often represents conflict of interest. For example, environmentalists protested the appointment of Anne Gorsuch as head of the Environmental Protection Agency, exclaiming, "Well, if that isn't the fox guarding the chicken coop!"

The fox on the prowl furnishes us with grist for oblique political and social commentary. Just as Reynard, that celebrated trickster of the great European animal epic, was a formidable tool in the hands of medieval satirists, the fox has also performed ably for contemporary satirists in this country.

In the Afro-American tradition of "signifying," the archetypal encounter between the fox and the geese supplies a biting commentary on interracial relations. In 1923 A.W. Eddins collected a story in which the fox ambushes a goose, who insists that she has a right to a hearing in court before he eats her. The story, as Eddins conveys it, concludes:

And so dey went to cote, and when dey got dere, de sheriff, he was er fox, en de judge, he wus er fox, and der tourneys, dey wus foxes, an all de jurrymen, dey was foxes, too.

End dey tried ole sis goose, en dey 'victed her and dey 'scuted her, and dey picked her bones.

Now my chilluns, listen to me, when all de folks in de cotehouse is foxes, and you is jes er common goose, der ain't gwine to be much jestice for you pore nigger.[52]

The association of foxes with lawyers and their ability to circumvent the law is a common motif in folk traditions. Afro-American accounts contain warnings about the law, maintaining that it is likely to break agreements that it makes with the powerless. The fox, who gets caught by his own scheme in "The Fox and the Lawyer," (sung by Johnny Miles when he was in a state penitentiary) failed to read the signs from the outset:

Fox and a lawyer, two schemin' men,
Hired by de lawyer, fox had a den,

He went a-runnin', catch him one hen,
He was surrounded by bad dogs an' men.
Fox told de lawyer, "Didn't think it fair;
Just me, one only, find so many of you there. . ."[53]

Another fox and goose anecdote, collected by Henry Davis as an embedded text in 1914, illuminates extralegality from a different angle. A man who wanted to go hunting managed to convince a dubious constable that his quarry was in season. A black man who witnessed the discussion later told the hunter a story called, "The Fox and the Goose." In the story the fox tried to coax a suspicious goose down from a tree, telling her that all the animals had outlawed predation at a recent town meeting. The goose was nearly convinced, when suddenly they heard a hound dog approaching, obviously on the fox's trail. Puzzled by the fox's hasty retreat, the goose reminded the fox of the new law. "Yes," the fox replied, over his shoulder, "But some of the animals around here ain't got much respect for the law."[54]

The complex asymmetry between the fable and the situation is brilliant. The fox deals directly with his quarry, not with the law. The fox, who parallels the hunter, is really the animal with no respect for the law, because he takes the law into his own hands. The oblique message to the hunter was that he should not have been dealing with the law at all. Bargaining with the constable was as risky as a fox trying to bargain with a hound commissioned to protect the goose.

In this hound that clearly represents the law we see the practical underpinning of the foxhunt—the protection of domestic animals—articulated as the protection of the established order, with the fox cast in the role of outlaw. Elsewhere he is cast as lawyer and as judge.

"The fox is the lawyer of the animal world," said Cleophas Vigil, a storyteller from New Mexico. In one of Vigil's stories Sister Rattlesnake, trapped under a fallen rock, persuades Señor Coyote to remove the rock. Her long confinement has made her ravenous, and instead of being grateful to Señor Coyote, Sister Rattlesnake prepares to make a meal out of him. In desperation Señor Coyote hails Señor Fox, who happens to pass by, and asks him to judge the situation. The fox listens carefully to the story and feigns incomprehension. "I think I could understand it better if I could see exactly what happened," he says, "Sister Rattlesnake, could you please get back under the rock, so that Señor Coyote can lift it off of you again?" The rattlesnake obliges, but this time she remains rockbound, and coyote departs in relief with the fox.[55]

The Allegorical Fox on the Run

The Five-Day Deodorant company featured an advertisement several years ago in which an animated fox successfully eluded a pack of hounds by fastening one five-day deodorant pad to each foot. (The fact that the glands beneath the tail are the strongest source of the "foxy" odor had no bearing on the commercial's message.) The fox, like many Americans, is an animal on the go, and the more he is pressured by whatever hounds happen to motivate him, the more he sweats. The commercial does not suggest that the fox go into hiding, rather it offers a cosmetic solution to a problem that, if commercials are telling the truth, strikes terror into myriad human hearts: if we smell like the animals that we are, we will be socially ostracized. The commercial illuminates a tiny facet of a broader conflict.

Despite the back-to-nature movement we continue to be uncomfortable with the conflict between social and natural law, as the story of Señor Coyote and Sister Rattlesnake shows. The natural law, wherein we find "every man for himself," if implemented leads to cultural destruction. The social contract, with its golden rules, can lead to self-destruction. The fox, having been cast as judge, as lawyer, and as outlaw, as predator and as prey, plays both sides of the law. While he is the underdog or the outlaw we pull for him, but when he is in charge we get nervous. A fox in the political arena is not a philosopher king or an enlightened despot. He makes us uncomfortable because we are not always sure which side he is on. He may be ingenious, but he is also devious. Opinions of him are likely to conflict.

The fox has a venerable history as an emblem for lawyers and political and military leaders. Circe called Ulysses a fox and Christ returned the Pharisees to Herod, saying, "Go and give that fox this message...." It seems that politicians still try to follow Machiavelli's advice: "The prince must be a lion, but he must also know how to play the fox."

Since the early days of our nationhood we have watched in fascination while foxes play leading roles in our political arenas and military theaters. In American history this metaphor has been applied and developed in the political arena for three centuries. In the seventeenth and eighteenth centuries it was more insulting to be called a fox than it is now, as the examples of the Swamp Fox, the Desert Fox, and the Red Fox of Kinderhook show.

British general Banastre Tarlton was not trying to pay General Francis Marion a compliment when he first called him a fox. Having pursued Marion for thirty-five miles through treacherous swampland, Tarleton is said to have abandoned the chase with the words: "Come my Boys! Let us go back, and we will find the Gamecock [General Thomas Sumter], but as for this damned old fox, the devil himself could not catch him."[56] Some of Marion's biographers claim that, as news of the incident spread, the Whigs delightedly emended the disparaging phrase into the more swashbuckling "Swamp Fox," and that his followers began to sport fox tails from their caps. Heider points out, however, it is more likely that, in Marion's time only his enemies would have called him a fox.[57]

Two centuries later another fox in a different climate led another British general on a chase across North Africa. Forty years after World War II, Field Marshal Erwin Rommel, whose tactics in North Africa earned him the name of the Desert Fox, is as much a hero to British and American audiences as he was to the Germans and Italians with whom he fought. His biographers carry the metaphor through in their descriptions of him. "From the moment he first came under fire, he stood out as the perfect fighting animal," writes Desmond Morris, "Cold, cunning, ruthless, untiring, quick of decision [and] incredibly brave."[58] In *The Trail of the Fox*, David Irwin characterizes him as:

> a general, small in stature, with a vulpine cunning and a foxy
> grin, confounding time and time again a vastly superior enemy.
> He was regarded as a modern Hannibal, running rings around
> his foes, bewildering them, demoralizing them, and snatching
> victory after victory.... He outwitted, bluffed, deceived and
> cheated the enemy. It was said that his greatest pleasure was to

trick his opponents into premature and quite often needless surrender.[59]

Rommel's methods were indeed foxlike. (Incidentally, he had a pet fox when he was a child.) Though the Allies had a three to one advantage over him in terms of numbers and equipment, he baffled the British Secret Service by lying to his own superiors and allies, turning the enemy's spy network to his advantage. "His deception plan...shows us the genius of the Desert Fox," writes Samuel W. Mitcham:

> Rommel continued to play his game of duplicity with the Italians. This was Erwin Rommel at his most cunning. Just before the offensive started, he told General Gambarra, the Italian chief of staff in North Africa, that there would be no major offensive. "A small foray. A mere skirmish—you might call it a commando raid—is to be carried out." Gambarra considered this so insignificant that he failed to pass the information on to Rome, just as Rommel had calculated.[60]

The man who gave Field Marshal Montgomery a run for his money and whom General Patton was obsessed with defeating is to-day held in high esteem in Britain and America. That his death came about because he joined a conspiracy against Hitler when he grew intolerant of Nazi atrocities has enlarged and enhanced his profile in North America as well as in Europe. His heroism and ingenuity are the subject of an American film *The Desert Fox*.

The fox has also provided a rich cluster of metaphors for American political commentary. The theme of the fox chase underscored Martin Van Buren's entire political career. As an aspiring young lawyer in the early nineteenth century, Van Buren manifested a cleverness that earned him the somewhat dubious title of "the red fox of Kinderhook." One of his biographers, Alexander Holmes, noted:

> What Davy Crockett says of him—"If he could gain an object as well by openness as intrigue, he would choose the latter."—seems to have been a solemn fact. Not for nothing was he called the Red Fox of Kinderhook. No trail he laid ever went straight to his destination, and many a time the pack yapping at his traces was left barking up the wrong tree. When he decided to be Secretary of State, he confounded his rivals by resigning from the Senate

and running for governor of New York. When he deemed it time to make himself Vice President, he feinted off in another direction by resigning the State Department. . . when the pursuers finally caught up to him, he was calmly sunning himself in the position he had originally chosen.[61]

Van Buren's machinations caught up with him in his campaign against William Henry Harrison in 1840. Taking a pot shot at Harrison's perceived provincialism, a pro-Van Buren newspaper stated that Harrison, if offered two thousand dollars and a barrel of hard cider, would probably retire for good to a log cabin on the banks of the Ohio River. Harrison's campaign managers turned the hard cider and the log cabin into symbols of honesty, launching the hard cider campaign, in which Harrison was often featured as a frontiersman trapping a red fox whose face was Martin Van Buren's (fig. 6.5). Van Buren was eventually trapped, (fig. 6.6), and his presidency is analyzed by James Curtis in a book entitled *The Fox at Bay*.[62]

The Case of the Foxy Lady

To shift our fox-on-the-run paradigm from the realm of political conquest to the realm of romantic conquest, the fox chase has been made to yield numerous interpretations of male-female relationships. In the romantic arena, where our need to find a mate links us more with other mammals than do our power struggles in the political arena, the chase provides a grid for exploring the varied permutations in male-female relationships.

"Venery," of course, has two meanings. One has to do with sexual love, the other with coursing for game. "Venery" and "venereal" spring from the Latin root that gave us Venus, the goddess of love, and, according to Webster, both have to do with sexual love. Venus, interestingly, springs from the Indo-European "wenos," meaning desire, from the base "wen" meaning "to strive for, to attain." The second definition given for venery relates it to the word "venison": "the act or practice of hunting game; the chase."

Sexual interpretations of the fox chase are well known. Maureen Duffy, in her protest against hunting for sport, deplores the ritual enactment of sexual fantasies at the expense of animals. She offers an explicit interpretation of these fantasies, as she reads them. Any

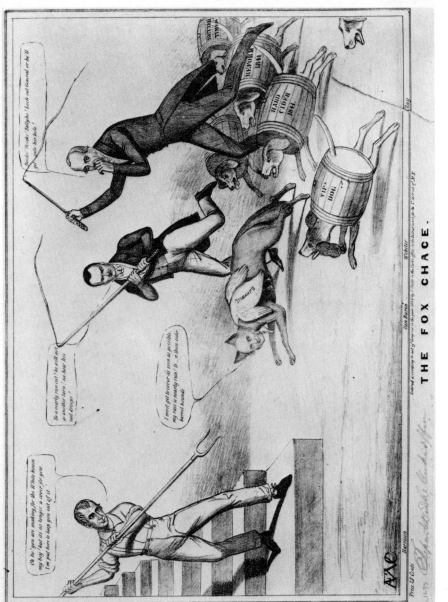

6.5. "The Fox Chace," political cartoon from the Library of Congress, Prints and Photographs division, presidential file.

6.6. "Old Jack in the Last Agony and the Fox Caught in a Rat Trap," political cartoon from the Library of Congress, Prints and Photographs division, presidential file.

hunt, she explains, consists of two parts: the hunt and the kill, which are equivalent to the build-up and the orgasm. She then argues that different quarry have different gender values. While hares are traditionally feminine, foxes are masculine:

> The fox and the otter both have prized tails, and no great insight is needed to divine what they represent. Even the folklore characters of these animals are phallic: the fox with its cunning, the otter in its playfulness. Their body shape isn't hard to see as a phallus and both are traditionally sexy beasts and dwell in holes.[63]

The fox chase, of course, has no fixed meaning, and the allegorical fox can be masculine or feminine. The popular song, "Fox on the Run," now an American bluegrass standard thanks to the Country Gentlemen, was first performed by the English rock group Manfred Mann. The protagonist casts the story of his unrequited love in terms of a fox chase. He was tempted, we are told, by a woman he met in a drinking establishment. Because of this affair he is now a fugitive, an unfortunate rake perhaps, pursued by an ambiguous pack of hounds that represent, in some way, his downfall.[64]

So far all of the foxes we have considered are masculine. In fact, the fox in nature is generically masculine, referred to as Reynard, Charley, Mister Fox, old man fox, and "the boss." Even if the actual fox in question is a female, foxhunters and trappers speak of him as a male. Thus we may be astonished to discover, as Nunn Balew did, that King Devil is actually a vixen.

Female canids in general seemingly have little to recommend them. Both "bitch" and "vixen" have connoted ill-tempered women for centuries. They have been applied as terms of contempt in general, regardless of the referent's disposition. Anti-languages that reverse the meanings, using "bitching" in an admiring way for example, depend upon the derogatory sense for their impact. In English-speaking cultures it is insulting to be called a bitch or a vixen.

In "Fox-Hunt," a short story by William Faulkner, the wealthy Harrison Blair is consumed with hatred for the vixen he pursues on horseback across his Carolina preserve. His wife, whom he also despises, clearly resembles the fox at various levels in the story. While Blair is pursuing the vixen, his friend Steve Gawtry is pursuing Blair's wife, a woman whom an onlooking youth says is:

> Just like a fox. I be durn if I see how that skinny neck of
> hern.... Like you look at a fox and you wonder how a durn
> little critter like it can tote all that brush. And I once heard him
> [Blair] say...something to her that a man don't say to a woman
> in comp'ny, and her eyes turned red like a fox's and then brown
> again like a fox."[65]

Blair catches the vixen, trampling her to death with his foot, as his
wife gives herself in the woods to Gawtry. While the onlooking
youth sees her as "that remote and inaccessible she," Blair's wife is in
fact a trapped woman, stalked, in the person of her husband, by
"the tragic and inescapable shape of her ruin."

This image of a persecuted vixen contrasts sharply with the
"foxy" lady—a figure similarly endowed with beauty and mystery,
but who above all controls her own destiny. She is to be wooed, not
simply pursued. Fox Photo company recently sought a woman to fill
a "foxy lady" spot in a television commercial. In their search they
had to define the image:

> As many as 70 dancers were tested for the part, which required a
> middle-America look and an extremely photogenic woman with
> an acting ability to be able to relate to an invisible fox while
> dancing.[66]

In the commercial, designed to sell people a technique for producing
images, the foxy lady dances with the animated fox that is the company's logo (fig. 6.7).

This uniquely American image, however, did not come from
middle-America. It is an Afro-American term, a legacy of the jazz
scene. In Robert Gold's *A Jazz Lexicon* we find the definitions:

> fox, n. [by analogy with both the beauty and the cunning; some
> currency esp. among Negro jazzmen since c. 1958...] Fox: a
> beautiful girl.[67]

The noun sprang from the adjective. The 1942 *American Thesaurus
of Slang* defined "foxy" as "stylish, chic," noting its currency "especially among Negro jazzmen since 1925."[68] The term achieved a national prominence in the 1960s. Robert Gold cites a sentence
published in 1961 in *The Sound*: "I mean all the studs in fancy duds
and foxy chicks togged to the bricks is gonna be there."[69]

The American "fox" exists at counterpoint to the English "vixen"

6.7. "Fox Photo Fox and Foxy Lady." Courtesy Fox Photo, Inc.

that for centuries has suggested a shrewish woman. The foxy lady is irresistibly attractive, but there is something mildly unattainable about her. She is a dream woman, to be eternally pursued and never completely caught. "No tears, no fears, no ruined years," sang the Doors, of the "Twentieth Century Fox," "No clocks; She's a Twentieth Century Fox":

> She's the queen of cool, and she's the lady who waits,
> Since her mind left school, it never hesitates;
> She won't waste time on elementary talk,
> She's a Twentieth Century Fox.[70]

While she is not a harlot, neither is she a wife and mother. She is certainly not as innocent as the Fox Photo commercial portrays her, her sensuality being much vaunted. "Foxy" is phonetically linked to "sexy," a link that is exploited in rhymes and in rock 'n' roll. Children

from St. John's Island in Georgia perform a handclapping game to
the following rhyme, which gives an ambivalent message about being foxy:

> *Group:* Oolay, oolay, who thinks she's bad?
> Oolay, oolay, who thinks she's bad?
> *Tiny:* I think I'm bad cause Tiny's my name
> And love is my game
> That's why the boys follow me,
> I am sexy as can be
> *Group:* Bad—she thinks she's bad
> *Tiny:* Bad—I know I'm bad
> *Group:* Foxy—she thinks she's foxy
> *Tiny:* Foxy—I know I'm foxy
> *Group:* Child, hush, cause you nakedly blush
> And your teeth need brushed
> And your toilet needs flushed.[71]

The game was taught to the children by their great-grandmother, Janie Hunter, who said that when she was a child a word like "hand-
some" would have been used rather than "foxy."[72]

Jimi Hendrix pursued his foxy lady in a rock 'n' roll song in the
late sixties:

> You know you're a cute little heartbreaker—Foxy!
> You known you're a sweet little lovemaker—Foxy!
> I wanna take you home
> I won't do you no harm
> You got to be mine, all mine
> Foxy lady!
>
> Here I come, Baby,
> I'm comin' to getcha!
> Aw! Foxy Lady—
> You look so good—Foxy!
> You make me feel like singin'!
> Foxy Lady![73]

The Afro-American image of the fox as a beautiful and self-
possessed woman reverses a number of elements in the English image of the fox. The term "fox," often applied to the male of the
species, is made to connote a woman who is not at all like the vixen
so disparaged by white men. She is beautiful, mysterious, and thor-

oughly in command of her male suitors. The masculine fox that the English have systematically hunted and destroyed emerges out of the black community as a strong, desirable woman, who, whether black or white, is assured of the upper hand.

The Fox As Cultural Trickster

The fox never achieved the magnitude in Native American trickster cycles possessed by Coyote, Raven, or Wolverine. We might wonder why a creature that is perceived as such a trickster in the natural world never made it into that pantheon. What is the connection between an animal's natural behavior and its work as a cultural trickster?

The fox in the Advest commercial (fig. 6.4) did not exactly serve to endorse the product. The company's use of a real fox ironically highlighted the discrepancy between the image of the fox and the fox as he really is:

> Advest and agency folk alike, expecting a foxy creature, flawlessly trained as well as glossy and perky, got a bit of a surprise on the day of the shoot. "The fox had cataracts and couldn't see very well—we had to touch up his eyes in the print ad," remembers Judith Johnson, Advest's senior vp/marketing. "We also found out that the fox couldn't be shot from far away because it looked like a rat! We didn't realize how small foxes are."[74]

There is no fox in the American trickster literature to rival Reynard, that scourge of the medieval European animal world. In fact, in several modern American trickster cycles, the fox is the trickster's foil, the reversal of his natural self. The prototype of the dumb fox, provided by Aesop in the story, "The Fox and the Grapes," was resurrected in the 1940s by cartoonist Frank Tashlin. The Fox and Crow series, inspired by Old-World animals, anticipated the animated enmity of their New World substitutes, Roadrunner and Coyote. For more than twenty years Americans slapped their thighs over the antics of a chiseling, Brooklynese crow, always at the expense of the vainglorious, dimwitted "Foxie." The crow succeeds repeatedly by playing upon the fox's incurable vanity. Thus the archetypal wily flatterer is fooled by his own tricks, administered by his traditional prey.[75]

And, of course, Brer Fox meets his nemesis in Brer Rabbit.

We could say that this is simply happenstance, that trickster figures are in fact interchangeable, and that tricksters in literature have little to do with their animal prototypes. For example, a number of motifs in the Reynard the Fox cycle reappear in the Brer Rabbit stories. Thus, both Reynard and Brer Rabbit find themselves trapped in buckets at the bottom of wells (fig. 6.8); both manage to escape by persuading a larger animal to jump in the bucket at the top of the pulley. (Thus Reynard dupes Dame Ereswine the wolf, and Brer Rabbit dupes Brer Fox.)

Brer Rabbit and Reynard are not interchangeable, however, for the listener's awareness of the behavior of the fox and the rabbit in the wild is essential to an understanding of the stories. Both tricksters are lawbreakers. Brer Rabbit violates the natural law. The larger creatures that are normally his predators don't stand a chance against his cunning. He represents the triumph of a social order in which the underdog, the hero of Afro- and Native-American tales, has turned the tables on the top dogs, via the fox that symbolizes their brand of justice.

Reynard, on the other hand, troubles the audience by maintaining natural law while violating the social contract. He uses his cunning not only to elude predators, which is fair, but he turns it against those whom he would devour. It seems unfair that the deck should be stacked so heavily in his favor. That Reynard cruelly dispatches Kyward the hare and that Brer Rabbit brutally kills Brer Fox suggest that the cycles exist not as parallel universes, but as boxers in a ring, opposing sides of an argument over where to draw the line between nature and society.

Like shadows moving in the murky depths of a crystal ball, a welter of conflicting images take shape and then dissolve in the fox: sacred and profane, man and woman, dog and cat, human and beast, dupe and con-man, Afro-American and Anglo-American, English and Anglo-American, lawyer and outlaw, predator and prey, and order and chaos. The fox signifies illusion, whether he is hiding his scent from the hounds, sending Bruin to a false bee tree, or setting Brer Rabbit up with a Tar Baby. When taken as the sum total of his images, he resembles the trickster described by Paul Radin:

> Trickster is at one and the same time creator and destroyer, giver and negator, he who dupes others and who is always duped

6.8. Tricksters in the well: Brer Rabbit and Brer Fox by A.B. Frost, from *Uncle Remus* (New York: Schocken Books, 1974), p. 79 (first published in 1880) and Reynard the Fox and Dame Ereswine by W. Frank Calderon, from *The Most Delectable History of Reynard the Fox* (New York: Schocken Books, 1967), p. 205.

himself. He wills nothing consciously. At all times he is constrained to behave as he does from impulses over which he has no control. He knows neither good nor evil yet he is responsible for both. He possesses no values, moral or social, is at the mercy of his passions and appetites, yet through his actions all values come into being.[76]

Reynard the Fox is on trial throughout much of the medieval epic. Unlike the goose in the Afro-American story he is well matched to the prosecution. He is on trial not only for being a predator, but for disguising his intentions. He is the source of all disorder in the kingdom, yet those caught in his maelstrom have only themselves to blame: they know he is a liar, yet they believe him.

He is on trial, actually, for being himself—a creature who prompts us to admit with Jack Davis, who for seventy years has chased him all over South Jersey: "Foxes are rightly named—they're foxy!"[77]

NOTES

I am especially grateful to Jack Davis, Norman, Caroline, and Freeman Taylor, John Earlin, Donald Pomeroy, Leon Hopkins, and Milton Collins, for taking me on fox chases and for sharing their enthusiasm for foxes with me, and to Tom Brown who is a great credit to the South Jersey Fur-Takers Association. I owe special thanks to Gerald Parsons for sharing his rich and varied thinking on wildlife and human behavior, and to Steven Oaks for his many critical readings of the manuscript. Thanks also to Marvin Kranz of the Local History and Genealogy Reading Room at the Library of Congress for his help in interpreting the Martin Van Buren cartoons; to Mike Licht of the Archive of Folk Culture; to Barre Toelken and Jay Mechling for encouragement and helpful suggestions; and to Judith Gray and Dorothy Sarah Lee of the Federal Cylinder Project for giving me Native American leads.

1. Ernest P. Walker, *Mammals of the World,* 3rd ed. (Baltimore: Johns Hopkins Univ. Press, 1975), 1156.

2. E.D. Ables, "The Ecology of the Red Fox in North America," in *The Wild Canids,* ed. Michael Fox (New York: Van Nostrand, 1975), 216–37, 233.

3. Richard Harlan, *Fauna Americana: Being a Description of the Mammiferous Animals Inhabiting North America* (Philadelphia: Anthony

Finley, 1825. rpt., New York: Arno Press, 1974, ed. Keir B. Sterling), 87.

4. Konrad Lorenz, *King Solomon's Ring* (New York: Thomas Y. Crowell Company, 1952), 22.

5. William S. Hamilton, Jr., and John O. Whitaker, Jr., *Mammals of the Eastern United States* (Ithaca, N.Y.: Cornell Univ. Press, 1979), 265–69.

6. Walker.

7. Harriet Arnow, *Hunter's Horn* (New York: Avon Books, 1949), 120.

8. Howard J. Stains, "Distribution and Taxonomy of the Canidae," in *The Wild Canids,* 3–26.

9. For more background on the scientific positions see Fox, ed., *The Wild Canids,* and Maxwell Riddle, *The Wild Dogs in Life and Legend* (New York: Howell Book House, Inc., 1979).

10. Lydia T. Black, "The Nature of Evil: Of Whales and Sea Otters," in *Indians, Animals and the Fur Trade: A Critique of Keepers of the Game,* ed. Shepard Krech III (Athens: Univ. of Georgia Press, 1981), 109-54.

11. John Lawson, *A New Voyage to Carolina* (Chapel Hill: Univ. of North Carolina Press, 1967), 130. Reprint of 1709 London edition.

12. G., "The Red Fox," in *American Turf Register and Sporting Magazine,* Oct. 1829 (Baltimore: J.S. Skinner), 74-75.

13. Ibid., 9.

14. Peter Kalm, *Travels into North America* (Barre, Mass.: The Imprint Society, 1972), 146-47.

15. Edmund Leach, *Claude Lévi-Strauss* (New York: Penguin Books, 1976), 40, and "Anthropological Aspect of Language: Animal Categories and Verbal Abuse," in *New Directions in the Study of Language,* ed. Eric Lenneberg (Cambridge: M.I.T. Press, 1964), 52.

16. J. David Henry, "Fox Hunting," in *Natural History Magazine* (Dec. 1980): 61-69.

17. J.N.P. Watson, *The Book of Foxhunting* (New York: Arco Publishing Company, Inc., 1977), 36.

18. Maurice Burton, "Dog-Fox and Cats," in *London Illustrated News,* April 2, 1955, 612.

19. Fieldnotes, April 1979 and Nov. 1980.

20. P., "The Red Fox," in *American Turf Register and Sporting Magazine,* Dec., 1829 (Baltimore: J. S. Skinner), 198. Dogs and red foxes cannot mate, according to scientists.

21. Spencer Fullerton Baird, *Mammals of North America: The Descriptions of Species Based Chiefly on the Collections in the Museum of the Smithsonian Institution* (Philadelphia: J.B. Lippincott, 1859; rpt., New York: Arno Press, 1974, ed. Keir B. Sterling), 130.

22. Julie Holland and Tony Tolleson, "The Music of the Hounds!" in *Ebbtide* (Dec. 1980), 37

23. Jack Scott, "The Fox—Neither Devil nor Angel," in *Sports Afield* (Jan. 1978), 62f.

24. Interview, Velma Wallis, July 1, 1984.

25. Reverend J.G. Wood, *Animate Creation: Popular Edition of "Our Living World"* (New York: Selmar Hess, 1898), vol. 1, 271.

26. *The Cabinet of Natural History and American Rural Sports* (Philadelphia: J. V. T. Doughty, 1830-33; rpt., New York: Arno Press, 1978), vol. 2, p. 26.

27. Jerome B. Robinson, "Decoy Dogs," *Sports Afield* (Aug. 1981), 64-65.

28. Ibid., 106, and Gerald Parsons, personal communication.

29. Pat Sedlak, *The School-Boy Trapper* (Belle Vernon, Penn.: Pat Sedlak, 1960), 106. And interview, Tom Brown, Feb. 1984.

30. Ibid.

31. Interview, Tom Brown, June 1985.

32. Black, 123.

33. Conversations with Gerald Parsons, Paula Johnson, and Tom Brown indicate that this incident is probably well known among trappers in the Middle-Atlantic region.

34. Wood, 267.

35. Geoffrey Chaucer, "The Nun's Priest's Tale," lines 3377–3386, in *The Complete Poetry and Prose of Geoffrey Chaucer*, ed. J.H. Fisher (New York: Holt, Rinehart and Winston, 1977), 306.

36. The song has many British and American variants. The one cited is "The Fox," sung by Burl Ives on *Folksongs by Burl Ives*, edited by Alan Lomax, with texts and notes by Kenneth S. Goldstein, Stinson Records SLP-1.

37. George Caines, *New York Term Reports of Cases Argued and Determined in the Supreme Court of that State* (New York: I. Riley, 1814), vol. 3, 175.

38. Watson, *The Book of Foxhunting*, 24.

39. Oscar Wilde, "A Woman of No Importance," Act I. See Venetia Wells Newell, "The Unspeakable in Pursuit of the Uneatable: Some Comments on Fox-Hunting" *Folklore* 94(1983):86-90, for a discussion of contemporary foxhunting in England, its relationship to social hierarchy, and recent conflicts between foxhunters and farmers. For a historic ethnography prompted by Leach's observation that "foxhunting is a barbarous ritual" (Leach, 60), see James Howe's, "Fox Hunting as Ritual," in *American Ethnologist* 8(1981):278-300, esp. p. 294.

40. *Burlington Almanac*, 1789.

41. Harriet Arnow, 121.

42. Folklorist Barre Toelken brought this anecdote to my attention.

43. Gerald Parsons formulated this contrast in conversation.

44. J.N.P. Watson, *The Book of Foxhunting* (New York: Arco Publishing Company, 1977). See the glossary at the back.

45. David Lyne, "What Are They Saying?: A Study of the Jargon of Hilltopping," M.A. thesis, Univ. of Kentucky at Bowling Green, 1976.

46. Mary Hufford, "Foxhunting in the Pine Barrens," in *History, Culture and Archeology of the New Jersey Pine Barrens*, ed. John Stinton (Pomona, N. J.: Stockton State College, 1983), 222–34.

47. Holland and Tolleson, 35.

48. Ibid., 34.

49. Hufford.

50. Michael Licht surveyed some of this music, with special attention to diatonic harmonica pieces in his paper, "Trailing the Fox Chase," presented at the Society for Ethnomusicology meeting in Bloomington, Indiana, in 1980.

51. Reverend Boddy C. Perry, "A Refuge from the Frustrations of Life," *Hunter's Horn* (April 1978), 34.

52. A.W. Eddins, "Brazos Bottom Philosophy," in *Coffee in the Gourd*, ed. J. Frank Dobie (Dallas: Southern Methodist Univ. Press, 1923), 51. In 1978 I heard John Davis, a Philadelphia-based storyteller and musician, use this story to teach school children about "signifying," an Afro-American speech genre that conceals a message from its target, usually a person within earshot, by using oblique language.

53. "The Fox and the Lawyer," Archive of Folk Culture, Library of Congress. Recorded sound collection. Collected by John A. Lomax in 1934 from Johnny Miles at the State Penitentiary in Raleigh, North Carolina.

54. Henry C. Davis, "Negro Folk-Lore in South Carolina," *Journal of American Folklore* 23(1914): 243.

55. Interview, Cleophas Vigil, July 2, 1984.

56. Hugh F. Rankin, *Francis Marion: The Swamp Fox* (New York: Thomas Y. Crowell, 1973), 117.

57. Karl G. Heider, "The Gamecock, the Swamp Fox, and the Wizard Owl: The Development of Good Form in an American Totemic Set," *Journal of American Folklore* 93(1980): 13.

58. Desmond Morris, *Rommel: The Desert Fox* (New York: Harper and Row, 1965), 16-17.

59. David Irwin, *The Trail of the Fox: The Life of Field-Marshal Erwin Rommel* (London: Weidenfeld and Nicolson, 1977), 4-5.

60. Samuel W. Mitcham, Jr., *Rommel's Desert War: The Life and*

Death of the Afrika Korps (New York: Stein and Day, 1984), 27.

61. Alexander Holmes, *The American Talleyrand* (New York: Harper and Row, 1935), 23.

62. James Curtis, *The Fox At Bay: Martin Van Buren and the Presidency, 1837-1841* (Lexington: Univ. Press of Kentucky, 1970).

63. Maureen Duffy, "Beasts for Pleasure," in *Animals, Men and Morals: An Inquiry into the Maltreatment of Non-Humans* (New York: Taplinger Publishing Company, 1972), 116.

64. Tony Hazzard, "Fox on the Run." Bluegrass version performed by The Country Gentlemen on their album *Sound Off*, produced by Rebel records.

65. William Faulkner, "Fox-Hunt," in *Collected Stories of William Faulkner* (New York: Random House, 1950), 587-605.

66. Tom Bayer, "Shades of Gene Kelly—The Fox and the Lady Dance," *Advertising Age*, July 12, 1982, 48.

67. Robert Gold, *A Jazz Lexicon* (New York: Knopf, 1964), 111.

68. *American Thesaurus of Slang* (London, Ont.: Constable, 1942).

69. Gold, 112.

70. The Doors, *The Doors*, Electra 74007.

71. Sung by Tiny and Shawdy of Saint John's Island, July 1984.

72. Filmed interview with Janie Hunter, by Steve Zeitlin and Marjorie Hunt, July 1984, in the collection of the Smithsonian Institution's Office of Folklife Programs.

73. Jimi Hendrix, *Are You Experienced?*, Reprise 6261.

74. Debbie Seaman, "Agency Uses a 'Ratty' Fox to do a Lion's Job," in *Adweek*, July 18, 1983, 2.

75. See Joseph Jacobs, ed., *The Most Delectable History of Reynard the Fox* (New York: Schocken Books, 1967), and Joel Chandler Harris, *Uncle Remus* (New York: Schocken Books, 1974).

76. Paul Radin, *The Trickster* (New York: Greenwood Press, 1972), xxiii.

77. Interview, Jack Davis, Oct., 1979.

The Coyote

THERESA MELÉNDEZ

The landscape is bleak and arid: a series of ragged mountain peaks divides the horizon in purple and reds as a familiar sound speeds toward us. The roadrunner stops his blur of runs, jumps, and beeps to look over his shoulder. In determined pursuit, flying toward the roadrunner in yet another outrageous contraption comes the coyote—Wile E. Coyote, to be exact. We know Wile E. will blunder again, that his clever intentions to trap his prey will fail, that he is doomed to Saturday-morning deaths—plastered flat against the canyon floor, squashed under an avalanche of boulders, or blown to pieces by his own dynamite trap—and we also know that he will emerge once again, fully recovered in scrawny body and indomitable will, to continue his struggle for existence against all odds. This Warner Brothers cartoon character is a well-known figure to American audiences, a figure who is clearly the villain in the battle between predator and prey in the animated film, but who also represents the underdog against the obnoxiously invincible opponent, thus engaging our sympathies as well as our laughter. For most North Americans, this caricature of a coyote is perhaps their only acquaintance with the animal and the figure that has become a varied and complex symbol of paradox, contradiction, and, above all, of survival in American culture.

The propensity of Coyote, animal and folkloric character, to endure all hardships brought about either by his own nature or by a hostile environment, to survive victoriously the vagaries of existence, is due primarily to his inhabitance of liminal regions, that is, boundary areas between socially categorized positions in nature or culture.[1] In fact and fiction, Coyote is characterized by a wide variety of traits. As animal, he has been called avaricious and generous, cowardly and brave; he is seen as dangerous in his predatory habits and beneficial as a carrion-eater. His mournful howl has long been emblematic of the desolateness of the West in its romantic renderings in film, art, and literature, while in actuality, most sheep and cattle ranchers have decried his presence in their land. Coyote can be trickster, cultural hero, and deity; both foolish and wise, creating order and disorder, a secular and a sacred figure, he holds a prominent position in the native oral narrative traditions. His voracious appetites and slippery ways have made him dear to poets and scholars alike. Animal or fictional character, comic buffoon or wise god, he stands as intermediary along the borders of our concepts. Because he is neither simply the one nor simply the other, he falls between the two, at the interstices of orderly classifications; he is ambiguous. As such, Coyote has great freedom and power because he can create his own order. Living at the threshold of neither-nor, he establishes meaning through the juxtaposition of contradictory elements which, seen singly, seem distinct enough, but whose clear-cut divisions are blurred when forced by Coyote's intrusions to be seen as points along a continuum.

Coyote fascinates and attracts us because of this rich range of meanings and because his sometimes foolish, sometimes wise, behavior seems to mirror our own imperfect nature. And because of our shortcomings, we need a special vision of the world that will enable us to endure. Coyote survives through the power of his comic spirit that, like all comedy, encompasses the trivial acts of everyday existence, such as satisfying nutritional and sexual needs, as well as the significant events of one's life, the working out of social identity, the relationship between creature and creator, the nature of the world. Except that in comedy, as in Coyote's wanderings, the trivial may become the significant (and vice versa). Sexual appetites impede our human philosophic quests, as well as Coyote's, merging (in our many roles) as undifferentiated Desire, so that we become, like Twain's description of the coyote, "a living, breathing allegory of

Want." Or, our bumbling attempts to understand life, which we proudly call science or philosophy or religion, lead us to a pratfall when our own limitations pull us up short. For unlike tragedy, comedy has no heroes moving towards a specific, directed goal, the playing out of one's fate. Comedy is based in ancient revels for the celebration of community values rather than individual ones. Like Coyote, it displays a spectrum of values from ritualistic union, as in marriage or feasts, through social satire and on to the grotesque, as in black humor.

One of Coyote's most salient traits, his hunger to possess, to know, to question, attacks everything indiscriminately in the quest for satisfaction. The comic expresses itself by revealing the chaotic at the edges of our structured existence, whether it is the lack of control over our bodies or the failure of our social institutions. So that when Coyote loses parts of his body, as he does in some of his adventures, or when he is unable to repress his antisocial desires, threatening conventions or higher authorities, he is reflecting the inherent fragility of our human condition. The comedic perspective shows us the importance of experiencing disorder in the very process of establishing order. What Coyote knows is that there are many fates available, various orders to be investigated, possibilities we may ignore only at the expense of our survival.

As a natural animal native to North America, the coyote was most probably an open plains animal originally, but its versatility and its adaptable nature have considerably extended its range. Even in its biological sphere, the coyote is what some naturalists call an "edge animal"; that is, its range can be determined by the amount and the type of "edge" terrains available, such as glacier moraines, forest fire clearings, or logged-off lands in former forest areas. As human civilization encroached upon its natural territory, its migration to these "edges" would also have depended on the availability of a food supply. As game would increase or livestock be introduced into a particular area, the coyote would follow. At the present time, the coyote is found in almost all open areas of the continent, from the far reaches of Alaska to Costa Rica in a north-south range of nearly 7500 miles. Certainly it inhabits all states west of the Mississippi and has been recorded intermittently in some eastern and southern states as well. In Mexico and Central America, the coyote is restricted to semi-forested, arid country along the Pacific Coast, while in Canada, it has extended its range from the prairie into the woods.

Nineteen subspecies of the coyote are recognized; it usually has litters of from five to nine young; and it subsists mainly on carrion, rabbits, rodents, insects, and some vegetable food, although some domestic livestock and poultry also make up its food. And because of its wide distribution, its fertility, and its abundance, it is considered one of the most destructive carnivores in the country.[2] Thus, the coyote's history is marked by violence (both by and against it), as well as by its having inspired a remarkable gamut of emotions, from profound respect to affection and contempt.

The coyote existed as character and symbol in American and Mexican Indian oral literatures and cultures long before the European colonization of the "New World" began. In fact, one of the earliest archaeological finds, dated from 11,000 B.C., and collected in the northern part of the Valley of Mexico, is an artifact in the shape of a coyote, carved out of the vertebra of an extinct species.[3] One can only speculate what moved that early artisan to carve such a piece. It is not likely that it formed part of a religious rite since the oldest figurines are usually female and associated with agriculture and fertility rites. Perhaps the impulse was simply the same force that moves any artist—the aesthetic appeal of the animal or the power it represents.

To the European newcomers on the American continent, the coyote was also a curious find and interesting addition to their scientific knowledge. Not only were new peoples found in America, but also a variety of plant and animal life previously unknown. As Joseph de Acoma in 1570 noted, "[there are] a thousand different kindes of birdes and beasts of the forrest, which have never been knowne, neither in shape nor name; and whereof there is no mention made, neither among the Latins nor Greeks, nor any other nations of the world."[4] This astounding newness of species is what drove the early travelers, conquerors, and settlers to remark on the coyote, even when considering its similarity to their wolf and fox, for which it was often mistaken.

The coyote made its first appearance in the Old World in the sixteenth century when the Spanish conquerors and missionaries were still underestimating the validity and the endurance of native cultures. One such priest, Fray Bernardino de Sahagún, began collecting the historical and natural lore of the New World in his ethnographical work entitled *The General History of the Things of New Spain* (1547–77), in which he described the coyote's physical characteristics in detail, such as its alleged power to stupefy its prey with its breath. The author included a tale of a grateful coyote who is rescued from a snake by a traveler. Upon its release, the coyote brings several hens to the man in token of its thanks.[5]

Although this incident conforms to a well-known motif of the Grateful Animal (B381) in folk literature, this alleged trait and other similar folkloric beliefs attach themselves to the reputation of the coyote in many natural histories. Because Sahagún's work lay dormant in manuscript until 1830, Francisco Hernández's *History of the Animals and Minerals of New Spain* (published in Latin in Rome, 1651) was the first printed description of the animal:

> The coyotl, which certain people think to be the Spanish fox, others the Adipus (jackal), and which others regard as a distinct species, is an animal unknown to the Old World. . . . It is a persevering revenger of injuries and, remembering prey once snatched from it, if it recognized the thief days afterward it will give chase. Sometimes it will even attack a pack of its own breed and if possible bite and kill them. And it may avenge an injury and exact a penalty from some troublesome man by finding out his dwelling place with great perseverance and care and killing some of his domestic animals. But it is grateful to those who do well by it and commonly signifies its good-will by sharing a bit of prey. Looking to its medical value, they say that the pain of extracted teeth may be allayed with the tail of a coyotl.[6]

But it is not until 1780 when Francisco J. Clavijero published his *History of Mexico* in Italian that the coyote got much notice. Oddly, in Buffon's widely circulated and very influential *Natural History of the World* (1749-1804), considered the authoritative text of the time, there is no mention of the coyote.

The Spaniards recognized the new species and referred to it by its indigenous name, *coyotl*, later transformed to coyote. In the language of the Mexica Indians, Nahuatl, *coyotl* seems to be derived from the root *coyo-n*, "to be(come) dug out or to be(come) a hole," apparently deriving its significance from either the coyote's piercing cry or its habit of digging out a den.[7] And interestingly, many early Mexican hieroglyphs depict the coyote with a hole through its body, perhaps also signifying its hunger (fig. 7.1). The early Anglo-American explorers often mistook it for a fox or species of wolf and called it a variety of names: prairie wolf, wolf of the plains, burrowing dog, and brush wolf or jackal. The Lewis and Clark journals of their expedition to explore the unknown Louisiana Territory (1804-1806) record the first good Anglo-American description of the animal, although somewhat inaccurately depicting its behavior: "The wolves are very abundant, and are of two species. First, the small wolf or burrowing-dog of the prairie which is found in almost all the open plains. . . . They live and rear their young in burrows, which they fix near some pass or spot much frequented by game, and sally out in a body against any animal which they think they can overpower; but on the slightest alarm retreat to their burrows, making a noise exactly like that of a small dog."[8]

It was not until the 1820s that biologist Thomas Say, sometimes known as the father of American zoology, in an expedition to the Rocky Mountains, described and gave the coyote its scientific name, *Canis latrans,* the "barking dog," even though colloquially it was known as the prairie wolf for years to come.[9] According to E.T. Seton's *Lives of Game Animals* (1929), the earliest form of the word found in English print was "cuiota," found in F. W. Beechey's *Narrative* (1831).[10] But Hamilton Smith in 1839 called it the "caygotte," from which the Mexican subspecies later received its name: "The Caygotte of the Mexican Spaniards and most probably the Coyotl of the native Indians, is a second subspecies, but slightly noticed by travelers. Mr. William Bullock observed it near Rio Frio, in the Mexican Territory, and was informed by muleteers, then with him, that it was the Caygotte, a very fierce kind of wolf."[11] Although Audubon mentions the prairie wolf several times in his *Quadrupeds of America* (1852), not much is known about its behavior until the late nineteenth century, with the exception of travelers' observations from their sightings of the animal.

Many travelers, recording their impressions of new territories, were taken by the surprising behavior of the coyote. The accounts which follow are often a mixture of fact and feeling and point out the ambivalent impressions with which the coyote was met. An Irish fur trader, Ross Cox, wrote in 1831 of his journeys along the Columbia River and noted the abundance of the prairie wolf who, he said, preferred to travel in numbers: "Two or three of us have often pur-

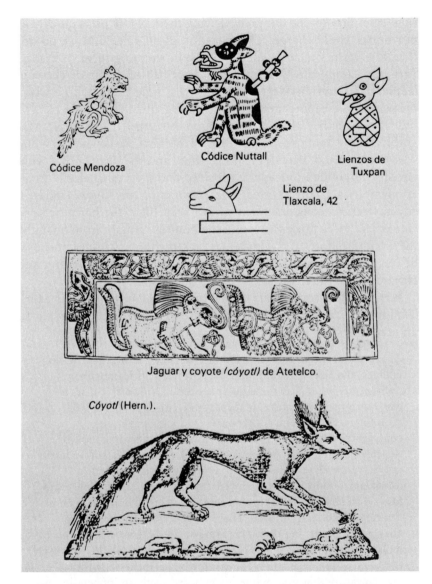

Códice Mendoza

Códice Nuttall

Lienzos de
Tuxpan

Lienzo de
Tlaxcala, 42

Jaguar y coyote *(cóyotl)* de Atetelco.

Cóyotl (Hern.).

7.1. Coyote representations in Nahuatl codices, murals, and Hernández's *History*. From César Macazaga Ordoño, *Diccionario de zoología nahuatl* (México: Innovación, 1982), 36.

sued from fifty to one hundred, driving them before us as quickly as our horses could charge. The skins are of no value and we do not therefore waste much powder and ball in shooting them."[12] Francis Parkman, along the Oregon Trail, described its habit of chewing leather: ". . . a grim-visaged, but harmless little brute, whose worst propensity is creeping among horses and gnawing the ropes of rawhide by which they are picketed around the camp."[13] And Susan Magoffin, on the Santa Fe Trail in 1846, wrote that the coyote's howling was "a mixture of cat, dog, sheep, wolf, and the dear knows what else. It was enough to frighten off sleep and everything else."[14] In an anonymous account entitled *The Hounds of the Jungle* (1868), a coyote occurrence is documented in Costa Rica; the narrator says: "He is said to be descended from the hounds brought from Spain by the Conquistadores. . . . He cannot be tamed to any useful purpose; he has not the faintest idea of gratitude or affection; cunning and cowardice are the main features of his character."[15]

Perhaps the most famous traveler among them, however, is Mark Twain, who chronicled his first glimpse of a coyote in *Roughing It*, an account of his journey from Missouri to Nevada in 1861:

> Along about an hour after breakfast we saw the first prairie-dog villages, the first antelope, and the first wolf. If I remember rightly, this latter was the regular *coyote*. . . . And if it *was*, he was not a pretty creature or respectable either, for I got well acquainted with his race afterward, and can speak with confidence. The coyote is a long, slim, sick and sorry-looking skeleton, with a gray wolfskin stretched over it, a tolerably bushy tail that forever sags down with a despairing expression of forsakenness and misery, a furtive and evil eye, and a long sharp face, with slightly lifted lip and exposed teeth. He has a general slinking expression all over. The coyote is a living, breathing allegory of Want. He is *always* hungry. He is always poor, out of luck, and friendless. The meanest creatures despise him, and even the fleas would desert him for a velocipede. He is so spiritless and cowardly that even while his exposed teeth are pretending a threat, the rest of his face is apologizing for it. And he is *so* homely![16]

Twain goes on speaking contemptuously of the coyote's habits, matched only by his contempt toward the desert, "the most rocky, wintry, repulsive wastes that our country or any other can exhibit," and the Indians, "the wretchedest type of mankind I have ever seen," although he later makes a disclaimer about these feelings.[17] During the same period, naturalist Elliott Coues similarly notes the coyote's hunger, in a less vicious description: "He compels a certain degree of admiration, viewing his irrepressible positivity of character and his versatile nature. If his genius has nothing essentially noble or lofty about it, it is undeniable that few animals possess so many and so various attributes, or act them out with such dogged perseverance. . . . The main object of his life seems to be the satisfying of a hunger which is always craving; and to this aim all his cunning, impudence, and audacity are mainly directed."[18]

The want and hunger of the coyote had also been noticed by the ranchers and sheepowners of the developing West, where American society would go on to pay back the coyote's destructiveness many times over. In 1825, Missouri became one of the first Western states to legislate a bounty act on the animal, and during the years 1860 through 1885 an extensive killing campaign against the coyote was instituted and carried on primarily by the "wolf poisoner," who sought the wealth its pelt (and the wolf's) brought: between 75¢ and $1.50 per skin. The campaign extended across the wide range of the coyote's habitat on the Great Plains from Canada to Texas. In one winter alone (1861–62), three thousand wolves and coyotes were documented as having been poisoned and pelted. After the federal government began the systematic destruction of predatory animals in 1915, fur prices also increased, so that prior to World War II, coyote pelts produced more than a million dollars annually. It is estimated that from 1915 through 1947, almost two million coyotes were killed.[19]

Even today, department stores, at least in the West, regularly run advertisements in newspapers and on television in which coyote furs are offered alongside more traditionally valued luxury furs. Woolgrowers and game men join the federal government in destroying the coyote with guns, snares, poison, and hounds, hunting them at times by air or with a trap called the "coyote-go-getter," a kind of cyanide gun. In 1982, Newsweek ran an article on what it called the "longest war in the American West," the war between sheep ranchers and coyotes. A federal judge recommended that the Environmental Protection Agency rescind its ban on Compound 1080, a powerful poison with no known antidote. Introduced in 1950 and then banned in 1972, the poison killed thousands of coyotes through baited carcasses, but did little to reduce the general coyote population, although it did affect hundreds of bear, eagles, and badgers found dead near the poisoned bait, and thereby countless others in the food chain.[20]

However deplorable the actions of ranchers may be, their thoughtless killing is motivated for economic reasons and not simply for sport, a motivation that apparently inspires many hunters. The gruesome statistics may be found in the records of state game commissions, although these records tell us little of how one can enjoy the alleged sport.

When C. Hart Merriam made the first revision of coyotes' species classification in 1897, he presented his findings at the Biological Society of Washington. He enjoyed there, between himself and a more famous person, Theodore Roosevelt, then Assistant Secretary to the Navy, what spectators called an ardent discussion on the various forms of the coyote.[21] A few years later in *Scribner's*, Roosevelt enthusiastically described his thrill at hunting wolf and coyote.[22] François Leydet in his *The Coyote: Defiant Songdog of the West*[23] recounts the many letters he received and the long conversations he had with ranchers and others who indignantly cry out against those who side with the coyote in their battle. It is estimated that half a million or more coyotes are killed every year. And even so, the coyote survives.

In his memoirs, John Lame Deer, a Miniconjou Sioux born in 1903, uses the case of the coyote to represent white man's exploitation of America generally and points out the major difference between Native Americans' treatment of the coyote and that of America's more recent inhabitants:

> To us, life, all life, is sacred... [Coyotes] are our natural garbage men cleaning up the rotten and stinking things. They make good pets if you give them a chance. But their living could lose some man a few cents, and so the coyotes are killed from the air. They were here before the sheep, but they are in the way; you can't make a profit out of them. More and more animals are dying out. The animals which the Great Spirit put here, they must go. The man-made animals are allowed to stay—at least until they are shipped out to be butchered. That terrible arrogance of the white man, making himself something more than God, more

than nature, saying "I will let this animal live, because it makes money"; saying, "This animal must go, it brings no income, the space it occupies can be used in a better way. The only good coyote is a dead coyote." They are treating coyotes almost as badly as they used to treat Indians.[24]

Native peoples do not readily treat "nature" as something separate from themselves. Everything has a right to its place in the world and everything exists for some purpose, and not always necessarily is that purpose translated as what is good for man at a particular time in history. Only in recent times has modern science come to substantiate the Native Americans' intuitive understanding that we live in a precariously balanced ecological system that can be destroyed by man's carelessness and ignorance, or "arrogance," to the detriment of all life on earth.

In Native American oral literatures, the coyote as natural animal is subsumed within the creative archetype of Coyote, embodying coyote-like traits of resourcefulness and endurance as well as considerable power and influence. Here, Coyote is at his most complex; he may be deity, cultural hero, mediator, transformer, trickster, dupe— and true to his slippery ways, not easily classified and categorized by non-Indian peoples. In the oral genres that scholars have divided into myths, legends, chants, or tales, Coyote is present as central character wherever the coyote as animal is also found. Coyote in these literatures goes about establishing and destroying order in whatever mode is most useful to the cultures. He has many names, as is appropriate to one who has many roles, and is as holy and heroic or as bawdy and foolish as necessity deems. And in this case, necessity is often cultural model or example, for one can learn from Coyote how *not* to be or what *can* be.

Early ethnologists and anthropologists of the nineteenth and early twentieth centuries came upon Coyote when collecting materials on native cultures for primarily linguistic reasons, and, as a consequence, coyote myths and tales were often purged of Coyote's more bawdy exploits, or translated into Latin so that general readers would not be offended. More serious were the problems of interpretation that arose because cultural contexts were not usually recorded or studied in these collections. Yellowman, the Navajo story-teller, told Barre Toelken that Coyote stories "are not funny stories," even though much about the story may be funny, and that Coyote does foolish, good, or terrible things because "If he did not do all those things, then those things would not be possible in the world."[25] Coyote tales, Yellowman indicates, present us with the basis for analyzing social and natural orders—Coyote's inversions or subversions of norms, while comic in themselves, are directed toward another end. They offer us the range of possibilities inherent in all choices, thus forcing us to deliberate upon our motivations, the consequences of our actions, and especially, our static conceptions of society and the world.

Until recently, scholars generally thought that Coyote existed in two modes: the sacred myths in which Coyote was cultural deity who inhabited a pre-human world of spirit-animals and the secular tales where Coyote lived a more profane and often ribald existence as a trickster-dupe with animal and human attributes. Now this distinction has been found to be not so clearly marked as had been thought.[26] In whatever form, Coyote continues to exert a wealth of multivalent symbolic influences in traditional literatures, oral narratives, language, and culture.

Coyote figures prominently in oral literature as deity or trickster character ranging from the Plains, throughout the Southwest, along the Pacific Coast, and especially in the northwestern region of the United States. Perhaps his most well-known role is that of Trickster, a figure of indeterminate appearance whose most salient characteristics are his wanderings, his voracious appetite, and his unbridled sexuality. In this role, he is among the oldest of mankind's imaginative creations, for Coyote as Trickster does not stand alone. Trickster appears in different forms, not only in Native American cultures, but also in African and European ones, as hare, raven, spider, fox, or *picaro* (rogue) and confidence man, and even as Prometheus or Hermes in classical Greek mythology. (For example, in the Winnebago trickster cycle, Coyote is only a minor figure who has some run-ins with Trickster; Coyote, in this case, does not embody the Trickster's character and the latter does manage to shame Coyote so that he never again appears among people.[27]) Wherever he is found, Trickster exhibits his traits boldly: his pluralistic nature as a combination of god, man, or animal; his power as a shape-shifter with the ability to transform or be transformed; his cunning and fondness for deceit, which causes malicious or foolish consequences for himself and others or inadvertently brings about some good.

Coyote stories are properly told in winter, when the season is right for the many tales told about this bold adventurer who is rarely subdued. The following overview of these narratives merely introduces us to the many facets of Coyote's ambiguous character, but what may be noted is his presence in various social realms. He crosses the boundaries of what Western culture classifies as sacred or secular, evil or good, culture or nature. For example, among the Kiowas, Coyote is known as Old Man Coyote, an influential person who, even so, may be tricked and who always tricks in return. Among related Sioux peoples, the Mandan and Hidatsa have tales of Coyote as First Creator, who, finding himself in dangerous circumstances, is rescued by traditional rivals, through his unconquerable trickery. His role as divine figure does not prevent him from exhibiting his talent for deception.

In the Southwest, Coyote is the cultural hero or the trickster figure. Among the Zuni, Coyote is again both. Their account of the beginning of creation tells of a people who sought the center of the earth, its "heart," as the most suitable place to live. With the help of Water-Strider, the Holy Twins founded Middle Place, where Zuni live. At this place emerged all of the sacred things, including the Coyote Society, the *Saniyakya* with yucca wreaths around their heads. Through their priestly songs, the Coyote Society brought about the fine rain that is necessary for life, and for this reason, according to the story, it is "singled out/as the most extraordinary, most wonderful group/at the beginning" and the reason also why prayers are still offered to the Saniyakya during winter solstice. In Zuni, "sani" is the more esoteric term for Coyote, while "suski" is the everyday term. In a tale of "Suski and the Junco," Suski, or Coyote, hunting for food for his children, comes upon Junco, a bird, who is winnowing seeds and singing a song. So that he might get seeds for his children in a similar manner, Coyote asks Junco to teach him the song. Three times she does so, and each time Coyote loses the song. After the fourth time, Junco becomes weary of his carelessness and disguises a rock as herself. When Coyote is not able to get the disguised rock to teach him the song once more, he attempts to bite her (it) and in so doing, breaks all of his back teeth. Although this tale seems to explain how the coyote lost his molars, such tales are not usually meant to be etiological; instead, according to the narrator, "It just teaches how the coyote is being very foolish."[28] While Coyote, like other creators, has the power to give life to the people, he is not exempt from the business of living. He must learn about life, as all creatures do, by experiencing it, by making mistakes and accepting the consequences. Both wise and foolish, Coyote pre-empts neat classification.

Among the Papago and Pima from Arizona, Coyote is a foremost meddler; yet, his antiquity gives him certain privileges. Nothing is too sacred or too important or such a secret that he can't get involved, often to his shame and detriment, but also to some good end as well. After Elder Brother or First Born, Coyote is the second creature to be created by the union of the sky and the earth. He immediately begins to make his presence known: after First Born brings the animal and plant life out of darkness, all agree to call the light-giver "sun," except for Coyote who likes to be different and wants it called "light." Similarly, when corn is given to the people for the first time, all plant corn in accordance with the rules laid down, finding the proper land and time, and also singing the correct song for a good harvest. Only Coyote, who is lazy and doesn't care about conventions, plants corn while singing his own song; as a consequence, what he reaps instead of corn is the plant called "coyote tobacco" that grows along the arroyos. In other tales, it is Coyote's son who is the main mischief-maker, inheriting his father's propensity for trickery, but none of his wisdom. He is vain and distrustful and most of all, egotistical. He doesn't believe in following the customs of the people. He tricks and steals and is deceived in return. As Imitator, he foolishly believes that copying others will gain him their advantages, whether it's snake's eating habits or skunk's spraying habit. Coyote must learn again and again that each person has an appropriate talent that is not necessarily suitable for others.

Although Coyote sometimes tries to do good after his own fashion of course, his means are not always in step with his ends. Helping First Born recreate people out of clay after the Flood has destroyed most life, Coyote laughs as he purposely makes partially formed or misshaped people. But his cunning ways have also allowed him to trick secrets out of other first people, such as Bean Child and Turtle, thus bringing important food stuffs, mesquite beans and saguaro seeds to mankind, or creating beauty—the Milky Way—by accidently scattering the corn meal he has stolen from Heaven. One such tale ends: "This is why Coyote is good for something for people. . . . And, because he was a survivor, and saw many things and suffered much and knew the earth everywhere from the beginning until now, he was a very wise person."[29]

In another native language from Arizona, Yavpe, Coyote tales also depict him in his guise as the Imitator, an imprudent role, as the variants of his name denote: "desert dog," "Mr. Coyote the Fool," or "Mr. Foolish One"; but his idiosyncrasies sometimes have serious and significant implications. In the following narrative, in free translation from the original, Coyote brings death into the world permanently:

> The people said they wanted there always to be flowers. Coyote said, "This will not be. . . (there will be flowers) only in the Springtime (when the earth becomes warm)." The people said that when a person died, they wanted him to return to life. Coyote said, "This will not be. This will never happen. When they die, it's proper that they die." The people said they wanted to eat mescal just as it ripened. The people said that they wanted to eat mescal as soon as it was fit to eat. Coyote decreed, "Mescal shall be baked first." The people wanted to be living, thinking creatures. And so Coyote said, "They will be wild animals and roam about in the forests." The people wanted the sun to emerge and shine there (in the heavens) all the time, they said. Coyote, however, said, "Let there be night! When that occurs, we will sleep." After a while Coyote had a family and settled down with them there. His daughter took sick and died. Coyote cried and came around to the people's houses with his head bowed. "Pray for me! I want my daughter alive." When he said this, the people said, "Go away! You cry [now], but you formerly thought that when a person died, it was correct for them to die. So, your daughter is dead. It's proper therefore that she's dead and gone."[30]

Coyote has the power to make distinctions that affect the nature of the world: he defines the seasons of the year, life and death, the use of food, human and animal differences, night and day. By designating categories for the world he sees, Coyote creates order. The wielding of such formidable power, however, carries with it the attendant responsibility of accepting the consequences of one's actions. And perhaps more importantly, Coyote learns, along with his audience, that although establishing order may bring stability, happiness does not necessarily follow, that any ordered view of the world has limitations one cannot foresee. After all, in the story cited above, the creation of order also brought death.

In Mescalero and Navajo Apache cultures, both part of the Southern Athabascans, Coyote is holy, especially in emergence myths, and also plays the wandering trickster in many tales. Occasionally both capacities are combined, inadvertently benefiting mankind, as in the tale in which Coyote sets fire to the earth accidentally, thus securing fire for the people.[31] Among the Navajo, another benefit brought to the people through Coyote is health, since most illness among humanity is attributed to transgressions against the Holy People. "Coyoteway," a healing ceremony of the Holyway type, consists of a series of prayer-chants and other rites enacted during a period of several days in which the afflicted person is reconciled ceremonially with the Holy People, in this case, the Coyote People. The ceremony is accompanied by a series of sandpaintings that depict the central Hole of Emergence, because while their manifestations exist in the surface world as animals, the divine Coyote People live underground. The mythic-historical origin of the Coyoteway ceremony is said to have occurred during a cold winter snowstorm when a hunter, searching for food, came upon coyote tracks. The hunter followed the tracks to a ladder, set in the middle of a pond, on which the hunter descended to another world. There he found it was summer, and the kind people who fed and cared for him were the Coyote People, who, subsequently, showed him the procedures for the ceremonial. The story is important because not only does it depict the institution of Coyoteway, but also the general origin of healthy human beings in the surface world.[32]

In the Northwest, the mythic Coyote's trail is bright and strong, as he winds through the landscape, creating natural features such as rocks and rivers, naming plant and animal life into existence, and establishing particular cultures and customs. As a mythic being, Coyote exerts his powerful influence benignly or selfishly; he gives life, through actual creation or by securing foodstuffs, but just as often, his presence brings death. In a tale similar to the Yavpe story, the Nez Perce blame Coyote's impatient and selfish love for his wife for making death a permanent fixture in the world. As a transformer, he changes the earth in more specific ways, as when he metamorphoses a female chief of the Wishram into a petroglyph, or, because of his love for a beautiful star, falls from the heavens, creating Crater Lake in Klamath country. And this ability to alter shapes is, of course, extended to himself, so that he can become any plant or animal at will, often in the process losing parts of himself, whether it be eyes or penis. He transgresses taboos by having sex with his daughter, or by being lazy or disrespectful, but he always pays for his crimes in shame and ostracism. The trickster element in his character serves him well in most of his roles, procuring the satisfactions of Coyote's needs and desires in delightful and humorous ways. When Coyote ventures out beyond the socially respectable and finds his plans have backfired, the laughter at his inflated sense of himself reminds us of the weaknesses and frailties we have in common with him.

For the Lake Miwok people in northern California, Old Man Coyote in a pre-human age was a powerful personage who could both create and destroy life, and who indeed is the creator of humanity. In one tale, called "Fire, Flood, and Creation," Old Man Coyote is a doting and magical grandfather, who does many favors for his troublesome grandson, Bullet Hawk. As a result of Bullet Hawk's escapades, Coyote saves the world from fire by creating a flood, then sets about repopulating the earth with its many species of animal and plant life, and last of all creates human beings. In the Wishram culture along the Columbia River where Coyote is said to have originated, Coyote is a shape-shifter who oversees many of the great changes in the world through his clever transforming abilities, opening up the river, bringing salmon to the people, and inflicting or endowing others, as he sees fit. Similarly, among the Molala people, while Coyote is making the world, he sees to it that the Molala will become the best hunters of deer, just as he taught the Chinook the proper procedures for salmon fishing and rituals. In Chinook tales, Coyote has the amazing ability to dismantle himself when necessary, and to speak to his own excrements for advice. In these tales, although elements of the buffoon or trickster-dupe play a part in his management of the world and its people, Coyote is depicted as the wisest and most cunning of all creatures.[33]

The Northern Paiute tell tales of Coyote as a great trickster who breaks taboos or long-established friendships with little moral discomfort. Although he may suffer physically, Coyote always manages to survive the dire consequences of his misdeeds. In the tale of "Coyote the Eye-Juggler," for example, he loses his eyes while juggling them through the trickery of his friends who want to retaliate against his boastful ways. The friends take his eyes to a nearby camp where the people celebrate the capture by dancing over the eyes. After some desperate moments, Coyote disguises himself as an old woman who wishes to join in the dance. Making his way carefully to the center of the dance, he reaches for his eyes and runs away triumphantly. Or Coyote can be the voice of authority, as in "How the Animals Found their Place," in which Coyote ensures all the animals, as well as rocks and plants, their proper place in the world. For although Coyote can create disorder, he usually gets his comeuppance. Or he guides the circumstances himself toward order; ultimately harmony is restored, even though it may be a precarious one when Coyote is around.[34]

The Coyote figure is one of the most studied roles in oral literature, whether in order to understand Trickster's psychology (which Jung called that of a "collective shadow figure, an epitome of all the inferior traits of character in individuals"[35]) or from anthropologists' view of the trickster as a form of ritualized rebellion or licensed aggression. For Lévi-Strauss, Coyote's role in myth represents a mediation between two polarities. As a carrion-eater, the Coyote (as well as similar Trickster figures) functions as intermediary between the forces of life and death, represented as the herbivorous and carnivorous, respectively. As such, Coyote must retain elements of both forces, resulting in his ambiguous, contradictory character.[36] Barbara Babcock calls this ambiguity a necessary one, for better or worse, because it is the Trickster figure's privileged freedom and great creative force, demonstrated in its comic, antisocial behavior, that establish a sense of community in the culture.[37]

Relatively little is known about the role of the coyote in Mesoamerican cultures, but it is clear that the animal was an integral part of the symbolic systems of the early peoples, and one whose influence can be traced even today in the coyote lore that forms an undercurrent in many parts of Mexican culture throughout the southwestern United States or wherever Chicanos are found. The *Mexica* culture (or *Chichimec*), known to us popularly as the Aztecs conquered by Cortez in the early sixteenth century, had a rich civilization in which Coyote played an obscure role. Because of the enormous destruction of the buildings, the art work, and the books of the Mexica, it is difficult to piece together Coyote's significance in the culture. In the pantheon of gods, *Huehuecoyotl,* "Venerable Old Coyote," was the god of song and dance (fig. 7.2). His identifying insignia are a coyote mask and a musical hieroglyph coming from his mouth; various codices show him playing a musical instrument made of tinkling shells or beating on a drum. Huehuecoyotl is associated closely with *Xochipilli,* "the Flower Prince," who represents a young god of abundance and pleasure: patron of those involved in games, song, flowers, dance, and art. Xochipilli is sometimes known as *Macuilxochitl,* "Five Flowers," a music god and patron of blind people, who in this form carries musical instruments and wears the ear of a coyote around his neck.[38] Since in Nahuatl, a highly metaphoric language, "flower-and-song" represents poetry, the coyote could also be associated with the making of poetry. Among the varied motifs of clay stamps collected, which were used to mark poetry, and paper and skin as well, one motif is of a coyote emerging from a flower (fig.7.3). It is tantalizing to imagine the symbolism behind such a representation, called Coyote Flower.

Music formed an essential part of religious ceremonies among Native Americans and was also used in warfare to confuse the enemy with the loud distraction of beating drums and shrill whistles. Singing and dancing were arts carefully taught to the youth and were community enterprises enacted in the solemn festivities of the gods. Thus, the Mexica seemed to have placed Coyote as the god of song and dance, not only for his playfulness and wit, but also for his astuteness and aggression. Because music was an event of such great community participation, not simply an individual pastime, Coyote must have been an intimate of all manner of people, from high priest to dancer, ball-player, and artisan.

Another figure in their mythology was *Coyotlinahual,* "Coyote-Sorcerer," who appears in a legend as an evil deity who disguises Topiltzin Quetzalcoatl, priest-ruler in the tenth century A.D. Coyotlinahual is said to have been the god of the feather workers who founded Amantlán, where his image stood adorned with gold, plumes, and dressed in the skin of a coyote.[39] But a *nagual* (or *nahual*) is traditionally the spirit animal, the soul or the "double" of a person who can assume its shape to perform evil deeds without recognition. As Coyotli*nahual,* then, Coyote becomes the conjurer, the transformer, who can disguise not only himself but others as well. As a shape-changer, Coyote must have been extremely powerful.

7.2. Huehuecoyotl, god of song and dance. The character's face emerges from a coyote's open nostrils, and he is adorned with turquoise and quetzal feathers, symbolizing the green color of spring. From Nigel Davies, *The Aztecs*, 50.

7.3. Clay stamps of coyote motifs. From Jorge Enciso, *Sellos del antiguo México* (México: Innovación, 1947), 109.

And "Fasting" or "Hungry Coyote," *Nezahualcoyotl*, was the name given to the Chichimec prince of Texcoco who initiated the culture's Golden Age. He was a patron of the arts, composed poetry, and was famous for his orations.[40] Sahagún records three proverbial phrases in which the coyote also figures. The first one, "Cuix tleuh yetinami in coyotl" (Does a coyote carry his fire around with him?), is said by someone who bolts down his food, cooked or not, as if he were ravenous, or told to another cooking a meal which one wishes to share. Another phrase is: "Quin ni nicoyotl: ma ica niquitta" (When I am a coyote, I shall see it), implying that someone is being untruthful or boastful, and that only the old and wise can perceive the truthfulness of the other. The last saying, "Canin mach coyona- cazco" (When, perhaps, in a coyote's ear? or, Tell it to the coyote!), is used to rebuke a person who rudely criticizes another, or to some- one who refuses to understand instructions.[41] In these sayings, the coyote appears to have had traits similar to those of the North American Coyote: hungry and impolite, but also wise and old.

In modern day Mexico, Coyote as divine figure has given way to other influences, although Frances Toor in her *Mexican Folkways* describes the Coyote Dance of the Yaquis still practiced in her times. Three men dressed in coyote skins and beating a hunting bow with a sonorous reed cane dance to the beat of a drum. Imitating the body movements of the coyote, the dancers move forward to regular beats and backwards to irregular beats, while the drummer sings in Cahíta: "Crow, crow, outside, outside, he comes, not playing, playing." The Coyote Dance, says Toor, is performed at fiestas for patron saints and at funeral ceremonies for Yaqui soldiers, village officials, and other dancers.[42]

Coyote still reigns, however, in popular Spanish usage, where once again Coyote is many things to many people. In the Spanish spoken in Mexico and the United States, the word "coyote" has an interesting variety of meanings. Santamaría's *Diccionario de mejicanismos* gives us at least six besides the actual animal: a street vendor, a lay attorney, an intermediary, creole, a regional pastry, and a beverage.[43] Among horsemen, "coyote" refers to a particular color of horse, and used as a verb, *coyotear*, it means to con, to hassle, or to hide from legal authorities. The term has been used both by and against the Mexican Indians. In colonial times, "coyote" referred to a person of a particular mixed ancestry in the socioracial terminology used to uphold the hierarchical class structure,[44] but it also was an Indian term of contempt towards the Spaniards. And it came to signify the larger class of people of mixed bloods, the *mestizo*, who were social and political outcasts in the rigid colonial system.[45] Curiously, it can now simply mean indigenous or native. Today the term "coyote" is still used derogatorily for a child of Mexican-Anglo parents in the Southwest. But when used affectionately, it refers to the youngest child in the family, stemming not from *coyotl*, but from another Nahuatl word, *xocoyotl*, meaning the youngest.[46]

Both Spanish and non-Spanish speakers along the United States-Mexican border are familiar with "coyote" used to mean the smuggler engaged in the profitable job of bringing people over the border illegally and—recently found in a Texas border newspaper as well as in *The Wall Street Journal*—as the black-market vendor of Mexican money. In addition, the migrant labor contractor, often exploiting workers, is called a "coyote," as is the person whom Santamaría calls the "lay attorney," who with no legal training sets up a fraudulent business to prey upon the vulnerable. A woman who is accused of tempting and deceiving men is called a *coyota* (which a civil liberties organization of prostitutes convening in San Francisco has picked up as its name, COYOTE: "Call Off Your Old Tired Ethics"). But when someone is spoken of being *muy coyote* (as an adjective, very coyote), it can also mean the person is astute and shrewd.

Both popular and folk songs reflect the uses of "coyote." In "La coyota," the female singer-narrator decries her reputation as a temptress, while "El corrido del coyote" is a ballad that relates the adventures of the comic but valiant coyote in folk tales, a figure with which the singer identifies.[47] Another song, "El coyotito," collected in the early part of the twentieth century, is a farewell song of lament for the transitoriness of all things, including love, and in which the singer ironically compares himself to the coyote who "loves them and leaves them."[48]

In Mexican folk narratives from both sides of the border, usually a mixture of European and indigenous elements, Coyote is found occasionally as a mediating figure and more commonly as a trickster-dupe. Coyote usually receives the raw end of the deal, as in the tale about the coyote and the burro. The coyote has tricked a burro carrying his master's food supplies into allowing the coyote to steal them. Because the burro is beaten for the loss of the food, he seeks revenge. Finding the coyote's den and lying before it, the burro opens his anus wide enough to disclose his intestines. Attempting to eat the "meat," the coyote enters the burro's body through the anus. The burro closes it, capturing the coyote who is then taken to the burro's master and skinned alive.

As a mediator, Coyote functions as a helpful agent to the hero-victim, usually in order to display his wit and cleverness. A tale rare in print demonstrates both attributes, the tale of coyote as "other." The tale narrates the encounter of two coyotes on a hillside. One, introducing himself says, "Yo soy coyote" (I am coyote), but the other one replies that he is *not* a coyote. "Yo soy otro" (I am other), he argues. To prove his point, the second coyote wagers that men working nearby will agree with him. As the first coyote runs by the men, they shout, "Allá va un coyote" (There goes a coyote), but when the second one passes them, the men say, "Allá va otro" (There goes [an]other). And of course, the coyote wins his bet; he becomes Other. Coyote refuses to define himself, even to another of his kind, for he has the power of the word, and he can become anyone or anything he wishes.[49]

Coyote has worked his way into English usage as well, especially in the Southwest where Coyote is a popular name for many natural features such as mountains, creeks, springs, and arroyos. California, Arizona, and Texas each sports a Coyote Peak or Coyote Creek or Coyote Lake, while New Mexico, which has traditionally emphasized its tricultural heritage, boasts of at least four settlements, three creeks, two canyons, an arroyo, a draw, and a valley called Coyote, handily beating out the other states.

Some of the motivations for such place names must have been derived from observing the coyote's natural behavior. For example, in the Great Salt Lake Valley of Utah, Mormon pioneers built "coyote houses," which were cellars dug into the ground and used as living quarters until a more permanent home could be made. Coyoteville was a California boom town in the 1850s named after the tunnel method of mining then in use, which was said to resemble the building of coyote dens, and Coyote Wells, California, reputedly was so named because of the method used by coyotes to dig holes in search of water.[50] In addition, because of the coyote's well-known traits of speed and agility, the animal has been adopted as mascot by a high school in Wichita Falls, South Dakota; and a women's track team, "Los Coyotes," in San Antonio, Texas, proudly wear T-shirts with a picture of the coyote. Marc Bekoff in his *Coyotes: Biology, Behavior, and Management* remarks that the coyote's success as a predator is noted in bumper stickers in the West which say, "Eat lamb—10,000 coyotes can't be wrong."[51] The coyote is a popular subject for southwestern post cards which feature the animal as an emblem of the desert. And at least one popular beverage is named after it as well— "Coyote Coffee," described in a menu as a "wild Southwestern combination of coffee and chocolate liqueurs."

Many full-length books have been devoted to coyote lore and natural behavior, among which are J. Frank Dobie's *The Voice of the Desert* (1947), Joe Van Wormer's *The World of the Coyote* (1964), Hope Ryden's *God's Dog* (1975), François Leydet's *The Coyote: Defiant Songdog of the West* (1977), and numerous natural histories. These studies in large part speak to the importance of the coyote in white American oral traditions of the West. In the 1930s, Lillian E. Barclay also studied coyote lore and collected the many references to the animal in the Southwest's popular literature. She found several poems praising the coyote's characteristic howl as the voice of the desert, as in E. T. Seton's "The Coyote's Song" or E. A. Brinninstool's "The Desert Serenader." She noted that writers have made the coyote a "super Dr. Jekyll and Mr. Hyde," cataloguing his sometimes contradictory and often unpleasant traits, but that, notwithstanding his reputation as predator, he typified the independent spirit of the West and Southwest.[52]

A brief survey of early twentieth-century Western literature reveals that the coyote is made a symbol of the outcast or the fierce individualist who is misunderstood by society, as in Whitman Chambers's *Don Coyote* (1927) and James Roberts's *The Coyote* (1925), neither of which has the actual coyote represented in it.

In more recent Anglo-American literature, the coyote character is drawn less from the natural animal than from the Anglo interpretation of Coyote in American Indian cultures. Gary Snyder, the well-known poet, explains that the fascination of modern writers with Coyote is derived from two main concerns: (1) white America's identification of its heroic self-image with the expansion of the western frontier and, hence, with the coyote as the frontier's "protector spirit," and (2) a later identification in the 1950s and 60s with the antiheroic trickster image of Coyote.[53] Native American writers have often criticized writers such as Jerome Rothenberg and others, who present a strongly one-sided view of Coyote, choosing to emphasize his antisocial behavior and his more obscene antics over his revered role as wise and benevolent leader.[54]

Modern Chicano writers have also portrayed Coyote in his trickster guise, not as a symbol of unbridled freedom and irresponsibility, but as a character type that they use to explore the effect of ambiguous or oppressive cultural norms and social structures. Luís Pérez in *El Coyote/The Rebel* (1947) writes about a young *picaro*, the literary analogue of the trickster, who fights in the Mexican Revolution and migrates to the United States, ever avoiding confrontations and ever falling into disillusionment. Mario Suarez uses the trickster figure to depict the effects of nationalism in the short story "Los Coyotes" (in *Festival de Flor y Canto*, 1976) about two Chicano con men who prey on their community during World War II. In the *actos* of the Teatro Campesino, the coyote figure is the migrant labor contractor, who works both sides, management and labor, to exploit non-unionized farmworkers. Sergio Elizondo, in "Coyote, esta noche" (from *Rosa la Flauta*, 1980), narrates the adventures of a bilingual coyote, a witty trickster cognizant of his historical role and able to fool both men and domesticated animals.[55]

Clearly, it is in contemporary Native American literature that Coyote enjoys the full range of his cultural heritage. A recent special issue of *Coyote's Journal* (unnumbered, 1982) exemplifies his endowment. Recalling traditional tales, Louis Oliver's "Grandfather Coyote and the Yellow Dog" (116–18) represents him as an amusing but also feared and respected personage, while Joseph Bruchac in "Writing About Coyote" holds the memory of Coyote, both mythic and actual, within him until ready and "less eager/ to hurl crazy power" and returns the gift of poetry Coyote has given him (58–59). Carol Lee Sanchez's poem from *Through the Microscope* speculates on Old Coyote's return: "Grandfather's coming back one day/to tell us another dream" and perhaps also to "tell us/Why/we are" (123–26). Both Peter Coyote and Peter Blue Cloud question the white poet's use of the archetypal Coyote, who, for Peter Coyote, hunts like the rest of us "enduring value and/knowledge" (45–46). Blue Cloud's dialogue with Coyote on power and magic ends with these lines:

> Coyote, coyote, please tell me,
> Who you belong to?
>
> According to the latest
> survey,
> there are certain persons,
> who,
> in poetic or scholarly guise,
> have claimed me
> like a conqueror's prize.
>
> Let me just say
> once and for all
> just to be done:
>   Coyote
> he belongs to none. (56–57)

Novelist and Pulitzer Prize winner N. Scott Momaday's *House Made of Dawn* (1968) also invokes Coyote's ambiguous, sacred/ profane character in his portrayal of Tosamah, Priest of the Sun. And in Leslie Silko's fiction and poetry, Coyote is reinterpreted to represent not only the mythic trickster and negative example, but also contemporary tricksters, replete with traditional attributes of craftiness and sexuality. In "Coyote and the Stro'ro'ka Dancers," Silko re-creates a traditional Laguna tale in which coyotes form a live animal chain, mouth to tail, down a cliff in order to prey upon the dancers below. When one coyote farts and disperses the chain, all fall to their death, leaving the skins for the dancers to wear as neck-pieces in their traditional costumes. But in "Toe'osh: A Laguna Coy-ote Story," the coyote-chain tale, as well as other traditional tales, is woven around contemporary trickster stories of the Laguna's deal-ings with politicians and other white men; instead of falling to their deaths, the coyotes fall among the whites. And in her comic, master-ful short story, "Coyote Holds a Full House in his Hand," the La-guna Indian protagonist, a lazy and lustful contemporary analogue of Coyote's, tricks all the Hopi clanswomen into letting him caress them intimately, in retribution for his having lost his lady love to a Hopi man. The narrative is told from the trickster's point of view, slowly revealing his sly character, overtly dim-witted and slow but, in actuality, ingenious as he takes advantage of the circumstances presented to him.[56]

Coyote and poet Simon Ortiz are occasionally difficult to distin-guish from each other in Ortiz's many pieces on Coyote. In "Two Coyote Ones," the poet-persona tells a story of "real Coyote luck" about a blonde in a pick-up and with a ginger cake who felicitously approaches him one night while he is sitting beside a campfire; the poem ends with Coyote telling a story about sitting at a campfire and being approached by a blonde in a pick-up.[57] This close associa-tion of himself with Coyote the storyteller seems to lie at the core of Ortiz's reason for writing. When asked why he wrote, his response was ". . . Because Indians always tell a story. The only way to con-tinue is to tell a story, and that's what Coyote says." Coyote is the ele-mental self, inextricably tied to the natural world: "Breaking thin ice from a small still pool/I find Coyote's footprints./Coyote, he's al-ways somewhere before you."[58]

And indeed it appears that Coyote *is* always before us. His pres-ence both as natural animal and artificial human creation is at least as ancient as the Mexican coyote artifact from 11,000 B.C. and as re-cent as our imagination and his endurance allow. As predatory killer, victim of man's cruelty, symbol of Western independence and exploitation, trickster-deity, and most especially, creative force, the coyote will continue to survive as long as we do, or perhaps longer. For this overview only skims the surface of the persistence and the variation of Coyote in American culture and offers no explanation of why his stronghold on the continent has been so complete. Coyote appears everywhere as unconquerable. We can only say, along with "Gogisgi" Carroll Arnett:

> You get tired of
> hearing from
> Coyote, right?
>
> Well, he's long
> since tired of
> hearing from
>
> you too,
> you too,
> pilgrim.
>
> Live on, like
> Coyote
> does,
>
> on and
> on and
> on.[59]

NOTES

1. See Victor Turner's discussion of liminality in *The Ritual Process: Structure and Anti-Structure* (Ithaca, N.Y.: Cornell Univ. Press, 1969), 94–130, and further developments in his *From Ritual to Theatre: The Human Seriousness of Play* (New York: Performing Arts Journal Publications, 1982); also Edmund Leach, *Culture and Communication* (Cambridge: Cambridge Univ. Press, 1976), 33–36.

2. Stanley P. Young, "Part I: Its History, Life Habits, Economic Status, and Control," *The Clever Coyote* (Lincoln: Univ. of Nebraska Press, 1951), 11–45, 79–81, 124–30. Part II (229–316) is written by Hartley H. T. Jackson.

3. Eric Wolf, *Sons of the Shaking Earth* (Chicago: Univ. of Chicago Press, 1959), 49.

4. Cited in Alfred W. Crosby, *The Columbian Exchange* (Westport,

Conn.: Greenwood, 1972), 12, from De Acosta's *The Natural and Moral History of the Indies* (1570).

5. Fray Bernardino de Sahagún, *Historia general de las cosas de nueva españa*, vol. 3 (México: Jose Porrua, 1969), 225–26.

6. Cited in J. Frank Dobie, *The Voice of the Coyote* (Lincoln: Univ. of Nebraska Press, 1947), 259n, from *Nova Plantanum, Animalium et Mineralium Mexicanorum Historia* (Rome, 1651).

7. Mauricio Swadesh and Madalena Sancho, *Los mil elementos del mexicano clasico* (México: U.N.A.M., 1966); J. Richard Andrews, *Introduction to Classical Nahuatl* (Austin: Univ. of Texas Press, 1975).

8. Elliott Coues, ed., *History of the Expedition under the Command of Lewis and Clark*, 3 vols. (1893; rpt., New York: Dover, 1965), vol. 1, 297.

9. Young, 232.

10. Cited by Lillian E. Barclay, "The Coyote: Animal and Folk Character," *Coyote Wisdom* 14 (Austin: Texas Folklore Society, 1938), 39–40.

11. Young, 308.

12. Ross Cox, *The Columbia River* (Norman: Univ. of Oklahoma Press, 1957), 239.

13. Young, 124.

14. Cited in Dobie, 28.

15. Young, 24.

16. Twain, *Roughing It* (Avon, Conn.: Heritage, 1972), 25–26.

17. Ibid., 97–99.

18. Coues, "The Prairie Wolf or Coyote, *Canis Latrans*," *American Naturalist* 7, no. 7 (1873): 384–89.

19. Young, 5–7, 115–19; Dobie, 44.

20. "War on the Range: Sheep 1, Coyote 0," *Newsweek*, Nov. 8, 1982, 81–82.

21. Young, 232–33.

22. Theodore Roosevelt, "Wolf Hunt in Oklahoma," *Scribner's* 38 (Nov. 1905): 513–32.

23. Françoise Leydet, *The Coyote: Defiant Songdog of the West* (San Francisco: Chronicle Books, 1977).

24. John Lame Deer, "That Gun in the New York Museum Belongs to Me," in *American Indian Literature*, ed. Alan R. Velie (Norman: Univ. of Oklahoma Press, 1979), 231.

25. Barre Toelken, "The 'Pretty Languages' of Yellowman: Genre, Mode, and Texture in Navaho Coyote Narratives," in *Folklore Genres*, ed. Dan Ben-Amos (Austin: Univ. of Texas Press, 1976), 155; see Mary C. Douglas, "The Social Control of Cognition: Some Factors in Joke Perception," *Man* 3 (1968): 361–76, for the function of humor; Barbara Babcock-

Abrahams's introduction to *The Reversible World* (Ithaca, N.Y.: Cornell Univ. Press, 1978); and also Judy Trejo, "Coyote Tales: A Paiute Commentary," *Journal of American Folklore* 87 (1974): 66–71. For a discussion of age-differentiated responses to an African trickster, see Bruce T. Grindal, "The Sisala Trickster," *Journal of American Folklore* 86 (1973): 173–75.

26. For a survey of responses to the trickster figure, see MacLinscott Ricketts, "The North American Indian Trickster," *History of Religions* 5 (1966): 327–50; and for a thorough symbolic analysis, Barbara Babcock-Abrahams, " 'A Tolerated Margin of Mess': The Trickster and His Tales Reconsidered," *Journal of the Folklore Institute* 9 (1975): 147–86; and T.O. Beidelman, "The Moral Imagination of the Kaguru: Some Thoughts on Trickster, Translation, and Comparative Analysis," *American Ethnologist* (1980): 27–42.

27. Paul Radin, *The Trickster: A Study in American Indian Mythology* (New York: Schocken, 1956).

28. Dennis Tedlock, *Finding the Center: Narrative Poetry of the Zuni Indians* (Lincoln: Univ. of Nebraska Press, 1972), 284, 75–84; see T.T. Waterman, "Explanatory Elements in the Tales of the North American Indians," *Journal of American Folklore* 27 (1914): 1–58.

29. From Dean and Lucille Saxton, *Legends and Lore of the Papago and Pima Indians* (Tucson: Univ. of Arizona Press, 1973).

30. William Bright, ed., *Coyote Stories*, Native American Text Series No. 1 (Chicago: Univ. of Chicago Press, 1978), 151–61.

31. W.W. Hill and Dorothy Hill, "Navajo Coyote Tales and their Position in the Southern Athabaskan Group," *Journal of American Folklore* 58 (1945): 317–43.

32. Karl Luckert, *Coyoteway: A Navajo Holyway Healing Ceremonial* (Tucson: Univ. of Arizona Press, 1979).

33. Jarold Ramsey, ed., *Coyote Was Going There: Indian Literature of the Oregon Country* (Seattle: Univ. of Washington Press, 1977).

34. Ibid., 224–59.

35. C.G. Jung, "On the Psychology of the Trickster Figure," in Radin's *The Trickster*, 209.

36. Claude Lévi-Strauss, "The Structural Study of Myth," *Structural Anthropology* (Garden City, N.Y.: Doubleday, 1967), 202–28.

37. Babcock-Abrahams, " 'A Tolerated Margin of Mess' "; see, also, Turner's discussion of "communitas" in *The Ritual Process* and in his *Dramas, Fields and Metaphors* (Ithaca, N.Y.: Cornell Univ. Press, 1974).

38. Frederick A. Peterson, *Ancient Mexico: An Introduction to the Pre-Hispanic Cultures* (New York: Capricorn, 1959), 202–216.

39. Jacques Soustelle, *Daily Life of the Aztecs* (Stanford, Calif.: Stanford Univ. Press, 1961), 67.

40. Peterson, 79–97.

41. Thelma D. Sullivan, trans., "Nahuatl Proverbs, Conundrums, and Metaphors, Collected by Sahagún," *Estudios de Cultura Nahuatl*, 4 (México: U.N.A.M., 1963), 93–177.

42. Francis Toor, *A Treasury of Méxican Folkways* (New York: Crown, 1947), 334–36.

43. *Diccionario de mejicanismos* (México: ed. Porrua, 1978).

44. Magnus Mörner, *Race Mixture in the History of Latin America* (Boston: Little, Brown, and Co., 1967), 58–59.

45. Wolf, 237.

46. Cecilio A. Robelo, *Diccionario de aztequismos* (México: Fuente Cultural, 1904).

47. Ballad text cited in Dobie, 250–51.

48. John Donald Robb, *Hispanic Folk Music of New Mexico and the Southwest: A Self-Portrait of a People* (Norman: Univ. of Oklahoma Press, 1954), 308–9.

49. From my earlier study, "Coyote: Towards a Definition of a Concept," *Aztlan* 13 (1982): 295–307.

50. Young, 6; other place names taken from survey of geographical dictionaries.

51. Marc Bekoff, *Coyotes: Biology, Behavior, and Management* (New York: Academic Press, 1978), xiii.

52. Barclay, 36–103.

53. Gary Snyder, "The Incredible Survival of Coyote," *Western American Literature* 9 (1975): 255–72.

54. See Gerald Hobson, "The Rise of the White Shaman as a New Version of Cultural Imperialism," *Yardbird* 1 (1977): 85–95; and also Lawrence J. Evers, "Further Survivals of Coyote," *Western American Literature* 10 (1975): 233–36.

55. From my "Manipulating Ambiguity: The Coyote in Chicano Literature," paper presented at the MLA, 1980.

56. Leslie Marmon Silko, *Storyteller* (New York: Seaver, 1981), 229–65.

57. Simon Ortiz, "Two Coyote Ones," *A Good Journey* (Berkeley: Turtle Island Press, 1977), 100–2.

58. Simon Ortiz, "The Boy and Coyote," *Going For the Rain* (New York: Harper and Row, 1976), 88.

59. Arnett, *Coyote's Journal*, ed. James Koller, 'Gogisgi' Carroll Arnett, Steve Nemirow, and Peter Blue Cloud (Berkeley: Wingbow Press, 1982), 153.

Contributors

A childhood interest in folk music led DANIEL J. GELO to the study of folklore and anthropology. Holding a B.A. and doctorate in anthropology from Rutgers University, Gelo has published articles on New Jersey folklife and two books of arrangements of traditional Irish music. His current research is on animal symbolism in the ceremonial life of the southern Plains Indians.

ANGUS K. GILLESPIE is associate professor of American studies at Rutgers University. With an undergraduate degree in American studies from Yale University and his graduate degrees in American civilization from the University of Pennsylvania, Gillespie has done extensive fieldwork in the New Jersey pinelands. He became an avid armadillo fan while working as an NEH summer seminar fellow at the University of Texas, Austin. He was a Fulbright Lecturer at the University of the Philippines for 1985-86.

MARY HUFFORD is a folklorist and free-lance writer living in Washington, D.C. Since 1982 she has been a folklife specialist at the American Folklife Center, Library of Congress. From 1983 to 1985 she directed the Pinelands Folklife Project, a field survey of culture and environment in New Jersey's Pinelands National Reserve. She is currently working on a book entitled *Navigators in a Sea of Sand: A Geography of Pinelands Life.*

JAY MECHLING is professor and director of American studies at the University of California, Davis. With his undergraduate degree in American studies from Stetson University and his graduate degrees in American civilization from the University of Pennsylvania, he publishes widely in American studies, folklore, and popular culture studies. He is editor of *Western Folklore,* quarterly journal of the California Folklore Society, and he currently is writing on the animal-rights debate.

THERESA MELÉNDEZ is associate professor of English at the University of Texas at El Paso, where she teaches Chicano literature, Mexican folklore, medieval literature, and oral traditions. She has published in these areas and on the Spanish ballad. Her *El caballero burlado y la infantina* (Madrid: Ed. Gredos and Instituto Menendez Pidal, 1986) is part of the series *Romancero tradicional,* edited by Diego Catalan.

Freelance writer TAD TULEJA holds a master's degree in American studies from the University of Sussex. He writes frequently on popular culture, and from 1978 to 1981 contributed a column on American foodways to the New Brunswick, New Jersey, *Home News.* His most recent book is *Fabulous Fallacies* (1982), a compendium of popular misconceptions.

DAVID SCOFIELD WILSON is associate professor of American studies at the University of California, Davis. He earned his graduate degrees in American studies at the University of Minnesota. The author of *In the Presence of Nature* (1978), Wilson regularly teaches courses on nature and culture in America. He is presently working on a book, *Found in America,* which examines the symbolic treatment of an assortment of native North American flora and fauna.

Index

American Wildlife in Symbol and Story was designed by Sheila Hart; composed by Point West, Inc., Carol Stream, Illinois; printed by Thomson-Shore, Inc., Dexter, Michigan; and bound by John H. Dekker & Sons, Grand Rapids, Michigan. The book is set in 11/13 Sabon with Sabon display and printed on 60-lb. Glatfelter.

THE UNIVERSITY OF TENNESSEE PRESS: KNOXVILLE